Attitudes, Poverty and Agency in Russia and Ukraine

One of the main ideas behind this book was to trace continuities from the Soviet time to post-Soviet Russia. There are many similarities between Russia and Ukraine, indicating such a continuation. Russia and Ukraine had a lot in common in terms of culture, language and history, partly because of their common origin. After the dissolution of the Soviet Union, however, the two independent countries chose different routes of development. This makes it possible to distinguish between the effects of politics/reforms on the one hand and the impacts from the Soviet system on the other. After some more or less chaotic development paths in the 1990s, showing clear differences between the two countries, and before the contemporary conflict broke out in Eastern Ukraine (2013), they had once again more similarities in terms of political leadership and policies in general.

The chapters in this book focus on Ukraine and on two regions in Russia: Nizhny Novgorod and Archangelsk. Contributors look at attitudes towards poverty and poor people; strategies of the poor; and policies against poverty.

This book was published as a special issue of the *Debatte: Journal of Contemporary Central and Eastern Europe*.

Ann-Mari Sätre is Associate Professor in Economics and a senior lecturer/researcher at the Centre of Russian and Eurasian Studies at Uppsala University, Sweden. She specializes in the structure and performance of the Soviet/Russian economy. Her current research focuses on poverty, local development and women's work in Russia.

Ildikó Asztalos Morell is an Associate Professor in Sociology at Mälardalen University, Sweden. She is also a senior research fellow at the Centre of Russian and Eurasian Studies at Uppsala University, Sweden. Her research interests include gender and economic transition during and after state socialism, welfare systems and rural transition, with a focus on multiple marginalities in Hungary.

Attitudes, Poverty and Agency in Russia and Ukraine

Edited by
Ann-Mari Sätre and Ildikó Asztalos Morell

Routledge
Taylor & Francis Group
LONDON AND NEW YORK

First published 2016
by Routledge

2 Park Square, Milton Park, Abingdon, Oxfordshire OX14 4RN
711 Third Avenue, New York, NY 10017

Routledge is an imprint of the Taylor & Francis Group, an informa business

First issued in paperback 2017

British Library Cataloguing in Publication Data
A catalogue record for this book is available from the British Library

ISBN 13: 978-1-138-95764-0 (hbk)
ISBN 13: 978-1-138-30014-9 (pbk)

Typeset in TrebuchetMS
by RefineCatch Limited, Bungay, Suffolk

Publisher's Note
The publisher accepts responsibility for any inconsistencies that may have arisen during the conversion of this book from journal articles to book chapters, namely the possible inclusion of journal terminology.

Contents

Citation Information

The chapters in this book were originally published in *Debatte: Journal of Contemporary Central and Eastern Europe*, volume 22, issue 3 (December 2014). When citing this material, please use the original page numbering for each article, as follows:

Chapter 1

Attitudes, Poverty and Agency in Russia and Ukraine
Ann-Mari Sätre
Debatte: Journal of Contemporary Central and Eastern Europe, volume 22, issue 3 (December 2014) pp. 266–268

Chapter 2

Perceptions of Poverty in Small-town Russia
Alla Varyzgina and Rebecca Kay
Debatte: Journal of Contemporary Central and Eastern Europe, volume 22, issue 3 (December 2014) pp. 269–287

Chapter 3

Homelessness in Ukraine: Structural Causes and Moral Evaluation
Anastasiya Ryabchuk
Debatte: Journal of Contemporary Central and Eastern Europe, volume 22, issue 3 (December 2014) pp. 288–306

Chapter 4

Families' Ways of Coping with Poverty in Small-town Russia
Ann-Mari Sätre, Alexander Soldatkin and Alla Varyzgina
Debatte: Journal of Contemporary Central and Eastern Europe, volume 22, issue 3 (December 2014) pp. 307–328

Chapter 5

Single Men, Single Stories: Alternative Paths in the Transition from the Late Soviet to the Neoliberal Market Economy in the Light of Life Stories
Ildikó Asztalos Morell and Irina Tiurikova
Debatte: Journal of Contemporary Central and Eastern Europe, volume 22, issue 3 (December 2014) pp. 329–351

Chapter 6

The Ukrainian Power Elite and Poverty Reductive Efforts: An Inquiry into a Selection of Elite Members' Legislative and Philanthropic Initiatives
Tetiana Kostiuchenko and Hanna Söderbaum
Debatte: Journal of Contemporary Central and Eastern Europe, volume 22, issue 3 (December 2014) pp. 352–378

Chapter 7

Policies Against Poverty in Russia – A Female Responsibility
Ann-Mari Sätre
Debatte: Journal of Contemporary Central and Eastern Europe, volume 22, issue 3 (December 2014) pp. 379–402

Chapter 8

Searching for a New Approach to Face Poverty on the Local Level, a Case Study in a Small Russian Town
Nina Ivashinenko
Debatte: Journal of Contemporary Central and Eastern Europe, volume 22, issue 3 (December 2014) pp. 403–419

Notes on Contributors

Ildikó Asztalos Morell is Associate Professor of Sociology at Mälardalen University, Sweden, as well as senior research fellow at the Centre for Russian and Eurasian Studies, Uppsala University, Sweden. Her research interests cover gender studies, the study of rural transition including agrarian production forms and processes of social marginalization. Her main research focus is on Hungary during and after state socialism. Her major publication is *Emancipation's Dead-End Roads: Studies in the formation and development of the Hungarian model for gender and agriculture 1956–1988* (1999). She has been co-editor of several comparative volumes, such as *Gender Regimes, Citizen Participation and Agricultural Restructuring* (2008); *Gender Transitions in Russia and Eastern Europe* (2005); and *Bilden av ingenjören* (2013).

Nina Ivashinenko is Professor and Head of the Department of Economic Sociology at Lobachevsky State University, Nizhni Novgorod, Russia, and Head of UNN-ISEPN RAN joint laboratory for the study of the population's quality of life as a basis of social management. She is an honorary research fellow at the University of Glasgow, UK. Her research interests include economic sociology, quality of life, social insecurity and migration. Her key publications include *Groups of Poor and Prospects for Using a Participatory Approach as a Strategy for Poverty Reduction in Russia* (2012); *Economic and Social Cohesion of EU: Methodology of investigation* (2011); and *Social Politics and Economic Activity of the Population* (2002).

Rebecca Kay is Professor of Russian Gender Studies at the University of Glasgow, UK. Her research has explored gendered transformations in Russia since the early 1990s. More recently she has been researching experiences of social security, welfare and care in rural Russia. Her key publications include 'Rural Realities in the Post-Socialist Space' (2012, *Journal of Rural Studies*); *Gender, Equality and Difference During and After State Socialism* (2007); *Men in Contemporary Russia* (2006); and *Russian Women and their Organizations* (2000).

Tetiana Kostiuchenko is a PhD candidate in Sociology, and a lecturer in the Sociology Department at the National University of Kyiv-Mohyla Academy, Ukraine. Her dissertation is focused on the structure and particularities of the political elite network in Ukraine between 2007–2012. Her broader research interests cover two main issues: the role of various social groups in state functioning, and the application of network analysis as a research approach for studying interaction of social actors. In January 2012, she received an award for two publications in international peer-reviewed journals from the Marta Turchyn's Foundation.

Anastasiya Ryabchuk received her MPhil from the University of Cambridge, UK, and PhD from the Kyiv National University, Ukraine. She is currently teaching at the Department of Sociology at Kyiv-Mohyla Academy, Ukraine, and is a research fellow at the South African Research Chair in Social Change at the University of Johannesburg, South Africa. Her research interests include poverty, homelessness and urban marginality, labour and the labour movement, and qualitative research methods.

Ann-Mari Sätre is Associate Professor of Economics and a senior lecturer/researcher at the Centre of Russian and Eurasian Studies at Uppsala University, Sweden. She specializes in the structure and performance of the Soviet/Russian economy. Her current research focuses on poverty, local development and women's work in Russia. Her key publications include 'Paid and Unpaid Social Work in Russia. Is Women's Social Work opening up Opportunities for Empowerment Processes?' (*International Social Work*, 2014); *Vild kapitalism och gammal byråkrati. Om småföretagare i Ryssland* (2007); 'Women's and Men's Work in Transitional Russia. Impacts from the Soviet System' (*Post-Soviet Affairs*, 2001) and *Environmental Problems in the Shortage Economy: The legacy of Soviet environmental policy* (1994).

Hanna Söderbaum is a PhD candidate in the Department of Economic History at Uppsala University, Sweden. Her research is focused on the growth of 'giving', or 'philanthropy', among the political and business elites in post-Soviet Ukraine. The dissertation explores the self-representation and deeds of the established giving institutions. Her research interests include power elites, post-Soviet transformation and corporate social responsibility.

Alexander Soldatkin is Associate Professor in the Department of Economic Sociology at Lobachevsky State University of Nizhni Novgorod, Russia. He is a sociologist focusing on the issues of quality of life in contemporary Russia, especially in urban context. His current research concentrates on socio-technological aspects of quality of life and on migration to and from smaller cities and towns. His recent publications concern socio-economic aspects of poverty in small towns.

Irina Tiurikova is a candidate of Science and a lecturer in Social and Political Philosophy at the Institute of Social and Political Sciences, Northern Arctic Federal University in Archangelsk, Russia. Her research interests include multiculturalism and migration studies, issues of democracy and social justice, and gender studies.

Alla Varyzgina is a Sociologist PhD candidate in the Department of Economic Sociology at Lobachevski State University of Nizhni Novgorod, Russia, and a researcher at the UNN-ISEPN RAN joint Laboratory for the Study of the population's quality of life as a basis of social management. Her current research focuses on poverty and strategies of overcoming poverty in Russia. Her most recent publications include (in Russian) *Strategies of Overcoming Poverty of Families with Children: Applying to social services agencies* (2012); *Stigmatization of Poverty as an Obstacle to Social Relationship* (2013); *Efficiency of Strategies of Overcoming Poverty of Poor Families* (2013); and *The Efficiency of Low-income Families' Appeal to Socially Oriented NGOs* (2014).

Attitudes, Poverty and Agency in Russia and Ukraine

Ann-Mari Sätre

One of the main ideas behind this special issue was that we wanted to trace continuities from the Soviet time to post-Soviet Russia. There are many similarities between Russia and Ukraine, indicating such a continuation. Russia and Ukraine had a lot in common in terms of culture, language and history, partly also because of their common slavic origin. After the dissolution of the Soviet Union, however, the two independent countries chose somewhat different routes of development. This makes it possible to distinguish between the effects of politics/reforms on the one hand, and impacts from the Soviet system, on the other. After some more or less chaotic development paths in the 1990s, showing clear differences between the two countries, and before the contemporary conflict broke out in Eastern Ukraine (2013) in the early years of the second decade of this century, they had once again more similarities in terms of political leadership and policies in general.

The various papers, which were presented during eight workshops in 2011–2013, financed by a grant from the Swedish Institute, provide the primary source to this special issue. Seven of the contributions have been developed into separate articles to be published in this Special Issue, two on Ukraine and five on two regions in Russia: Nizhny Novgorod and Archangelsk.[1] Two of the articles concern attitudes towards poverty and poor people (Varyzgina and Kay; Ryabchuk). Two concern strategies of the poor (Asztalos Morell and Tiurikova; Sätre, Soldatkin and Varyzgina), while three of the articles focus on policies against poverty (Ivashinenko; Kostiuchenko and Söderbaum; Sätre). One common pattern concerns the tendency to return to attitudes which were dominant under socialism, when citizenship was defined in a way based on work. If you did not work, you did not contribute to the building of socialism. Not to work was illegal, it was considered deviant. In the 1990s, when everybody was poor in the aftermath of the perestroika processes, it was considered legitimate to be poor. However, the mass unemployment that some researchers waited for did not happen, soft budgets continue to be both a Russian and a Ukrainian practice and overemployment remained an accepted practice in both state institutions and private firms. In addition, attitudes changed back towards earlier ones. In the 2000s, as a significant number of people were able to start firms and in other ways pull themselves out of poverty, it became unacceptable to be poor, and the "blaming the victim" mentality reappeared. Attitudes to poverty are crucial as they feed into both strategies and policies to meet problems of poverty in politics as well as society in general (Varyzgina and Kay; Ryabchuk). Hence, the supporting role of institutions is especially important when considering the possibilities for poor people themselves to take actions (Ivashinenko; Sätre et.al.). The demise of the Soviet Union led to clear reductions in social services. Although social welfare provision has increased since then, in both countries, the fragile system for social policy is a still existing common feature in them. The necessity of solving the worst social problems at least was high, however, and as one solution, the state and business made new kinds of unwritten deals on combatting social problems and poverty. Some of the responses to the shortcomings of social policy are highlighted (Ivashinenko; Kostiuchenko and Söderbaum; Sätre). One difference appears to be the opening up of new opportunities for the poor in Russia to benefit from National Programmes, focused on healthcare, housing, education and agriculture, implemented by the Putin administration with the help of incomes from oil and gas exports. All the contributions take the effect of transformation into account in their analyses.

Social Welfare and Combatting Poverty — A Female Responsibility

It is well-documented that female politicians were commonly responsible for social policies in the Soviet Union and that women continue to take this responsibility at all political levels in post-Soviet Russia and Ukraine. It also seems clear that female officials view women's organizations as potential allies in the social sphere, being potential providers of social services, and filling gaps in the badly shredded Russian safety net.

In terms of gender, we found two tendencies. On the one hand we hear about the feminization of poverty. Women have lower wages, more women than men have incomes below the poverty line, women are the ones who work as social workers, and who have very low pay, they do most of the unpaid work within households, it is quite evident that single parents most of the time are women. Women were the first to lose their jobs following the closing of work places in the 1990s. In both Russia and Ukraine, it is clear that gendered segregation on the labour market continues from the Soviet time. This continuity is quite remarkable, despite all the talk that women should not take jobs as long as men are unemployed, and that women should be relieved from their double burden.

But there is also another tendency pointing at women having often a capability of coping with transformation, being responsible for finding solutions to everyday problems within households as well as in their local surroundings. In the post-Soviet space, women have persisted and developed "entrepreneurial skills" that they used to have in the Soviet time. We have also seen that men have difficulties in fulfilling expectations of being the main breadwinner, failing in attempts to build up businesses, or simply failing to cope with new life circumstances (Asztalos Morell and Tiurikova).

The writers hope that this special issue will give readers new insights into interesting tendencies of poverty and into policies to reduce poverty in Russia and Ukraine, which will stimulate more systematic analyses of differences and similarities between post-Soviet countries.

Note

1. I would like to express my sincere thanks to Nina Ivashinenko for inviting me to participate in her research team at Nizhniy Novgorod Scientific Research Centre for Economics, Society and Science (EON), at Lobachevsky State University of Nizhniy Novgorod. Three contributions (and to a part also a fourth one) are based on a Russian project on poverty in the Nizhny Novgorod region in 2010–2012, in which Ivashinenko (project leader), Kay, Sätre, Soldatkin and Varyzgina, all took part.

Perceptions of Poverty in Small-town Russia

Alla Varyzgina and Rebecca Kay

The paper reviews some of the perceptions and categorizations of poverty found through a study of participatory approaches to poverty reduction in provincial Russia. It draws on theorizations of poverty as a subjective reality which is socially constructed and maybe differently perceived by different subsections of the population. The paper argues that perceptions of poverty matter, because they feed into both formal categorizations of need and entitlement to assistance or support and more informal, cultural understandings of impoverishment which may be morally and emotionally inflected.

Introduction

Poverty has been studied by sociologists, economists, anthropologists, geographers and many others for a long time. Over the years, there have been considerable developments and debates regarding the concept itself and the most useful ways of studying it. Early studies which focused primarily on economic and absolute measurements of poverty (Rowntree 1901) have subsequently been contested by others arguing for the need to explore in more depth the experiences of poor people from a variety of social, cultural and economic perspectives (Beresford et al. 1999; Lister 2007). This has included increasing acceptance in both academic and policy circles of poverty as a relative phenomenon (Townsend 1954). Amartya Sen's influential capabilities approach brought a sharp focus to debates surrounding the different ways in which poverty both affects and constrains livelihoods, well-being and agency and related this directly to pertinent questions regarding the development of effective strategies for poverty reduction (Sen 1985; Deneulin and McGregor 2010).

Further pursuit of debate and theorization of poverty as at least in part a socially constructed and culturally experienced phenomenon has often led to heated disagreements and controversies. Lewis' introduction of the concept of a "culture of poverty" in the 1960s had a perhaps unintended impact on policy debates in the USA at the time, supporting an ideologically driven view of poverty as "pathological" and transferable between generations due to the dysfunctional values and behaviours of poor people themselves (Goode and Maskovsky; 2001, 10). Diverting attention away from the structural causes of poverty, and its perpetuation, such theories were also critiqued for focusing on passivity, dependency and the negative aspect of poor people's agency, rather than giving attention to political and collective action on the part of the poor (Goode and Maskovsky; 2001, 14). As such, they contributed to much longer standing processes by which the poor are divided into "deserving" and "undeserving" categories, facilitating criteria for and, importantly, exclusions from eligibility for programmes of public support and assistance (Fraser and Gordon 2002). As Howe has pointed out, a particularly important, and pernicious, aspect of such definitions of deservingness and the moral categorizations of respectability, responsibility and contribution upon which they draw, is that these are often at least tacitly acknowledged and shared by those experiencing poverty as well as by welfare officers and other members of the community (Howe 1998). A critical analysis of locally inflected attitudes towards and understandings of poverty therefore provides a significant contribution to attempts to understand the workings of a welfare support system, both in relation to how it is conceived through policy and implemented by professional and bureaucratic personnel (cf. Lipsky 1983) and in relation to how it is experienced and understood by those living in poverty themselves.

Historically, many of the above debates and the empirical studies which they have inspired and/or drawn upon have focused on either West European and North American contexts or on the countries of "the developing world". However, in the aftermath of the collapse of communist regimes in the Former Soviet Union and Eastern Europe, there has been increasing scholarly and policy interest in issues relating to poverty and ways of dealing with it in these parts of the world also. Whilst initial approaches were dominated by statistical measurements and analyses (Korchagina, Ovcharova, and Turuntsev 1998; Shevyakov and Kiruta 2001; Ovcharova 2003; Korchagina 2005; Migranova and Korchagina 2013), more recent studies have challenged "official designations" of poverty due to their over emphasis on measuring monetary incomes and expenditures and failure to take sufficient account of other aspects of poverty such as access to public services and impacts on health and other "capabilities" (Rimashevskaya and Ovcharova 2001). Other researches (Bondarenko 2005) studied changes in perceptions of poverty during the time. Bondarenko points out differences in attitudes to poverty in the 1990's and the 2000's. In the first case, poverty in mass opinion had a very close connection to the economic situation in Russia in general and was a result of external, not personal reasons. Poverty was widespread (Bogomolova and Tapilina 2005), and at that time to be poor was a kind of norm or standard. In the 2000's the attitude towards the poor changed and moved to a relativistic one, in terms of deprivation. The division between "deserving" and "undeserving" poor came into sight.

A growing body of research in recent years has begun to interrogate the meanings and definitions of poverty and marginality in Russian and other "post-socialist" contexts from both historical and contemporary standpoints. Thus, Khlinovskaya-Rockhill's study of state provision of care for children removed from their families in both Soviet and post-Soviet contexts explores intersecting definitions of poverty and "deviance" which both transcend and inform processes of political, economic and institutional change (Khlinovskaya-Rockhill 2010). Stephenson's work on homelessness raises similar questions and concerns about the interlinking of social, cultural and economic exclusions and the designation of certain categories of the poor as "subhuman" (Stephenson 2006). Bringing insights from the local level, anthropological studies of poverty and social assistance across a range of post-socialist rural contexts have explored the ways in which constructions of poverty and need shape access to both formal and informal forms of poverty relief and service provision (Kay 2011; Thelen et al. 2011; Schwarz 2012).

This article aims to contribute to this growing body of work exploring attitudes towards and understandings of poverty, not simply for the purposes of an academic interest in unpicking and critiquing "discourse" (cf. Goode and Maskovsky 2001, 15), but rather more significantly, in order to shed light on the ways in which such understandings shape the experiences of families and individuals living with, or on the verge of poverty. The article draws on the findings of a research project exploring "Participatory approaches to Poverty reduction: perspectives from small-town Russia," for which fieldwork was conducted in a small-provincial town of Nizhegorodskaya oblast in November 2011 (the first stage of the research took place in an earlier project: "Participatory approaches to Poverty reduction: mechanisms of public participation" conducted in the city of Nizhny Novgorod in 2010) (cf. Ivashinenko 2011; Varyzgina 2012). The article draws primarily on interview data from 35 semi-structured, in-depth interviews conducted with local residents and families experiencing poverty, professionals from local social service structures, leaders of charitable and other nongovernmental organisations as well as representatives of the local administration.

Defining Poverty

Our study revealed that there was neither a shared and clear definition of poverty nor consensus about how best to reduce or overcome it amongst respondents, including those directly employed in services and structures designed to contribute to poverty-relief programmes. This lack of clarity and consensus may in part stem from an absence of public debate at both national and local levels. This is reflected in media coverage where as a recent study has found, there is much commentary on the widespread nature of poverty and generalised discussion of the problems in overcoming it, but scant if any attention to the actual causes and consequences of poverty, nor to detailed discussion of social policy initiatives (Teodorovich 2009, 452). As McKendrick et al. point out:

> Although it would be naive to attribute public attitudes towards poverty and public support for antipoverty initiatives solely to the mass media, it is important to acknowledge the pivotal role of the mass media in reflecting and influencing public ideas of poverty. (McKendrick et al. 2008, 7)

In the absence of media coverage or discussion, local residents and specialists alike struggled to judge the extent of poverty locally, confining themselves instead to generalisations and vague assessments such as "Living standards in our town are generally pretty low" (social pedagogue in a school).

This vagueness seemed in part to stem from an acknowledgement of the inadequacy of "official" definitions of poverty based on calculations of regional subsistence minimums and artificially established minimum wages, which have long been far too low for families to live well on. Some respondents, especially those with professional insight into the workings of the welfare system, did refer to these officially defined thresholds either in discussing poverty more generally or in explaining their own circumstances; however, there was often an implicit criticism in these discussions, as well as vagueness and confusion about the precise levels of thresholds:

> Well, the official version is that they are people whose income falls below the subsistence minimum. The subsistence minimum in Nizhegorodskii region is now round about 5600 rub for a working person. (Staff member, Local administration)

> The way it works out my family fits the criteria, because I'm not earning at the moment, I don't have any income at all, we have two small children, and my husband earns 15,000 rubles a month. If we're supposed to have about 6500 rubles per person in our region, then we are below the poverty line. (Lawyer-private entrepreneur, not currently claiming any benefits)

Other respondents rejected such official definitions more explicitly, sometimes pointing out that attempts to define poverty in absolute terms were out of date. They did not however use standardised definitions of relative poverty as the situation of those with incomes falling below 60% of average per capita incomes either[1]. Instead, respondents attempted to explain poverty in intuitive and often personalised terms.

Aware that many of those, who might fall above these official poverty thresholds, were nonetheless struggling to get by, respondents drew on more open understandings of poverty illustrating their observations with examples from their own experiences and those of neighbours and acquaintances. In doing, so they tended to avoid using a specific terminology of "poverty" (*bednost')* or referring directly to people as "poor" (*bednye*). If used, all these terms were referred to in the context of generalised discussions, but not when describing specific situations or people. In these more specific contexts "professional" respondents tended to use the official definition of "people with low income" (*maloimushie*). As shown in Table 1 below, both professionals and other respondents also used a range of terms referring either to people's economic and social circumstances or to their belonging to other social categories deemed synonymous with experiences of poverty.

Looking at these different categories and descriptors for poverty again, it is possible to discern four main tendencies in discussions of poverty:

- Poverty as lowered consumption, deprivation.
- Poverty as misfortune.
- Poverty as a disease and a source of danger to society.
- Poverty as stigma.

Amongst these tendencies, the first two are relatively objective and non-judgmental, the second two are much more subjective and introduce moralising discourses and value judgments to discussions of poverty as pathological and socially threatening. There is hardly any correlation between perceptions of poverty and the categories in which the interviewed fall. Teachers, social workers, unemployed, families and individuals living with or on the verge of poverty as categories do not seem to have any peculiar opinion towards poverty. All the four discourses can be represented amongst the different

Table 1. commonly used terms for describing those experiencing poverty

Terms describing circumstances	Terms using other social characteristics and identities as synonyms for poverty
Low-income citizens; Low paid; Those who live less well; People in difficult circumstances; People in impoverished circumstances; People with incomes below the subsistence minimum; People living below the lowest standards; People in need; People in need of assistance; The deeply needy; Families with limited income; People with lots of problems; Those below the poverty line; Those who are badly dressed	Families with many children; Young families; Single-parent families; Problem families; Families registered with social services; Elderly, Pensioners; Unemployed; Homeless; Alcoholic

categories of the interviewed. The following sections explore each of these tendencies in more detail.

Poverty as Lowered Consumption, Deprivation

The majority of our respondents described poverty in objective terms as an experience of material deprivation, a lack of financial and other resources and a lower standard of living. Many of them offered rather detailed descriptions of the ways in which families with low incomes were forced to restrict their consumption of goods or services. Here, poverty was defined not only in terms of low income or low consumption of objects and services, but also in terms of low quality nutrition, restrictions or lack of access to education and health care, poor housing conditions and problems with indebtedness.

> If a member of staff should notice for instance that a family is really so poor, then of course they will definitely call them up and offer to help them with clothing or maybe give them vouchers for hot food. Where there are situations like this of desperate need of course. (Professional working with children with disabilities)

> We can't afford to install PVC windows in the house, because it is very expensive, really expensive. We don't want to take out another loan. We can't pay off the debts we already have. (Mother, low income family)

In this sense our respondents reflected the arguments of Ocharova and Rimashevskaya (2001) and others that poverty cannot be measured in terms of income alone, but must take account of individuals' and families' wider access to goods, services and opportunities. Families on the edge of poverty may be forced to save on accommodation costs, nutrition, clothes or footwear. Other studies have shown that such families spend less money on holidays and leisure time and sometimes are simply unable to take holidays at all. In Klimova's study of the working poor this was the case for 50% of respondents (Klimova 2004). Such restrictions on consumption might also be seen to feed into Sen's understanding of poverty in terms of capabilities and the relationship between poor people's access to material, psychological, physical and social resources and opportunities (Sen 1985). The restricted capabilities that flow from restricted consumption do not only define their present circumstances but also circumscribe their opportunities and resources to change these circumstances for the future.

And yet, impoverished families and individuals also strive to meet the consumption norms which they see around them, perhaps as a way of inscribing their belonging to, and staving off exclusion from the wider society. Thus, several of the families we interviewed explained that as well as restricting spending in areas which might be considered fundamental such as housing or clothing, they also, on occasion, indulged in what might be viewed as non-essential spending, almost by way of compensation. Thus the same respondent who describes above the family's lack of resources for improving their housing by installing PVC windows, went on to explain:

> Yes, we have to restrict ourselves in many ways. We don't exactly live it up. We haven't got any spare for that. We don't spoil ourselves, but if we want to try something, we'll buy a little taster of something we've been really longing for. (Mother, low-income family)

Such practices might be seen to reflect Veblen's theories of "conspicuous consumption" as a striving to replicate the lifestyles and consumption of those with higher social status and greater economic security. (cf. Veblen 1994, 84)

In this sense, there was also an aspect showing tendencies to define poverty in terms of consumption which was relative and comparative. For our respondents, poverty was defined not so much in relation to someone's ability to meet the consumption norms of the rich, or even the comfortable, but rather as consumption below their own, or what they perceived as "average". Poor families were not excluded from the same desires and aspirations as everyone else, but they were unable to participate fully due to constrained resources (cf. Davidova 2003, 88–96). Respondents very rarely alluded directly to "wealth" or "poverty" as fixed categories, but rather were inclined to make statements like, "life is good for some people, for others it is difficult." In making such comparisons, people often used their own families as a standard, describing and defining poverty as "those who live worse than we do". Interestingly in this way, they maintained a perception or representation of their own family as "normal" or "average," even where in some cases they too may have been coping in rather constrained circumstances, or even have per capita incomes which would see them officially designated as "poor." This reluctance to categorise one's own experiences as poverty will be returned to below in the section on poverty as stigma.

Poverty as Misfortune

For a significant subset of our respondents, poverty was viewed primarily as the result of misfortune, a consequence of external circumstances that people could not themselves control, for example the state of the national economy, fire damage to one's house, redundancy etc. Understanding poverty in this way has deep historical roots in Russian culture (Teodorovich 2009, 10). Indeed, the words "poverty" (*bednost'*) and misfortune or trouble (*beda*) are etymologically linked. In the early period of post-socialist transformations studies in a number of countries found that poverty was viewed in this way as a widespread misfortune, imposed on people as victims of the "transition process" and as such, unequivocally the responsibility of the state. (Falowska 1997 cited in Studenna 2010, 196). And yet, more recent studies have revealed that as the immediate crisis of transformation has passed and increasing stratification in these societies has resulted in greater differentiation, new "neoliberal" understandings of poverty as individualised and pathological also converge in sometimes mutually reinforcing ways with an emphasis on labour participation and contribution from the era of state socialism (Kay 2011; Thelen et al. 2011).

Nonetheless in our study, respondents did continue to recognise poverty, at least in some instances, as the consequence of circumstances beyond the individual's control. Redundancies and wage insecurities brought about by the closure of the town's major industrial employers for example, were seen to have affected many and in a rather arbitrary fashion. As one professional (from the district centre for social—economic monitoring) explained, "There are problems everywhere. Firstly, two of our big factories have closed down. That means people lost jobs and wages." Other examples of poverty as misfortune described in interviews included several references to homelessness as the result of fire in the town's many wooden houses, and the loss of a breadwinner through ill health, death or divorce. In cases of this nature, families were commonly viewed as deserving of support and assistance and charitable actions as well as informal collective assistance were often mobilised.

> If someone is in trouble, everyone in school helps out. Last winter there was an accident – a house burned down, an old, wooden one. It happened at night and the people ran out into the snow, barely dressed. They didn't manage to take anything with them from the house. First, teachers and kids from the school brought things for them. Then when everyone else in our settlement got to know about it, we had a collection and they started to bring more things. When someone experiences a misfortune, everyone helps out. It's the done thing. (Social pedagogue, local secondary school)

Redundancy was also generally viewed as a misfortune both for the person directly affected and for their families. However, as explored in more detail in the following section long-term worklessness, especially where this is accompanied by addiction and other social or family issues are often viewed with considerably less sympathy.

Losing a job was described by many as synonymous with an experience of poverty. And yet, statistics show that at least 50% of the poor in contemporary Russia can best be described as "working poor," in other words those whose work is precarious and poorly paid (Bobkov, Zinin, and Rasumov 2004, 40). Our respondents certainly also related to the image of the working poor and frequently offered examples from amongst their acquaintances of kindergarten teachers, school teachers, public-sector employees, all of whom they saw as experiencing poverty due to circumstances beyond their control, namely the structure of wages and the wider economic situation in the country. As one school teacher explained,

> People can work from dawn till dusk, at two different jobs, but they don't have the right qualifications and so the jobs are low paid. Or it might be a worker in the public sector, on a middle or low pay scale. They find themselves in difficult circumstances which are basically beyond their control. (School teacher in smaller rural settlement)

Dedication to a low paid job and a reluctance to seek alternative employment was not regarded as evidence of laziness or dysfunction, although the overt rejection of such interpretations by respondents may suggest that they are not so uncommon.

> If someone has low wages, it doesn't mean that they are lazy. They might work hard from dawn till dusk and still have a low income. So it's hard to see how they can get out of this situation? (School teacher, social pedagogue)

Such assertions seem to tally with the self-perceptions and self-representation of the working poor themselves who do not see themselves as lazy or personally responsible for their predicament but rather as members of the "deserving poor" often associated with taking an active, rather than "passive" position through employment and other engagements (Howe 1998; Kay 2011).

Where poverty is interpreted in these ways, responsibility for finding solutions is placed squarely in the realm of the state and government. As one trade union leader put it:

> To be honest, responsibility for family poverty is a state responsibility. Heads of local administration, governors, the government should deal with it... It should be solved by the state and through the use of government resources at a local, federal, municipal level. Clearly defined steps need to be taken. The first thing to solve is the minimum wage." (Trade Union Leader)

As explained above, even a permanent job is not enough to guarantee sufficient income in order for a family to escape an experience of poverty (Bobkov, Zinin, and Rasumov 2004, 15) and a low wage "trap" keeps people fully occupied in one or several jobs, in some cases impacting negatively on their health or family relationships and reducing their capabilities to engage in other activities which might mitigate long- term family poverty. And yet, respondents agreed that unemployment was an even more serious problem.

For most of our interviewees, there was a strong automatic association between unemployment and poverty. Amongst the professionals interviewed, unemployment was often raised as the most significant factor influencing not only poverty but a wider and connected range of social issues in the town.

> As they say, trouble always comes in threes. It works out like this: there are redundancies, then there are problems at home, parents are lost, or heaven forbid something happens to a child. Everyone's situation is different, but they come to us and their eyes are so empty. We try to support them, to get them to take themselves in hand. You have to feel sorry for people. Obviously it is not their fault that all this has happened, but then all these other problems

> start coming down on them too. It's a shame for everyone. (Employment center section leader)

Thus, loss of employment can quickly become associated with wider patterns of social insecurity and exclusion, where those without work are not seen as making a useful social contribution and quickly lose social status and respectability (cf. Kay 2011). This can make redundancies and periods of unemployment, especially where they are protracted, difficult for people to accept. Whilst redundancy itself may be seen as an external misfortune, the problems it brings with it such as psychological issues, family breakdown, alcoholism, loss of social contacts, social exclusion and apathy may be viewed more equivocally. Amongst our respondents, there was a degree of understanding of the difficulties of dealing with unemployment, especially in the longer term, and yet, the extent to which people are able to cope in socially acceptable ways significantly influenced assessments of "deservingness" and the apportioning of responsibility for one's own predicament.

> In our settlement for example, alcoholism is on the rise, it's just booming. And what's more women are drinking too, they are becoming drunkards. You see them walking about, they look in a right state. ... It's mainly people with low incomes. And what can you do? If there's no work to be had, you start getting into debt. I watched my neighbour fall to drink in just 3 years. Now he is a total alcoholic. He used to have a family: husband, wife, two children. They were a great family, with no problems. Everything was great. He worked, she worked, their sons were grown up, one got married, the other went to the army. But then there was some kind of conflict between them and his wife left. He took to drinking. He drank everything away, the house, the garage, the car, everything. (Lawyer, entrepreneur)

As stated above, unemployment in and of itself was generally viewed as an external misfortune, and even the pull to drink amongst those who had lost their jobs was sometimes viewed with understanding. Respondents interpreted this sometimes as a response to the psychological shock of redundancy and a temporary symptom of a person in need of assistance and support from those around them. However, quite the opposite was true of those seen as succumbing to heavy drinking as a life-style choice. Here, some far more judgmental attitudes towards poverty and its associated misfortunes came to the fore.

Poverty as a disease and a source of danger to society

Discussions of poverty with our respondents revealed different levels of emotional engagement with poverty and its various manifestations and experiences. Whilst some took a rather distant and analytical stance, others expressed feelings of empathy towards the poor. Yet others revealed highly judgmental attitudes, distancing themselves morally and socially from the poor who were blamed for their own predicament and viewed as rather threatening and dangerous. In the words of one young mother, "Where there's poverty, there's always someone who's a drunk, either the mother or the father, but one way or another" (*a young mother*). Here and elsewhere poverty was described not as the result of an external misfortune but as a symptom of deviance and pathology within the family and of poor people themselves. This was also the case in discussion with professional respondents. For example a psychologist who viewed poverty and alcoholism as closely interrelated, explained, "It's very closely linked to alcoholism. If you take the example of an alcoholic, then he is usually someone who has lost his job and lives on the verge of poverty if he's not already at rock bottom. These people are most often unemployed" (*Psychologist at NGO*). Families experiencing long-term unemployment, poverty and alcoholism were viewed by many respondents as social parasites, bringing problems to those around them and for the wider society. Whilst their needs might have to be met, this was seen as an undeserved form of assistance and a burden on society.

Echoing Lewis' theorizations of the "culture of poverty" (Lewis 1966) as transferable between generations, respondents sometimes also used references to disease, inherent weakness and even a risk of infection in describing poverty as a social scourge. Here, particular attention was paid to the upbringing of children in poor families, and whilst there may be some sympathy for the difficulties children experience, there were also many assumptions about categories of "problem families."

> I teach the 8th grade. I know there are 3—4 low income families in the class of which one is a large single-parent family. They live with just their dad, and it has to be said he's not much of a dad. There are some older brothers and sisters, but I teach the younger girls. They're a real problem. They have difficulties all the time with studying, and everything is just always somehow not quite right with them. There are low income families, and there are children from single-parent families. There are families where it's just Mum. That is Dad did his thing and disappeared off somewhere. You see other children, who have a mum and a dad, and you can see they are strong and sure of themselves. These children just aren't like that. They are already kind of "coming apart at the seams" or something. Maybe it's because mums who are trying to be both mum and dad are too domineering, maybe that's why they turn out so weak and weedy. (School teacher, small rural settlement)

Another professional respondent took this analogy of weakness, infection and pathology a step further specifically describing such families as "socially dangerous:"

> We don't have a specific institution to provide social assistance to these families. Basically for low income families, large families, those who as a rule have a low standard of living and other socially dangerous families. (Member of staff, rehabilitation center for disabled children)

Attitudes of this nature appear to resonate closely with views of poverty as deviance and the individualization of pathology and blame, which have been associated elsewhere with the discourses and policies of neoliberalism (cf. Goode and Maskovsky 2001; Kingfisher 2001). Indeed, they may well draw on new economic and political contexts. However, it is also important to point out that similar discourses particularly in relation to single-parents, alcoholism and worklessness can be traced through the period of state socialism, adding a degree of familiarity and continuity to such rhetoric which can make it all the more widespread and socially acceptable. (cf. Stephenson 2006; Khlinovskaya-Rockhill 2010)

Continuing this trend, questions of children and their upbringing were also specifically linked to issues of work ethic and a culture of employment, or its lack, which had particular connotations for views on deservingness and need in such families:

> The kids pick this up from their parents. They aren't taught from children, they don't see their parents working so they don't have any example to follow. Children from low income families aren't hard-workers; they don't know how to work, they don't have it in them. Children from better off families, they are the ones who work. They get it. They see their parents working and they work themselves. Children from low income families are lazy. That's why they are poor, that's where it all comes from. Even the children are lazy, very-very lazy. They want money, but they don't want to work for it. (Mother, low-income family)

An interesting point about this particular interviewee was that her participation in the study came about on the basis of a recommendation from a local charitable organisation where she and her family had been receiving assistance. Although she revealed little of her personal circumstances during the interview and constantly distanced herself morally from the low-income families who she saw as deviant and worthy of blame, her clothing and demeanour as well as the description of her family provided by the head of the charity, suggested her own circumstances were far from comfortable. Here, we see then an example of Howe's point that those experiencing poverty, or on the verge of it, are not immune to the wider moralising discourses and normative understandings of virtue which circulate in their social context (Howe 1998). Moreover, where poverty is stigmatised and poor families or individuals blamed for their own predicament, or worse still viewed as potentially threatening to the rest of society, the motivation to differentiate oneself and one's family from such a category is increased.

Poverty as Stigma

As demonstrated in the previous example, respondents were keen to distance themselves from experiences of poverty, and even those who expressed more generally sympathetic attitudes to the misfortunes of others, had no desire to be seen as part of this group themselves (Varyzgina 2013). Many respondents, who discussed the problems of impoverished fellow townspeople and families, emphasised in conclusion that they were not poor themselves, accentuating the point that they have nothing in common with the poor. Some explicitly commented on the difficulty of admitting to experiences of poverty, "They won't name themselves poor. As for myself, I won't call myself poor, because I don't want to be in such a category" (*Mother of large, low-income family*). Even those who were open about experiencing financial and other difficulties were reluctant to claim a label of "poverty" which is stigmatised and which, they explained, could lead others to distance themselves leading to further isolation and additional problems as a result. Families expressed particular concern about the impact this could have on children:

> It's easy to see the attitudes which other children have towards children from low-income families. They are scornful of them. There's a girl Sveta, she's from a low income family. They aren't all that nice to her. Firstly, she's not as well dressed; sometimes the zip on her trousers won't fasten, something must be broken with it. She went around with an open zip for days. I don't know what her parents are thinking of. Because you might not live well, but that doesn't mean that you should simply not look after your children properly. How can it be – not to notice your child's zip is broken? You can always fix it, sew on a new one. So they (the children) weren't very nice to her. They were like "don't sit next to us." I tell them they shouldn't be like that. How would you feel if somebody treated you that way? Would you like it? So I try to bring them in line. They do OK as long as I'm there, but once they're away from me .... (Leader of children's club, mother of young son, divorced, living with parents)

Other professionals, often teachers, pointed out that the question of consumption and the need to fit in with wider social norms in this sense, as discussed earlier, was also often a cause of concern for children and could complicate relationships between children and parents in families with restricted means. It was argued that whilst some children understood their parents' predicament and asked for very little, others tried to push their parents to give them things so that they would not fall behind in comparison to the consumption of their peers. For these children, poverty was already recognised as shameful and they sought to hide any issues from those around them.

> Children have definitely became more materialistic as you might say. Things matter to them. Almost everyone has a computer. But still there are families who can't afford it. And children, some of them are very ashamed of it. Some try to conceal the poverty of their family. Some children make demands on their parents: "give me it, buy it for me. I don"t want to look worse than the others'. Problems like that. And somehow it then grows into a bigger problem in the relationships between children and their parents. I've come across families like this. At first the parents try, they buy the children this and that, but then they don't know what to do. This is also where it all comes from. They don't have the money, but they try all the same, and in the end ..." (Teacher)

As this teacher points out, parents in low-income families can find themselves in an impossible set of circumstances. They do not wish to upset their children, or to expose them to stigma, ridicule or isolation from other children. They also strive to conceal their poverty and fear that teachers and others may see them as "bad" parents and undeserving families, because they are perceived not to care for their children properly or to fulfil the duties of good, respectable parents. As the teacher's commentary regarding the girl with the broken zip in the previous quotation shows, such censorious attitudes do exist. The stigma of poverty therefore puts added demands on constrained budgets and on the often limited time resources of low- income parents, and as such, may further reduce the capacities of these families to deal effectively with their circumstances.

Perhaps, nowhere was this more clearly demonstrated than in the reluctance of some of the most materially and financially insecure to seek, or even to accept assistance, particularly if this comes with a "label" of poverty. This was reflected in the first stage of research for this project, when interviews conducted in the social service departments in Nizhny Novgorod revealed a particular reluctance on the part of respondents to talk about benefit claims based on means testing or other categorizations of "poverty" and "need." By contrast those benefits that were viewed as entitlements based on contributions and positive identity categories such as old-age pensions, payments for veterans and entitlements for parents or children were discussed openly and claimed as a "right" rather than necessarily on the basis of "need." Similarly in interviews and more informal discussions which took place during the second stage of the research, respondents presented mixed attitudes to claiming benefits. On the one hand, some of the apparently most needy (based on their descriptions of their housing conditions, health concerns, ratio of wageearners to other family members etc.) were cautious about claiming benefits or accepting assistance, for example in the form of second-hand clothes for their children or vouchers for free meals, insisting instead "I can clothe my children myself!" On the other hand, respondents who certainly also experienced constrained circumstances, but were able to present themselves as "respectable" and "deserving" through their employment and/or family status, were much more assertive and open about claiming entitlements and pooling resources. For example a young mother, working as a production assistant at a local television station and living together with her husband, children and her parents explained that they had applied for child benefits, even though she saw the sums received as derisory.

> Sure we get free milk and dairy products for my son. We also get 100 rubles in child benefit. It's a laughable sum of money. And to get it you have to collect all sorts of references, proving that you are really in need. Social work specialists came to our home to inspect our housing conditions and see if we really are poor. They asked us if we manage our household separately from that of my parents. We said "yes, that's why we have two fridges" We stocked them

> up in advance so they were full of food. I don't know if they believed us or not. (Mother with a young son, divorced, living with parents)

This narrative is interesting in that it reveals both a confidence in this particular respondent in claiming her entitlements, but also the potential humiliations and uncertainties of the process involved. Moreover, the detail regarding the fridges adds an interesting ambiguity even to this case. Ensuring the fridges are well stocked is evidence that the two households are not interdependent and therefore must be separately means tested, but also demonstrates a certain level of "respectability" and "self-reliance" that proves "deservingness" even if it might run counter to claims of more desperate need. It is not difficult to imagine how such "performance" and "identity management" might be too challenging for others, particularly those who feel most precarious in their material and/or social status.

However, a reluctance to claim benefits might backfire for poor people or families as a way of achieving a more respectable or deserving status. Indeed, failure to claim benefits and entitlements was referred to by several respondents as the ultimate evidence of a "passive" and "lazy" response to poverty, which was heavily criticized.

> We try to work with families with low incomes, but they are too lazy even to apply for benefits. They say that they are busy, but we know them, they're just too lazy to get all the necessary documents together and to go and register. (Professional, social pedagogue in school)

> If a person doesn't want to help themselves, you can't make them, they just won't do anything. We know some families like that. Some of them are lazy, some just don't believe they will get anything. It depends on a person's nature, a willingness to achieve, a degree of persistence. (Young mother)

Thus, just as with the question of consumption and children's demands discussed above, families with low incomes and especially those experiencing more severe forms of poverty and social exclusion can find themselves in a catch twenty-two situation. Perceptions of "deservingness" demand an active stance, a willingness and ability to provide for oneself and one's family as far as possible and a particular performance of respectability and self-confidence. Those who feel unable to maintain this and withdraw from contact with social service structures, or seek to avoid making claims that might expose them and their families to unwanted scrutiny, may face further criticism for "passivity" and "laziness" falling further into a perceived category of "undeservingness" as a result.

Conclusions

This paper has reviewed some of the perceptions and categorizations of poverty found in our study of a smalltown in provincial Russia. We draw on theorizations of poverty as a subjective reality which is socially constructed and may be differently perceived by different subsections of the population. We argue that perceptions of poverty matter because they feed into both formal categorizations of need and entitlement to assistance or support and more informal, cultural understandings of impoverishment which may be morally and emotionally inflected. As such, poor people's access to support, both formal and informal, the extent of their inclusion in wider social structures and environments and the capabilities these forms of in/exclusion open or close for them are to some degree determined through perceptions of poverty, the attribution of responsibility and blame and concepts of deservingness and respectability.

The paper also makes it clear that certain values and moralities are often shared by those experiencing a range of degrees of material comfort or insecurity. As such, perceptions of poverty and representations (including self-representations) of the poor are shaped by an acute awareness of and wish to distance oneself and one's family from stigma, blame and social censure. What is also important here is that such representations feed into and inform interpretations of practices, including those related to consumption and claiming of benefits which have a direct further impact for the predicament of poor families both in the present time and in terms of their future prospects for improving their circumstances.

Acknowledgements

Field research in Russia has been organised and made together with Nina Ivashinenko, Alexander Soldatkin, Ann-Mari Sätre, and Margarita Lobanova. We want to express our gratitude to them and to several other persons who participated in research work in different important roles.

Funding

The authors greatly appreciate funding from the Nizhny Novgorod Scientific Research Centre for Economics, Society and Science (EON), the research collaboration grant from the Swedish Institute, and funding from the Lobachevsky State University of Nizhniy Novgorod.

Note

1. See for example: http://www.poverty.org.uk/summary/social%20exclusion.shtml, or http://www.jrf.org.uk/sites/files/jrf/poverty-definitions.pdf for standardised measures of relative poverty in European contexts.

References

Beresford, P., D. Green, R. Lister, and K. Woodard. 1999. *Poverty First Hand: Poor People Speak for Themselves*. London: CPAG.

Bobkov, V. N., V. G. Zinin, and A. A. Rasumov 2004. *The Policy of Wages and Salaries*. Report for the Project Coping Poverty, Employment Assistance and Local Economic Development in north-West Federal district, Moscow, 40. http://www.ilo.org/public/russian/region/eurpro/moscow/areas/gender/events/textwagesdeskrus.pdf.

Bogomolova, T., and V. Tapilina. 2005. *The Poor in Economic Stratification of Population*. Moscow: The Studying of Poverty Problems in Russia, 7–25.

Bondarenko N. 2005. "Poverty and Poverty Perceptions According to Mass Population Surveys." *Index* 21. http://www.index.org.ru/journal/21/bond21.html

Davidova, N. M. 2003. "Deprivation Approach in Poverty Evaluation." *Sociological Research* 6: 88–96.

Deneulin, S., and J. A. McGregor. 2010. "The Capability Approach and The Politics of a Social Conception of Wellbeing." *European Journal of Social Theory* 13 (4): 501–519.

Falkowska, M. 1997. *Społeczna definicja biedy, jej zasięg i przyczyny*. Warszawa. Cited in Studenna M. social exclusion problem in postindustrial society on the example of Polish and Ukrainian coal production centers. History and Modernity. Vip. No. 1 (11) 2010, 196.

Fraser, N., and L. Gordon. 2002. "A Genealogy of Dependency. Tracing a Keyword of the US Welfare State." In *The Subject of Care Feminist Perspectives on Dependency*, edited by E. F. Kittay and E. K. Feder, 14–39. Oxford: Rowman and Littlefield.

Goode, J., and J. Maskovsky, eds. 2001. *New Poverty Studies: The Ethnography of Power, Politics, and Impoverished People in the United States*, 10. New York: New York University Press.

Howe, L. 1998. "Scrounger, Worker, Beggarman, Cheat: The Dynamics of Unemployment and the Politics of Resistance in Belfast." *The Journal of the Royal Anthropological Institute* 3: 531–550.

Ivashinenko, N. 2011. *Diagnosis of Implementation of Participatory Mechanism for Poverty Reduction: Models and Reality*. Vestnik of Lobachevsky State University of Nizhni Novgorod. Ser. Social Sciences. 1 (21). N.Novgorod: NNGU, 23–31.

Kay, R. 2011. "(Un)caring Communities: Processes of Marginalisation and Access to Formal and Informal Care and Assistance in Rural Russia." 27 (1): 45–53.

Khlinovskaya-Rockhill, E. 2010. *Lost to the State: Family Discontinuity, Social Orphanhood and Residential Care in the Russian Far East*. Oxford: Berghahn Books.

Kingfisher, C. 2001. "Producing Disunity: The Constraints and Incitements of Welfare Work." In *The New Poverty Studies: The Ethnography of Power, Politics, and Impoverished People in the United States*, edited by J. Goode and J. Maskovsky, 273–292. New York: New York University Press.

Klimova, C. (April 8, 2004). Working Poor in Russia – A Paradoxical Regular Occurrence? FOM Data base. http://bd.fom.ru/report/cat/poor_workers/d041435.

Korchagina, I. 2005. "Poverty Level Indicators: Income, Expenses and Households' Accumulations." The Studying of Poverty Problems in Russia, Moscow, 26–38.

Korchagina, I., L. Ovcharova, and E. Turuntsev. 1998. *System of Indicators of Poverty Level in the Transitional Period in Russia*. Moscow: Russian program of economic research.

Lewis, O. 1966. "The Culture of Poverty." *Scientific American* 215 (4): 19–25.

Lipsky, M. 1983. *Street Level Bureaucracy: Dilemmas of the Individual in Public Services*. New York: Russell Sage Foundation.

Lister, R. 2007. "From Object to Subject: Including Marginalized Citizens in Policy Making." *Policy & Politics* 35 (3): 437–455.

McKendrick John, H., S. Sinclair, A. Irwin, H. O'Donnell, G. Scott, and L. Dobbie. 2008. *The Media, Poverty and Public Opinion in the UK*. Glasgow Caledonian University First published 2008 by the Joseph Rowntree Foundation, 72 pp. ISBN: 978-1-85935-667-8 (pdf) A pdf version of this publication is available from the JRF website www.jrf.org.uk

Migranova, L., and I. Korchagina. 2013. "Level and Quality of Life of Population of Small Towns in Russia (the example of Nizhegorodskaya region)." In *Participatory Approach in Improving the Quality of Life: Monograph*, edited by N. M. Rimashevskaya, and N. N. Ivashinenko, 38–120. Moscow: Publishing House of the Nizhny Novgorod State University.

Ovcharova, L. 2003. *Conception of Studying of Households Welfare and their Participation in Programs of Social Help: Project to Promote the Restructuring of the Social Welfare System*. Moscow: SPIL 3.2.1a/29.

Rimashevskaya, N. M., and L. N. Ovcharova. 2001. *Predlozheniya k strategii sodeystviya sokrashcheniya bednosti v Rossii: analiz i rekomendatsii* [Proposals for a Strategy to Facilitate the reduction of Poverty in Russia: Analysis and Recommendations]. Moskva, www.ilo.org/public/russian/region/eurpro/moscow/info/.../rep_ru_edit.pdf (data obrashcheniya: 20.08.2014).

Rowntree, B. S. 1901. *Poverty: A Study of Town Life*. London: Macmillan.

Schwarcz, Gy. 2012. "Ethnicizing Poverty through Social Security Provision in Rural Hungary." *Journal of Rural Studies* 28 (2): 99–107.

Sen, A. 1985. *Commodities and Capabilities*. Amsterdam: North-Holland.

Shevyakov, A., and A. Kiruta. 2001. *Economic Inequality, Standarts of Life and Poverty of Population of Russia: Methods of Measurement and Analysis of Causal Relations*. Moscow: RPEI.

Stephenson, S. 2006. *Crossing the Line: Vagrancy, Homelessness and Social Displacement in Russia*. Aldershot: Ashgate.

Teodorovich, M. 2009. *Poverty as a Social; Problem: Strategic Approach*. Nizhny Novgorod: Monograph, 452.

Thelen, T., S. Dorondel, A. Szöke, and L. Vetters. 2011. "The Sleep has been Rubbed from Their Eyes': Social Citizenship and the Reproduction of Local Hierarchies in Rural Hungary and Romania." *Citizenship Studies* 15 (3–4): 513–527.

Townsend, P. 1954. "Measuring Poverty." *British Journal of Sociology* 5: 130–137.

Varyzgina, A. 2012. Strategies of Overcoming Poverty of Families with Children: Applying to Social Services Agencies. Vestnik of Lobachevsky State University of Nizhni Novgorod. Ser. Social sciences. 2 (26) N. Novgorod: NNGU, 15–21

Varyzgina, A. 2013. "Stigmatization of Poverty as an Obstacle to Social Relationship." In *Participatory Approach in Improving the Quality of Life: Monograph*, edited by N. M. Rimashevskaya and N. N. Ivashinenko, 189–197. Moscow: Publishing House of the Nizhny Novgorod State University.

Veblen, T. 1994. *The Theory of the Leisure Class*. New York: Dover Thrift Editions, 84.

Transliteration

Bobkov V.N., Zinin V.G., Razumov A.A. Politika dohodov i zarabotnoi platy. Doklad v ramkah proekta MOT "Preodolenie bednosti, sodeistvie zanyatosti i mestnoe ekonomicheskoe razvitie v Severo-Zapadnom federal'nom okruge. — M., 2004. http://www.ilo.org/public/russian/region/eurpro/moscow/areas/gender/events/textwagesdeskrus.pdf

Bondarenko, N. Bednost I problem ee vospriyatiya soglasno massovim oprosam naseleniya \\ Index, №21, 2005 http://www.index.org.ru/journal/21/bond21.html

Tat'yana Bogomolova, Vera Tapilina. Bednye v ekonomicheskoi stratifikacii naseleniya \\ Izuchenie problem bednosti v Rossii . — M.: «Aleks», 2005. — 224 s., s. 7–25
Davydova N.M. Deprivacionnyi podhod v ocenkah bednosti // Sociologicheskie issledovaniya. 2003. 6. S. 88–96
Ivashinenko N.N. Diagnostika potenciala vnedreniya mehanizma obshestvennogo uchastiya dlya preodoleniya bednosti: modeli i real'nost' // Vestnik Nizhegorodskogo universiteta im. N.I. Lobachevskogo. Seriya Social'nye nauki. 1(21) N. Novgorod: Izd-vo NNGU im. N.I. Lobachevskogo, 2011 s.23–32.
Klimova S. Rabotayushie bednye v Rossii – paradoksal'naya zakonomernost'? \\ Baza dannyh FOM, 08.04.2004, http://bd.fom.ru/report/cat/poor_workers/d041435
Korchagina I., Ovcharova L., Turuncev E. Sistema indikatorov urovnya bednosti v perehodnyi period v Rossii. Nauchnyi doklad 98/04. Rossiiskaya programma ekonomicheskih issledovanii. M., 1998.
Korchagina I. Pokazateli urovnya bednosti: dohody, rashody i nakoplennoe imushestvo \\ Izuchenie problem bednosti v Rossii . — M.: «Aleks», 2005. — 224 s., s. 26–38
Migranova L.A., Korchagina I.I. Uroven' i kachestvo zhizni naseleniya malyh gorodov Rossii (na primere Nizhegorodskoi oblasti) \\ Participatorni podhod dlya povysheniya kachestva zhizni naseleniya. Monografiya. Pod obshei redakciei N.M. Rimashevskoi, N.N. Ivashinenko, Nizhnii Novgorod-Moskva: Izd-vo Nizhegorodskogo gosuniversiteta im. N.I.Lobachevskogo, 2013. 268s., s. 38–120
Rimashevskaya, N.M., and L.N. Ovcharova. Predlozheniya k strategii sodeistviya sokrasheniya bednosti v Rossii: analiz i rekomendacii. Moskva, 2001, s.9 www.ilo.org/public/russian/region/eurpro/moscow/info/.../rep_ru_edit.pdf
Ovcharova L.N. Koncepciya obsledovaniya blagosostoyaniya domohozyaistv i ih uchastiya v programmah social'noi pomoshi // Proekt sodeistviya strukturnoi perestroike sistemy social'noi zashity naseleniya, SPIL 3.2.1a/29. Moskva, 2003
Shevyakov, A. Yu., and A. Ya. Kiruta. 2001. Ekonomicheskoe neravenstvo, uroven' zhizni i bednost' naseleniya Rossii: metodi izmerenia I analiz prichinnih zavisimostei. Moskva: RPEI, 84 s.
Teodorovich M.L. Bednost' kak social'naya problema: strategicheskii podhod: Monografiya. – Nizhnii Novgorod, 2009. – 452 str.
Varyzgina A.A. Strategii preodoleniya bednosti sem'yami s det'mi: vzaimodeistvie s sluzhbami social'noi zashity naseleniya \\ Vestnik Nizhegorodskogo universiteta im. N.I. Lobachevskogo: Seriya Social'nye nauki. 2(26) N. Novgorod: Izd-vo NNGU im. N.I. Lobachevskogo, 2012, s. 15–21. ISSN 1811-5942
Varyzgina A.A. Stigmatizaciya bednosti kak prepyatstvie social'nomu vzaimodeistviyu \\ Partisipatorni podhod v povyshenii kachestva zhizni naseleniya. Monografiya. Pod obshei redakciei N.M. Rimashevskoi, N.N. Ivashinenko, Nizhnii Novgorod-Moskva: Izd-vo Nizhegorodskogo gosuniversiteta im. N.I. Lobachevskogo, 2013. 268s., s. 189–197

Homelessness in Ukraine: Structural Causes and Moral Evaluation

Anastasiya Ryabchuk

Homelessness is seen among the most visible forms of urban marginality in post-soviet countries. As changes in the labour and housing markets led to a growing number of the homeless in Ukrainian cities, social policy moved towards moral evaluation of the homeless individual as "deserving" or "undeserving" which is unlikely to resolve the problem of homelessness at a structural level. On the contrary, affordable housing and access to decent work as universal rights guaranteed to all should be among the priorities of state policy and non-governmental institutions alike.

Introduction

An old woman approaches me in the street, asking to help her find her home. "It should not be far, but I do not see it. It is a small house, not like these palaces". Her name is Katerina, she does not remember her age, last name or her address. All she has with her is a handkerchief, a pair of glasses and a bag of instant noodles. She says she does not have children and lives alone in the village. I take her to the police station where I write a report (using a standardised form) about "an elderly citizen approaching me with a request for help" and ask the policemen what will happen next.

This paper is based on ethnographic work conducted in 2003–2004 (participant observation as a volunteer in a Christian NGO providing food and clothing to the homeless in the streets of Kyiv, 60 interviews with the homeless) and 2008–2009 (visits to various organisations working with the homeless in Ukraine, interviews with social workers, discourse analysis of press publications and official websites of key ministries dealing with homelessness), in the framework of my PhD thesis at Kyiv-Mohyla Academy and Ecole des Hautes Etudes en Sciences Sociales.

Katerina's prospects are quite bleak. Had she just left one of the apartment blocks ("the palaces"), her relatives or neighbours would have by now noticed her absence and called the police. She is too old to walk long distances, so there can only be two options: either she lives nearby, or she was brought there by someone. Brought there? Yes, a policeman responds calmly to my surprise, this has happened many times before. Somebody finds and elderly lonely person in a village near Kyiv, where land is expensive. They make her sign papers of giving the house as a gift or selling it for a symbolic price. Then they just take her to Kyiv and leave her in the street for police to pick her up and place her in a grim Soviet-style retirement home, where she will die in a year or two.

What surprises me most is not the housing affair scheme itself, but the calm matter-of-fact way of telling about it. The policemen are kind and polite, they offer Katerina some tea with biscuits, and they immediately start looking for phone numbers of social services and retirement homes. The housing affair is just taken as a given, as an independent variable. "This has happened many times before". And yet, the immediate function of the police is not to provide elderly homeless with tea, but to deal with these affairs, to punish the criminals and to prevent such situations from occurring in the future.

Another important issue is at stake here. In this story, the policemen are trying to help, and the homeless woman is perceived as "deserving" our support. But in a perspective that is based on moral evaluation of the homeless individual, he or she is totally dependent on the goodwill of the benefactor—the policeman, the doctor, the social worker, the employment officer, etc. In another recent encounter, a homeless man, who was beaten up by the street children, asked me to call the ambulance, but it refused to take him. The doctors just looked at the dying man (he died a week later on the street), and began shouting at me: "You knew we would not take this *bomzh,* why call us? What if somebody dies while we're wasting our time here?"

When I protested, they began to describe the situation in hospitals with a lack of beds for all patients, lack of medications and low salaries for medical personnel. Again, the under-financing of the health-care system, where doctors with limited resources are forced to choose whom to help and whom to leave dying, is simply taken as a given.

Moral evaluation of the homeless will always include these alternatives of pity or condemnation, charity or repression, or mere indifference. In this framework, it is indeed for the concrete policeman or doctor to decide based on his or her moral criteria whether to be kind, indifferent or aggressive at the encounter of a homeless person on the street. But the function of policemen or health care workers is not to evaluate the homeless as "good" or "bad", "deserving" or "undeserving"; it is to guarantee basic rights of housing, medical assistance, protection from crime. Why is it that moral judgment of the individual is the starting point in the construction of homelessness as a social problem?

The few sociologists who write about homelessness in post-soviet societies also tend to focus on the homeless individuals. They do list at least some of the major structural causes of homelessness, such as lack of affordable housing, lack of decent employment opportunities, flawed social policies towards the most vulnerable. But they spend most of their time defining homelessness, estimating the number of people on the street in a given city, classifying them, or producing ethnographic accounts of a typical day of the street homeless. These accounts contribute in many important ways to our understanding of the problem, but they take as a given the structural causes of homelessness during transition from a planned to a market economy, which I intend to problematize in this paper.

Instead of focusing on homeless individuals and on the moral evaluation of whether they are "deserving" or not (whether they should be given tea or beaten up, placed in social care on in gaol), In this paper, I focus on the social construction of homelessness in Ukrainian society. I look both at the material structures (the political economy of homelessness) and at the bureaucratic field where homelessness is being produced and reproduced as a social problem, reaffirming the current social order. My research is based on participant observation in the role of a volunteer of a Christian NGO serving food to the homeless in the streets of Kyiv between fall 2002 and spring 2004, 60 interviews with the homeless, conducted at the same time, 30 interviews with social workers and volunteers assisting the homeless, conducted in 2008–2009, and discourse analysis of press publications and official websites of ministries that deal with homelessness.

Homelessness and Lack of Affordable Housing

The first most obvious structural explanation of homelessness has to do with the situation on the housing market. United Nations declared the year 1987 as "Year of shelter for the homeless" in an attempt to draw the public attention to the millions of people in the world who have no home ("absolute homeless") as well as to a billion of insecurely housed and slum-dwellers ("relative homeless"). The second category included people whose housing does not meet the basic criteria of protection from elements, access to drinking water and sanitation, work and health facilities in vicinity to the dwelling, personal safety and stability, sufficient space to avoid overcrowding (Layton 2000, 25).

The line between the absolute and the relative homeless is rather artificial as they are often just different periods of insecure housing arrangements for most homeless people. Rather than staying on the street or in homeless shelters all the time, many of them spend several nights at their friends' and relatives' homes, rent out rooms in cheap hostels and sometimes even rent out flats for a few months. For instance, Oksana, one of my respondents, came to Kyiv pregnant with her husband, who found a job in construction industry. Just after she gave birth to a baby boy, her husband fell ill and died. Since she cannot work with such a young child, she turned to panhandling in order to pay for the little room in one of the suburbs of Kyiv. The landlady insisted that she pays for each night before 6 pm, otherwise she would go to the train station to find other guests for that room.

Oksana entered a vicious circle with work only possible if the child is in day care, municipal day care being available only for those registered in Kyiv, while registration is only possible in the case of a long-term work contract and enough money to pay rent by month and not by night. Her problem could be easily resolved with a combination of affordable childcare, job opportunities for single mothers and subsidised social housing. However, municipal construction of social housing has decreased by 21 times between 1990 and 2008, even as the total number of dwellings and their total surface has been on the increase. With so little social housing on offer, it would take more than a hundred years to provide housing for all those on the waiting list.

Another category in risk of homelessness consists of people living in dilapidated housing or in buildings that are unfit for permanent residence.[1] For instance, in the historic centre of Kyiv—on 32, Gogol Street—there is a rundown house where elderly people and families with children are forced to live in dilapidated communal flats for more than two decades. The house is too worn out to be reconstructed and must be torn down. In such a situation, according to the Ukrainian housing code, residents should be given flats of equivalent size in other buildings within the city limits. The city authorities were supposed to evacuate people from this house back in 1989, but this evacuation never happened. In Kyiv alone, currently there are 107 houses that were officially declared as unfit for living by the municipality, but where people continue to live for lack of other alternatives. They regularly write letters to city authorities, initiate court trials and protest events, but their demands for decent housing remain unanswered.

In Ukraine, over 40% of the population has to survive the cold without any centralised heating and one in ten was living with room temperature below appropriate level, 23% with frequent absence of electricity, 16% without running water (almost half without hot water), with cracks in the walls and leaking ceilings (over 16%), one in ten shares a room with two or more other people.[2] In Kyiv alone, as of 2006, there were more than one hundred apartment buildings that were officially declared "unfit for living", but were still inhabited. In addition to that, the homeless, migrant workers and other vulnerable categories find shelter in many of the evacuated buildings, and city housing authorities or private structures collect unofficial payments from them.

On some occasions, overcrowded living conditions lead to grown-up children kicking out their parents or other elderly relatives from their homes. Maria sold her house in the village and moved to live with her daughter when the daughter asked for her help in taking care of her young child. But when the child reached school age and Maria's help was no longer needed, Maria's daughter began to regularly kick her out of the overcrowded apartment of just

20 square metres for a family of four and force her to bring home money earned through panhandling:

> I had my own house and a garden in Cherkassy region, but my little granddaughter was often ill and I came to Kyiv to help take care of her. My daughter sold my house and let me sleep on a fold-out bed in the kitchen. I didn't mind, I've lived through the famine and the war, I can sleep anywhere and do any work. But my daughter became like a savage when a worker came to repair our gas stove and fined her for letting me sleep near the stove. He said it was a violation of some safety rules. But the flat was so small that there was no room to put me a bed anywhere. So my daughter threw out all my things from a balcony and kicked me out. Sometimes if I earn a lot of money from begging, I come and she lets me in, but if I don't bring enough, she won't let me in. She says I'm dirty and have too many things with me, overcrowding the flat. But I go to a public bath house to wash, and all my things are here in this bag! And she doesn't allow me to eat from their dishes or to go to their toilet.

One of the common explanations to overcrowding is that there is not enough housing in post-soviet societies, but average living space in Ukraine is 23 square metres per person (which would mean a small studio for a bachelor, a two-room flat of 46 square metres for a couple and a three-room flat of 70 square metres for a family with one child). The problem is not lack of living space for all, but uneven distribution of housing: in Kyiv, more than half of all recently built flats are of "elite" or "business" class, while flats of "economy" class constitue only 40% (even these "economy" flats cost at least one thousand euro per square metre and are unaffordable to most people, since average salary in the capital is just 400 euro a month.[3])

One specificity of the post-soviet housing market compared to Western societies is high risk of loss of housing due to housing affairs. "Homelessness and rising crime rates related to real estate are among the most dramatic consequences of the war over private property"—notes Michael Harloe (Andrusz, Harloe, and Szelenyi 1996, 12). He considers housing segregation a key factor of class differentiation in post-soviet societies. Gregor Andrusz adds: "as soon as housing became subject of legal commercial transactions, its market price skyrocketed and as a result it became object of criminal interest" (Andrusz, Harloe, and Szelenyi 1996, 61). He provides examples of affairs where sellers received nothing for their flats and ended up on the street or as "non-identified corpses" in the forests or next to autoroutes.[4] Semen Gluzman, the head of the Association of Psychiatrists of Ukraine, speaks of a typical housing affair scheme:

> Criminals often have good ties with the police and municipal housing services. There they get a list of potential victims who are not needed by anybody and can disappear without anyone noticing: the elderly without any relatives taking care of them, the alcoholics and drug addicts, mentally ill ... These are people who are unable to rationally think through all the legal details of selling their flats. They are easy to fool into selling their flat for a few coins, or even to offer it as a gift by signing some papers they can't even read. Among our patients there were a few such cases. There are even cases when relatives

> send their relatives to a psychiatric hospital and sell their flats in the meantime. Just to get a hold of their relatives' flats, they pay psychiatrists to sign papers that the patient has to be kept in a mental home, even if this is not the case and home care is a better option.

Furthermore, although nine in ten families privatised their flats in the 1990s, many of them are now unable to cover the costs of communal services like water, gas or electricity[5] and have to sell their flats and move to ever smaller dwellings with a high chance of being fooled along the way. And because of the privatisation of the majority of flats, now municipalities do not have enough housing stock on offer for the poor in risk of homelessness or those already on the street. As John Evans rightly notes, no matter how efficient are rehabilitation programmes for the homeless, they will not change much if at the end of the line the homeless are not offered any housing options (Evans 2003, 5).

Homeless as the Reserve Army of Labour

Unemployment is another obvious structural factor of homelessness, even though "unemployment" seems to be a very vague concept when trying to understand homelessness in post-soviet societies. Many people who are not officially employed are nevertheless working in the informal economy (which in Ukraine, according to different estimates constitutes between 30 and 50% of all economic practices). Some of those who are officially employed have wage arrears of six months or more, or earn a very low income, insufficient to pay for housing and other basic needs. Among those who are considered "productive" citizens (excluding the elderly, the handicapped as well as young children), the ILO defines many categories for the non-working population: not only the unemployed, but also students, caregivers and housewives, as well as the "desperate", who have stopped looking for work or think that no work is available for them (there was over quarter of a million people in this last category in Ukraine in 2010). And on the other extreme, there are those who do not need to work, because they can live from interest on their property or from financial assistance of third parties, and who will most likely never be at risk of homelessness under the present economic conjuncture.

As Mike Denning notes in his thought-provoking article "Wageless life",

> Capitalism begins not with the offer of work, but with the imperative to earn a living. Dispossession and expropriation, followed by the enforcement of money taxes and rent: such is the idyll of "free labour". [...] Unemployment precedes employment, and the informal economy precedes the formal, both historically and conceptually. We must insist that "proletarian" is not a synonym for "wage labourer" but for dispossession, expropriation and radical dependence on the market. You don't need a job to be a proletarian: wageless life, not wage labour, is the starting point in understanding the free market.

In the Ukrainian context, where up until 2004, three quarters of the population lived below the official poverty line (by 2010, this figure fell to 22%, but still constituted almost a quarter of the population) and where a third of almost 1.8 million officially registered as unemployed have been without work for more than a year (the average duration of unemployment in 2010 was 12 months, and those without work for more than a year do not receive unemployment benefits). It would be difficult to imagine these people as "not working". It is also not surprising that many of the homeless are doing some work to earn a living, even though this fact is often neglected by social workers, as witnessed by this quote by the director of Kyiv's only municipal homeless shelter:

> Social workers at the shelter now have more experience and accept only those who are in a really difficult situation. Earlier, construction workers used to live here, whole brigades of them. In one day they could make 100 hryvni [about ten euro]. They wanted to save on housing and that's why they would come to sleep here.[6]

While Karl Marx wrote about the market not recognising the unemployed worker ("The rascal, swindler, beggar, the unemployed, the starving, wretched and criminal workingman—these are figures who do not exist for political economy but only for other eyes, those of the doctor, the judge, the gravedigger, and bum-bailiff, etc.; such figures are spectres outside its domain."[7]), in the quote from the director of the homeless shelter we see a somewhat different trend of "doctors, judges, gravediggers and bum-bailiffs" not recognising workers in their homeless clients.

The few studies on the participation of the homeless in the labour market in post-soviet societies show that the majority of homeless work in order to satisfy at least part of their material needs. In a study conducted among the homeless of Yaroslavl (Zavialov and Spiridonova 2000), majority of homeless respondents worked from time to time and 19% had a stable job that nevertheless did not allow them to secure housing. Furthermore, only 4% of job refusals were due to a serious cause like alcoholism or drug abuse, there were almost no refusals due to lack of qualification (half of respondents had secondary education and a quarter—technical or higher education), while the majority of refusals were due to lack of housing (a vicious circle for the homeless). Similarly, in a study, conducted by "Doctors without borders" among their homeless clients in Russia, 46% declared that they worked part-time, almost two per cent worked full-time, and another 2,5% were receiving old-age pension (Gutov 2001).

Looking at the homeless as the reserve army of labour has several implications for our analysis. It allows to address situations when the homeless do have temporary and precarious jobs, when they participate in informal economic practices like garbage-collection and recycling, or when the permanently employed suffer from low wages that are insufficient to pay for housing and also end up on the street. Homelessness is thus not so much as a dysfunctional side effect of unemployment, but as a functional element of the capitalist labour market.

In 1990, ILO held an international conference in Moscow, entitled "In search of flexibility: the new Soviet labour market", where it promised to provide all necessary consultations on the creation of new employment opportunities, new sectors of the economy and new forms of property. The ILO stressed that wage regulation should be more flexible, that the harsh system of guaranteed employment should be abandoned and that unemployment should be recognised by the state "as a sad reality" (Standing 1991, 4–5). That same year, USSR indeed recognised the existence of unemployment. The Soviet state also admitted that in 1990 about 16% of work was performed outside the state sector and that in some regions of the country one in five workers will be forced to change jobs in early 1990s (Standing 1991, 2).

As a result of the transition of post-soviet societies to the free market economy, a reserve army of sub-proletarians appeared, who were struggling to survive and ready to take up any work offered. Survival strategies among the post-soviet unemployed and underemployed included growing own agricultural produce on their garden plots, barter exchange, petty trade on the street or in public transport or temporary informal employment. But as Ukrainian sociologist Natalia Tolstykh (2003, 83) notes, "Perhaps the only way to earn a living in the situation of unemployment is work in the informal sector, which only aggravates the level of social exclusion, for informal workers do not enter the sphere of judicial and social guarantees related to labour".

For the Ukrainian homeless, the most common survival strategies according to the NGO "Narodna dopomoha" consist in "agricultural work in summer months, work in construction (such jobs do not require long-term commitments and are paid right away), while for most homeless, the main source of income is in the collection of recyclable waste (mainly paper and glass)".[8] The homeless are often seen among the vendors of the unofficial flea market, selling items found in garbage bins. This market was created directly on the pavement of one of the working-class districts of Kyiv after the official one was torn down by the municipality in 2004 to construct a shopping mall. Being "unofficial" and lacking a permanent site to sell their goods, the vendors are being constantly harassed by the police and have to bribe the policemen by giving them between 2 and 5 hryvni [0.2–0.5 euro], which on less profitable days may amount to half of the daily earnings of a homeless vendor.

Many of the homeless have to work even after reaching retirement age, because without registration, they cannot receive their pension. For instance, 60-year-old Valentyna is constantly looking for temporary jobs in the Podil district of Kyiv:

> I went to a church, to sweep the ground and earn some money. I slowly swept and cleaned everything. But I earned just some coins. I am too old and almost blind now and cannot run everywhere like when I was young and worked in a café. I need something quiet and slowly-paced, so that I would not have to run, to break the glass ...

There are also those who lose their jobs and housing just a few years before reaching retirement age. Raisa lost her job in the wood industry in north-western Ukraine at the age of 51. She engaged in cross-border petty trade (her town was at the border with Belarus), then moved to Kyiv to sell vegetables in the street. After three years of work as a street vendor, she received a hernia from constantly carrying heavy boxes and then an inflammation of her legs and spent two months in a hospital. Upon leaving the hospital, she had neither work, nor housing and she was willing to take any job for a year before she would become eligible for a state pension at the age of fifty-five.

Some homeless show incredible creativity in adjusting their daily life and material needs to the meagre income-generating opportunities that are present. Two cases from my interviews reveal "contracts" that the homeless made with other poor workers to do their work in exchange for a place to sleep. Borys, a retired pensioner from a village in Central Ukraine, came to Kyiv after his old rural house became unfit for living. During the day, he collects bottles and buys food and vodka with the money he earns. In the evening, he takes the last suburban train to a small station in Kyiv region that is open 24 h a day. He asked the night guard whether he could sleep at the station under condition that he will not make a mess, with share some food and alcohol, and will help in case of emergency when night guard's assistance will be needed (so far, there were no emergency situations at the station and both the guard and Borys were able to sleep peacefully and seemed satisfied with the arrangement).

Similarly, Valia and Serhiy, who both lost their homes because of long-term unemployment, alcoholism and family conflicts, met on the street and made an arrangement with the street cleaner, who provided them a roof over their head and some stability with a predictable daily routine:

> I've lived for more than ten years with Seriozha. When we met, we began to think where to find a place to live. I knew a street cleaner who sometimes let me stay in the basement of one of the houses if I helped her clean the territory around that house. So we asked her, what if we will always clean up here instead of you, and you just let us live in that basement? We will guarantee cleanliness and order! There's not so much work: one or two hours in the morning and then we're free. It's good for her too: she doesn't need to do her work and she still receives her salary! And she's had no problems with us. So this is the contract that we made!

Following a parallel from Zygmunt Bauman's (2003) work, *Wasted lives*, one may say that Ukrainian homeless are degraded to the state of waste and often have no other option but to collect waste. In the Easter season of 2010, the NGO "Social partnership" (closely cooperating with Kyiv city council) initiated a "charitable event" entitled "Clean Thursday"[9], where the homeless cleaned up the waterfront of the Dnipro river, receiving 2 hryvni [0.2 euro] for a 50 litre bag of garbage. Not only was it profitable for the city administration to employ homeless cleaners at a much lower cost than they would pay otherwise for this work, but the homeless seemed grateful to have an opportunity to earn at least something and did not object to the event being presented as "charitable".

This readiness of the homeless reserve army of labour to gratefully take up any work that is offered is exploited by various so-called responsible or ethical businesses and social enterprises. For instance, in Chernivci, in the framework of a rehabilitation programme the homeless participate in the work of a social enterprise that specialises in cooking and preparing half-processed foods to cafes and restaurants in the city. Restaurants can order from this enterprise the services of vegetable-cutting, dough mixing, etc. while the use of the nearly free labour power of the homeless allows to cut on the price of the food.

The question of the use of homeless people's labour power is often raised in government programmes. During the meeting of the Lutsk city council dedicated to the prevention of deaths of homeless people in cold weather, participants agreed that

> The most important task is to create a special shelter for those citizens who live on the street. As the experience of neighboring cities (Lviv, Ivano-Frankivsk, Rivne) shows, the most reasonable solution is to create such a shelter in a rural area, in order not to "attract" the homeless to Lutsk. Furthermore, in such a case, those homeless citizens that will express their wish to remain in the center for a longer period, will have an opportunity to engage in agricultural labor, in such a way paying for their stay.

State officials sometimes also abuse their position to engage homeless and other vulnerable categories into slave labour. A journalist investigation by Lavryk et al.[10] revealed cases where policemen arrested homeless people in the street under pretexts of various administrative offences and sold them into slavery to isolated rural farms. Such abuse was revealed only after one of the slaves escaped and was picked up by the peasants. One of the judges in the city of Zhytomyr used the free labour power of those whom he condemned to several days or weeks of administrative arrest, by forcing them to participate in the construction of a house for his father. In Vinnytsia, workers of a detention centre for migrants used the labour power of a group of Somali asylum-seekers on various construction sites in the city.

Work is perceived by many NGOs as part of the "rehabilitation" of the homeless. For instance, in the community "Oselya" of the international movement "Emmaus", the homeless are expected to participate in the repair and sale of old clothes, toys and furniture, and thus to "regain a sense of self-worth" (the slogan of this community is "there are no things or people that are not needed"). "Just as an old broken item can regain life and continue to serve people if it is cleaned and repaired, so too the homeless can start anew and once again feel that they are needed in society and their work is valued"—explained one of the social workers.

Social Policy: From Universalism to Targeting, from Assistance to Repression

Analysis in previous sections of this paper showed the main structural causes of homelessness. These causes were readily acknowledged by social workers, bureaucrats and volunteers working with the homeless, and we can also see at least some level of awareness on behalf of the general public. But as changes in the labour and housing markets led to a growing number of the homeless in Ukrainian cities, social policy moved in the opposite direction. Universal programmes that take equality and socioeconomic rights as a starting point were replaced by targeting programmes for specific vulnerable social groups. The poor now have to prove that they are indeed poor and deserving of assistance.

Policies to guarantee right to housing and to employment are universal in the sense that they do not depend on personal qualities of recipients. Everybody, not just the homeless or some specific "deserving" groups of homeless, have the same basic human rights. But in Ukraine, the construction of social housing has decreased by more than ten times in the last twenty years and it would take more than a hundred years to satisfy the need of all who are now in the waiting list (if same quantities of social housing are constructed annually, and if nobody is added to the list). Furthermore, social housing that is constructed is immediately privatised by the recipients, and in some cases—resold at a market value. This practice turns social housing into precious gifts on behalf of the state to a small number of people, and a question of why these specific people (and not others) receive such gifts, becomes a question of social justice. Currently, 90% of housing is privately owned, while a universalist housing policy would presuppose an increase in the municipal housing stock in order to be able to provide affordable housing for rent to all who require it. And as far as the labour market is concerned, unemployment was recognised as a reality of late Soviet society back in 1990. Moreover, it was recognised a necessity for the capitalist market economy. Currently, the Ukrainian state has made an attempt to introduce the new Labour code that further reduces the rights of workers. Violation of labour rights has also become more common, and the informal economy grew to up to half of the total GDP. And small numbers of the unemployed, who are evaluated as "deserving", may be offered free classes to change or improve their qualification, or micro-credits to allow them to start their own businesses. In labour policies, as well as in housing policies, a focus on responding to concrete individuals' requests has turned the state into a charitable institution.

Additionally, targeting policies were developed to help specific groups that were defined as "vulnerable", among whom the homeless and those leaving prisons were lumped together and dealt with by a specific department of the Ministry of work and social policy. In case of homelessness, the person seeking help must first of all register at a special registration centre of this Ministry, pass a rehabilitation or a resocialization period of approximately three months (in the case of Kyiv, such a resocialization centre was created 40 km outside of the city in a former pioneer camp that was evacuated because of radiation from Chornobyl disaster). Otherwise, the homeless may only count on emergency shelter and free meals and clothing. In Kyiv, the only municipal homeless shelter can host 160 people, and only after they prove not to have any form of registration (so labour migrants would be immediately excluded), or contagious disease (considering that up to 80% of street homeless have tuberculosis, this homeless shelter is not an option for them), or to be under the influence of alcohol (another difficult requirement for many of the street homeless). In religious NGOs serving the homeless, the latter may be required to pray or repent and receive baptism in order to get food, clothing and basic medical service.

Social assistance programmes medicalize homelessness as a personal defect, and the homeless person has to be willing to engage in reintegration and adaptation programmes, where the social system is taken as a given. The homeless person also has to accept gratefully the goodwill of benefactors who are providing him or her with basic needs, instead of perceiving this provision as an obligation of the state and as his or her entitlement prior to any moral evaluation of individual deservingness. Both in state and charitable organisations, the homeless may be required to prove their desire to work. These targeting policies take as a starting point moral evaluation of the homeless individual rather than provision of universal guarantees to all, irrespective of whether somebody may be judged as "deserving".

A second component of social policy that begins with the moral evaluation of the homeless individual as "deserving" or "undeserving" is the growth of the penal state and the response to homelessness with assistance of police. In fact, Ministry of Internal Affairs is identified as one of the key ministries in social assistance programmes towards the homeless. Homeless people and beggars are often seen as threatening the "security" of upper- and middle-class citizens. As a result, the state that serves primarily the interests of dominant classes is more preoccupied with physical security in better-off areas than in improving living conditions in the poor neighbourhoods and in preventing homelessness.

As a consequence, police and private security are omnipresent in business and tourist areas such as the Independence square in Kyiv. Police has the right to arrest a person for up to 24 h to verify identity and for up to three months if a person has no documents or is seen drunk in a public space—a right that is often used against homeless or beggars to "clean up" the streets. People in shabby clothes are not allowed into large shopping centres and are chased away from elite residential areas. Tall fences, private security and surveillance cameras become all the more common. The homeless and the visible poor are stigmatised as criminals, and their behaviour is seen as illegal or antisocial.

By visible poor, I mean people who can be identified as "poor" based on their appearance and/or behaviour. They include the homeless and street people, unemployed youth from sleeping districts and people who come from villages and other poor areas of the country (identifiable by their accent, clothing style and behaviour). According to Lee, Farrell, and Link (2004, 42), the visible poor are stigmatised—"labelled or marked based on one or more attributes judged undesirable by in-group members". They are also "routinely avoided or treated as non-persons by domiciled passersby" (ibid.). Of course, the boundaries for such identification are never fixed but are socially constructed, and "excluded" groups may be different in different contexts. Lee et al. found that extreme exposure reduces sympathy towards the marginal groups and promotes avoidance of them: about ten per cent of city-dwellers they interviewed are even "altering where they go to shopping or entertainment or how they use public transportation because of the presence of homeless people" (ibid., 56). According to Wacquant (1998, 22), this is a type of poverty that causes discomfort "because it is visible, causes incidents and disagreements in public space and nourishes the diffused feeling of insecurity".

It is a known social fact that inequalities are a source of social tension, aggressive behaviour and crime. A logical conclusion from this fact would be that in order to decrease crime rates and feelings of insecurity, we should decrease the level of inequalities. On the contrary, the responses of the well-off population in the city centres are aimed at securing their privileged positions by keeping the poor out and making them invisible. Furthermore, in many countries, these are not only private responses (of the "Not in my backyard!" kind) but also public policies of the state. In particular, "zero tolerance" policies, first introduced in the United States, are now being copied as "best examples" throughout the globe: in Western Europe, in post-socialist countries and in the Third World alike.

"Zero tolerance" policies do not simply "spread" around the world: Wacquant (1998, 46) rightly notes that "they are flourishing because they meet the interests and feelings of authorities in the countries of destination". In well-off areas, where the presence of the poor is seen as a threat in itself, private security and "face control" are introduced to forbid the poor from entering. In Kyiv, the case of underground passages that were recently turned into shopping centres is especially interesting, because there was a change in major function (from a public passage to a semi-public shopping passage). It is an example of privatisation of public space in the Ukrainian capital—of course, people who do not intend to shop can still pass to the other side of the street as they used to, but several groups are excluded from passing. The homeless, the Roma, people under the influence of alcohol or drugs may be turned away by the guard. It is clear that the shoppers would not appreciate their presence, but how are these excluded groups expected to get to the other side of the street remains a question.[11]

Even when demands for security of the well-off residents of the city centres may be seen as legitimate, they definitely do not resolve the problems. Residents of apartment blocks in Kyiv often pay night guards to watch the entrances to their homes to prevent the homeless from entering and spending the night in the common hallways, on the stairwells or on the attics/basements.[12] This does not resolve the problem of homelessness, but instead leads to deaths of many homeless people in the streets during the cold winter (several hundred people died in the cold winter of 2006 in Kyiv alone, after which the state opened the first and only night shelter for the homeless).

Desire to clear the city centres from the poor is present not only among well-off individuals and private companies but also in public policies of the state. This tendency is more disturbing than private "initiatives", because the state by definition has to protect all of its citizens and not only those on the top of the social ladder. An example of such an attitude is "Operation 'Bum'" of the Transport Police at the train stations of Kyiv—places of high concentration of homeless people. People who look like they could be homeless are approached by policemen and asked to show documents and tickets to justify their presence at the station. Those without such documents are taken to the police station for further inspection and to check whether they have committed any crimes. In an interview to a TV news programme[13], a policeman said that this "operation" is good both for the passengers (who "are afraid of the homeless because they may steal their belongings and spread contagious diseases") and for the homeless themselves (who "get at least a temporary opportunity to spend a night in a warm place"— police station). Another example is the initiative of the Ministry of Social Policy of Ukraine to create a centre that would register the homeless. It is supposed to "identify the homeless and to provide them with access to social protection" but in reality contributes more to controlling the homeless through "identification" and "registration" than to preventing the problem.

Cooperation of state services with private institutions to control and contain the homeless is also highly problematic. A sector of economy is created that makes profit on social inequalities, insecurity and the fear of the "dangerous" poor and because the state supports their profitable initiatives instead of defending the rights of the poor citizens against such privatised forms of harassment and exclusion. Moreover, such a turn to crime control is "a mode of state action to compensate for political failures and retrenchments in other fields of social policy", notes Feldman (2002, 419). He also quotes Scheingold to support his oppinion: "while effective governance is increasingly out of reach, states in advanced capitalist societies develop diffuse, insistent, mutable, and, by some accounts, insidious iterations of disciplinary and punitive power. These capabilities are increasingly deployed as repressive surrogates for governance, that is, governing through crime control" (ibid.).

Increased crime control in cities usually means higher rates of imprisonment and over-representation of marginal groups in gaols (Wacquant 1998). This also means higher state expenses for maintaining prisons, which is done at the expense of decreasing state expenses for social programmes. Furthermore, when the poor leave the prisons after having served their sentence, they are confronted with a problem of having nowhere to go and no chances to find any work and to start a normal life. They either become homeless (among Ukrainian homeless at least a third are former convicts) or turn back to crime.

"Whenever the police comes to be considered as an alien force by the community it is supposed to protect, it becomes unable to fulfil any role other than a purely repressive one and, under such circumstances, it can only add to discord and disorder, often fuelling the very violence it is entrusted to curb" (Wacquant 2007).

Despite the fact that human rights are meant to be equal and guaranteed to every human being, in reality, they are differentiated based on one's position in society. Rights are not entitlements guaranteed equally to all, but become dependent on a series of other social factors—on class position, race or ethnicity, age, place of residence, levels of cultural and social capital. In post-soviet societies, "reduction of government services increased the misery of the poor while advancing the economy for the benefit of the upper middle-class professionals and wealthy investors" (Wright 2000, 34). Worldwide, "polarisation of the class structure ... combined with ethnoracial segregation and welfare state retrenchment, has produced a dualization of the metropolis that has consigned large sections of the unskilled labour force to economic redundancy and social marginality" (Wacquant 2007).

Such differentiation of citizenship often leads to serious violations of basic human rights of the poor. They are excluded from the semi-public places where they have to pay a fee to enter— many parks and sports facilities. They are excluded from cafes and supermarkets based on their appearance. For the homeless, this situation is especially acute, since they "might be so constrained that they are literally unable to do anything without infringing the rights of others" (King 2003, 667). They may end up having no place at all to eat, drink, buy food and clothes, sleep or simply sit down to rest.

Having analysed ways in which homeless people's rights are violated because they have no home, King (2003, 667—668) argues that housing should be seen as a freedom right and not a social claim: "all actions, be they urinating, love-making, reading a book or discussing philosophy are situated ... we must have a place to be". For Ukrainian homeless, such "places to be" often are public toilets, abandoned buildings or subways. Homeless people are seen as second-class citizens to be satisfied with minimum standards of life, which leads to creation of bad quality facilities that the homeless prefer not to use—unsafe, dirty and overcrowded night shelters. In Ukraine, social housing for poor families is given only in the distant sleeping districts, despite the fact that 7—12% of all housing being built in Kyiv goes to the city housing fund (according to the law). Such policies segregate the poor population of the city from the wealthy. In Kyiv, this segregation is reinforced by natural barriers—the historical city centre with the highest housing costs is situated on the hills of the right bank of the Dnipro river, while the working-class sleeping districts are on the left bank. Wealthy districts are safer, cleaner, better-kept and have better schools and general infrastructure. This is a proof of differentiated citizenship depending on the place of residence

And finally, the visible poor are excluded in the public discourses where they are seen as a problem for the state, for charities and for society in general. "Homelessness can be criminalised through discourse, by inaccurately describing the causes of homelessness and publicising those descriptions in newspapers, radio broadcasts and television shows. Institutional mechanisms can also play a role in this; for instance, laws have been created which specifically target the survival strategies of the homeless people. Through these means, the primary causes of homelessness—poverty, lack of affordable housing and lack of jobs with living wages—become obscured. If they were instead highlighted, they could challenge (though not necessarily successfully) the legitimacy of the existing social order" (Schiff 2003, 494). Schiff's conclusion is important: instead of criminalising poverty, developing countries that seek democratic transformations should highlight the root causes of existing social problems and be committed to change the existing social order and to fulfil its obligations towards its most vulnerable citizens.

Conclusions

Homelessness is seen among the most visible forms of urban marginality in post-soviet countries. At the same time, sociological analysis of inequalities and of structural causes of social problems such as homelessness or street crime is marginalised. A similar retreat can be seen in politics and public discourses where immense efforts are made to present these problems as the fault of the poor themselves and consequently to decrease social assistance programmes. This paper has analysed the major structural causes of homelessness in Ukraine in access to housing and in the labour market: privatisation of almost all available housing and decrease in the construction of social housing by more than twenty times in the last two decades, housing affairs, inadequate housing conditions and overcrowding, as far as housing market is concerned, and unemployment, underemployment and the phenomenon of the "working poor", and the place of the homeless as a reserve army of labour in the capitalist labour market.

After analysing these causes of homelessness, a logical conclusion can be made that in order to resolve homelessness at a structural level, affordable housing and access to decent work (following Labour code regulations and with salary above poverty level) should be among the priorities of state policy and non-governmental institutions alike. The right to housing belongs to basic human rights (paragraph 1, article 25 of the General declaration of human rights) and is guaranteed in the Ukrainian Constitution (article 47). Violation of this basic socioeconomic right leads to homelessness and inability to satisfy other basic needs, namely protection from unsatisfactory weather conditions, personal hygiene, regular rest and meals, safety and privacy, which are necessary for human existence. Right to housing should therefore be guaranteed by the state and a comprehensive policy should be developed. Similarly, as our prior analysis has shown, right to decent employment should also be guaranteed to all if we wish to prevent homelessness and other social problems. We see however two quite contrary tendencies in Ukrainian policy: a gradual shift from universalism to targeting and criminalization of social problems.

Wacquant (1998, 26) warns that one of the main causes of the degradation of social conditions and life chances of the urban poor is the "erosion of 'state social capital', that is, organisations presumed to provide civic goods and services—physical safety, legal protection, welfare, education, housing and health care—which have turned into instruments of surveillance, suspicion and exclusion rather than vehicles of social integration and trust-building". He also notes that "the punitive nature of street-level welfare bureaucracies ensures that their effect is more often disruptive than stabilising", arguing for the need to defend a strong social state instead of further criminalising poverty.

A focus on human rights and the need to create a democratic state that would respect them seems one of the possible solutions. Taking housing policy as an example, King (2003, 670) argues that "One of the key problems with housing policy is its relatively low political priority ... because housing as a social problem is all too frequently seen as particularist and concerned with a minority of population. [...] However, a discourse based on freedom rights concentrates on common features within a population by emphasising those basic elements which most take for granted, but which are impossible without access to housing. Hence, the stress is on what is common and universal to us all and not what separates or excludes certain groups or individuals". Access to work, medical assistance, education, transport, safe and well-kept public spaces, freedom of movement in the city can also be seen as freedom rights that the state has to guarantee to all.

Notes

1. According to the Social monitoring of the Institute of Sociology of the Academy of Sciences of Ukraine in 2010, almost a third of all respondents lived without sanitation or central heating (one in ten said their apartment was "very cold in winter"), a quarter had unstable supply of electricity, one in ten lived in overcrowded conditions (three or more persons per room) and the same number of people had leaking walls or ceiling.
2. Statistical data on housing conditions is taken from the Social Monitoring of the Institute of Sociology, Academy of Science of Ukraine and from the State Statistics Committee of Ukraine http://www.ukrstat.gov.ua.
3. High housing expenses also mean a need to save on other costs (food, medicine, clothing, transport, education, cultural and social life), forced co-habitation without a possibility to escape family violence or other conflicts, and a high risk of homelessness in case of illness, job loss or unpredictable expenses. This has lead Russian sociologist Tikhonova (2003) to list inadequate housing as one of the key factors of social exclusion.
4. According to the data of the Moscow Department for criminal investigations, at the end of 1994, 115 owners of sold flats were declared "disappeared". In 1993, there were 17 murders related to housing transactions, and in early 1994, there were already 50 such murders. Between January and June 1994, at least 500 persons ended up on the street because of housing transactions (Andrusz, Harloe, and Szelenyi 1996).
5. For instance, in Hungary, between 1989 and 1994, housing expenses rose by 50% and they continue to rise today (Polakov and Guillean 2001).

6. Published online at: http://gazeta.ua/index.php?id=137512 One should note that these construction workers are for the most part precarious day-labourers working in the shadow economy without work contracts or social guarantees.
7. Economico-political manuscripts of 1844.
8. http://www.homeless.net.ua/ua/researches.php
9. "Clean Thursday" is how Ukrainians call the day, when Jesus washed the feet of his disciples before being condemned to death. On this day, religious tradition encourages people to clean up their houses, wash themselves and all their clothes in order to prepare for Easter.
10. Published in a Ukrainian weekly magazine " Ukrainski Tyzhden" in October 2008, No. 41(50).
11. Other examples of such "privatisation of public space" are parks and green areas. Many small squares in the city centre of Kyiv have been turned into summer terraces of restaurants or cafés and you can only sit there if you order something.
12. A more extreme example of urban segregation and exclusion of the poor is seen in "gated communities". This a wide-spread (and widely criticised) phenomenon in countries like the USA (Low 2003) or South Africa whereas in Ukraine first gated communities are only beginning to appear in the last decade. In Kyiv such communities are presented as positive signs of city growth, prosperity and comfortable life. An advertisement of "Vozdvyzhenka" gated community proudly lists all the benefits of living "in the very heart of the city, but as if in a small peaceful XIXth century district, with private security, video surveillance, own kindergarten and elementary school, health and sports facilities ...".
13. A programme with the title "Transport police is conducting a prophylactic operation named 'Bomzh'" on 28 January 2006, online access at: http://5tv.com.ua/newsline/184/0/20300/.

References

Andrusz, G., M. Harloe, and I. Szelenyi, eds. 1996. *Cities after Socialism: Urban and Regional Change and Conflict in Post-socialist Societies*. Oxford: Blackwell. 356 p.

Bauman, Z. 2003. *Wasted Lives: Modernity and Its Outcasts*. Cambridge: Polity. 152 p.

Evans, J. 2003. "Building Partnerships in the Fight against Homelessness." *Homelessness in Europe: The Newsletter of FEANTSA* (Spring): 5–6. http://www.feantsa.org/spip.php?article1036&lang=en.

Feldman, L. C. 2002. "Redistribution, Recognition, and the State: The Irreducibly Political Dimension of Injustice." *Political Theory* 30 (3): 410–440.

Gutov, R. 2001. "Bezdomnye v Rossii: vzgliad na problem." [The Homeless in Russia: A View on the Problem – In Russian.] *Sociologichekoe Obozrenie* 5 (1): 102–113.

King, P. 2003. "Housing as a Freedom Right." *Housing Studies* 18 (5): 661–672.

Layton, J. 2000. *Homelessness: The Making and Unmaking of a Crisis*. Toronto: Penguin. 320 p.

Lee, B. A., C. R. Farrell, and B. G. Link. 2004. "Revisiting the Contact Hypothesis: The Case of Public Exposure to Homelessness." *American Sociological Review* 69: 40–63.

Low, S. 2003. *Behind the Gates: Life, Security and Pursuit of Happiness in Fortress America*. New York: Routledge. 288 p.

Polakov, V., and C. Guillean. 2001. *International Perspectives on Homelessness*. Westport, CT: Greenwood Press. 328 p.

Schiff, L. 2003. "The Power to Define: Definitions as a Site of Struggle in the Field of Homelessness." *International Journal of Qualitative Studies in Education* 16 (4): 491–507.

Standing, G., ed. 1991. *In Search of Flexibility: The New Soviet Labour Market*. Geneva: ILO. 440 p.

Tikhonova, N. 2003. "Fenomen socialnoj exclusii v usloviakh Rossii." [The Phenomenon of Social Exclusion in Russian Context – In Russian.] *Mir Rossii* 12 (1): 36–84.

Tolstykh, N. 2003. "Socialne vykluchennia v suchasnij Ukraini." [Social Exclusion in Contemporary Ukraine – In Ukrainian.] *Ukrainski Socium* 1 (2): 81–86.
Wacquant, L. 1998. "Negative Social Capital: State Breakdown and Social Destitution in America's Urban Core." *Netherlands Journal of Housing and the Built Environment* 13 (1): 25–40.
Wacquant, L. 2007. *Urban Outcasts: A Comparative Sociology of Marginality*. Cambridge: Polity Press.
Wright, T. 2000. "Resisting Homelessness: Global, National, and Local Solutions." *Contemporary Sociology* 29 (1): 27–43.
Zavialov, F., and E. Spiridonova. 2000. "Uroven i obraz zhizni bomzhej." [Level and Style of Life of the Bomzh – In Russian.] *Sociologicheskie Issledovania* 2: 62–68.

Families' Ways of Coping with Poverty in Small-town Russia

Ann-Mari Sätre, Alexander Soldatkin and Alla Varyzgina

This article analyses how poor families cope with poverty in provincial Russia. It draws on both survey data and interviews. On the basis of the survey, a factor analysis was carried out. This gives evidence to four common types of reactions to poverty. The article shows that being able to use rights, resources and relations is not enough to overcome poverty. Working more, while trying to reduce expenses just to cope, means that poor families are particularly vulnerable to changes that could start a downward process. The small percentage of those who succeed highlights the need for supporting structures. The paper argues that the supporting role of public authorities is especially important when considering the possibilities for poor people themselves to take actions.

Introduction

Transformation after socialism has, according to several studies, created large income gaps and removed social safety nets for ordinary people in Russia (Klugman 1998; Lokshin and Popkin 1999; Ovcharova 2008; Rimashevskaya 2004; Silverman and Yanowitch 2000; World Bank 2011; Yates 2004). Societal structures have disappeared and workplaces are not obliged to provide housing, child care, etc., as in the Soviet time, while individuals have to pay for services that they did not have to pay for previously. The situation some people end up with is chronic poverty, where expenses are constantly higher than income (Rimashevskaya 2010). Many Russian families are close to the edge of poverty, particularly younger families (Ovcharova 2008).[1]

In the 1990s, it was considered legitimate to be poor, as everybody was affected by the consequences of perestroika. The image of poverty has, however, changed since the Russian economy started to recover in the end of the 1990s. As it became visible that some parts of the population have been able to pull themselves out of poverty by their own actions, the demand for people to take active responsibility for their own life situations increased. This means that it has become feasible to study what strategies they have used. We would like to highlight the link between attitudes and strategies and to find out more about whether the change in attitudes towards the poor has also fed into strategies. Do people develop strategies to overcome hardships or do they just find ways of coping from day to day?

More specifically, the aim of the present paper is to analyse ordinary peoples' ways of dealing with hardships in the context of transition. Although low resources put a clear limit on strategies, we are not primarily interested in what resources people have access to, but rather how they use whatever means they have in their use. Therefore, the approach, here, starts from Sen's entitlement theory. According to his approach, a person's exchange entitlements are highlighted: the ability of people to break out of poverty depends on their ability to transform whatever income or assets they have into food and other necessities. Assets are, according to Sen (1984) classified into three categories: resources, including all kinds of capital (also social capital, human capital and cultural capital), rights, such as welfare entitlements, and relationships.

To study the effects of transition, we chose to focus on new groups of the poor, working or unemployed and after having children. Although earlier research on poverty in Russia demonstrates that there might be some potential for agency, it provides little guidance as to how agency could advance in the Russian context. The present study aims to provide a contribution in this field, using both survey data and interviews collected from families in a small Russian town.[2]

Based on the survey on families' strategies, a factor analysis was carried out. As we are interested in how poor families actually cope with hardships, the survey was complemented with interviews, which were conducted in a small provincial town of Nizhegorodskaya oblast in November 2011.[3] We have asked people above all how they survive and how they try to act to overcome hardships, and what resources they have used.

Previous Research on Household Strategies

In the literature on strategies and post-socialist transformations, a great deal of emphasis has been placed on how individuals and households use various strategies to improve their ordinary living conditions in post-Soviet contexts (Clarke 1999; Lokshin and Yemtsov 2001; O'Brien, Patsiorkovski, and Wegren 2004; Pickup and White 2003; Ries 2008; Walker 1998; Wallace 2002). In post-Soviet Russia, individuals or households have to deal with many uncertainties, which means that it is difficult to plan life. When wages are not high enough to cover basic expenses, all kind of means to get by are relevant. This could be to buy cheap clothes and cheap shoes, or to postpone any not immediately necessary expenditure, plot production or it could be to try to increase income through second jobs or the development of businesses. The choice of the family as the unit of analysis underlines the fact that adults in families make decisions collectively in some ways (Pickup and White 2003). There are various reform measures that each in themselves have presumably implied possibilities for some people to achieve prosperity and offered them the opportunity to leave poverty by means of their individual or family's agency (Sätre 2012). On the other hand, there are reforms that have led to losses of services that ordinary people previously received, such as being guaranteed a job, and thus a stable income, loss of access to free education, health care, child care and public transport (Lazareva 2009). Ordinary people have been affected by changes in the communal infrastructure and housing reform (Round and Kosterina 2005).

There are a number of laws that directly or indirectly transferred responsibility from the state to individuals or families (see Kravchenko 2008). Targets for support were diverted from families to general groups in the 1990s.The change from universal social rights to means testing also means that one has to prove to be part of the deserving poor. A new law on the monetization of social benefits, which converted in-kind benefits into cash allowances, was introduced in 2005.[4] This meant that ordinary people lost access to free local transport and local telephone calls, trips to sanatoria, free medicines and other benefits. Earlier research further shows that social networks based on family connection have fallen apart (Pickup and White 2003). Applying Sen's analytical framework, these are all examples of losses of entitlements which in turn might lead to losses of capabilities.

By strategy, we indicate a set of actions that are a matter of planning and not just for surviving for the next day, which, as emphasized by Walker (1998), could be seen as a lack of strategy altogether. But strategies are also about having alternatives. There has to be a matter of choice, where available strategies are limited by the resources families actually have access to (Avraamovoi 2003). We find the framework suggested by Sen (1984) useful here. He suggests that the ability of people to break out of poverty depends on their ability to transform assets into goods and services that they have a reason to value. Strategies are important in the post-Socialist context as they take into account the widespread informal ways to cope in the Soviet system, which might still be present in the post-Soviet period as well (Ellman 2000; Kim 2002). Families' strategies presuppose some form of agency, while also hinting at the need for various sources of income to cope with transformation (Wallace 2002). In line with Clarke (1999), we are, however, critical of the voluntarism implied by the concept of strategy. As we are focusing on the poor, it is presumably more adequate to talk about ways of coping with hardships.

Some of the earlier research works are written with reference to the 1990s when "everybody was poor", and "everybody was trying to survive" in one way or the other. Extreme conditions of uncertainty meant that alternative choices were limited. At the same time, the attitude towards poor was one of sympathy. Everybody was poor in the aftermath of shock therapy; it was accepted that you deserved any help or support from the state. But this has changed; as in the 2000s, it has been possible for some people to get out of poverty. What we have seen is a change back towards a blaming-the-victim mentality (Chebankova 2010). Policy-makers started to demand that people take responsibilities for their personal lives (Rivkin-Fish 2005). Simultaneously, the state transferred responsibility to families, while these as a result of reforms also faced rising costs for living. There is a system for compensation in the form of social benefits, unemployment benefits, subsidies for rents, etc., but there is no clear policy for supporting people in taking actions actually to change their situation. In this research, we wanted to find out information about actions that families take to deal with hardships.

There is a bulk of literature on household strategies, looking either at coping as a way to meet poverty, or at survival for the day. Many of these focus on how household strategies can be associated with Soviet norms. A few studies highlight how the survival of a collective spirit (Shanin 1999) or the paternalistic behaviour of employers (Granberg 2007) can facilitate the everyday life of poor people. The strategy then becomes one of relying on that these norms from the Soviet time actually survive.

Some studies focus on how connections (Gradoselskaya 2001; Ledeneva 1998, 2008; Tartakovskaya 2004) and inter-family networks can help people to combat or cope with poverty (Desai and Idson 1998; Ioffe and Nefedova 1997; Shubin 2007). Others pay attention to families' strategies for combining breadwinning and care, taking into account cut-downs in welfare services such as child care, free education and free medical care (Ashwin 2006; Kay 2006; Sätre 2012). There are also studies that take a more entrepreneurial perspective, looking at families strategies of relying on several sources of income, such as engaging in second jobs or moonlighting (Bobkov, Zinin, and Razumov 2004; Guariglia and Kim 2004; Kim 2002; Sätre 2001, 2010). Most of these are focusing on how people cope under conditions of uncertainty in the context of transformation. Few, however, look into strategies of changing these conditions or how to improve your situation.

Typology of Strategies to Overcome Poverty

The result of the factor analysis shows that actions to overcome or cope with poverty are unevenly distributed within the population of the small Russian towns under survey. Moreover, we can observe more or less sustainable constellations of behaviours, which we can interpret as "strategies" (See also Soldatkin and Varyzgina 2013; Soldatkin 2013). We present in Figure 1, the typology of strategies based on factor analysis of respondents' self-reported economic behaviour over the last five years before the survey (2006–2010). They are non-exclusive – typically, a family employs more than one strategy.

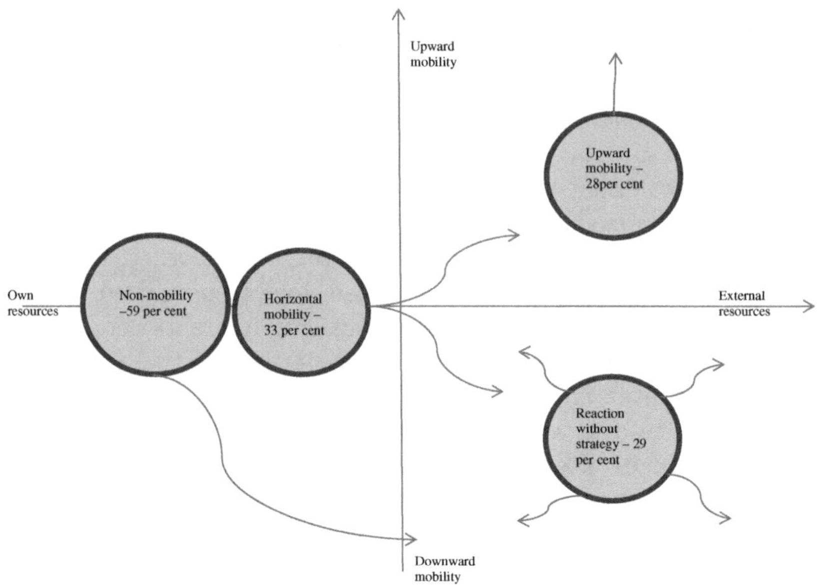

Figure 1. Typology of families' strategies

Non-mobility or Coping with the Use of Own Resources

The most widespread strategy is called *non-mobility or coping with the use of own resources* of the family. In practice, this means cutting down expenses on food, clothing and leisure (see Table 1). However, the opportunities for economizing cannot be limitless, and such families have to take actions to increase their resources. Some of them (29%) try to change job, some (23%) search for extra earnings. In 19% of the cases related to this strategy, jobless members of families started working. In brief, the strategy would, thus, be to remain on the same level of income, although costs for living are rising, by spending less and working more.

It should be noted that the prevailing strategy of economizing and reducing expenses is an element of all other strategies. It is the first action that a family takes when facing the risk of its well-being decreasing. For some families, enduring troubles may become a single or prevailing behaviour, and for others, it plays a supportive role, while other ways of action are oriented to improve family conditions.

Horizontal Mobility

The second of the alternatives could be defined as horizontal mobility. Typical actions within the frames of this strategy include changing jobs (or getting a job for the jobless), as well as changing occupation or profession. For some 30% of the households acting this way, labour mobility consists of finding extra earnings supplementing those from their primary job, while 28% accompany

Table 1. What actions did your family take over the last 5 years?

Actions in last five years	S1	S2	S3	S4
Non-mobility. Attempts to keep up status quo *with own resources (Strategy 1)*				
Economized on clothing and footwear	100	54	59	60
Economized on food	99	40	49	40
Economized in respect to leisure, vacations	98	55	57	67
Keeping up social status with horizontal mobility (Strategy 2)				
Changed job	29	86	30	39
Jobless got a job	19	45	22	23
Changed profession, occupation	12	39	10	15
Offered apartment, dacha and garage for rent	2	8	11	7
Reaction without strategy with the use of external resources (Strategy 3)				
Got material support from relatives, friends	15	25	63	23
Increased agricultural productivity of a smallholding	15	11	34	27
Got support from state or municipal social care	6	6	31	9
Sold property	6	13	15	12
Moved to a cheaper apartment (house), moved to live along with relatives	2	6	7	0
Got support from NGOs	1	1	3	2
Got support from authorities for starting own business	2	1	0	4
Upward mobility with the use of external resources (Strategy 4)				
Got in contact with useful people	11	17	21	65
Found extra earnings	23	30	24	54
Raised their professional and educational level	12	28	23	41
Got useful information	5	4	5	23
Started own business by themselves	2	8	0	10

their change of job with an improvement in their professional and educational level. A significant part (40–55% – see Table 1) of households employing this strategy also rely on economizing; however, most of them take steps in the sphere of employment and labour.

Reaction Without Strategy with the Use of External Resources

The core element of the third kind of behaviour (*reaction without strategy*) is reliance on material support from relatives and/or friends (63% of the households which adopt this strategy). Much more frequently than the others, such families also rely on benefits from municipal or state social care authorities (31% of families employing this strategy compared with 5–10% of the others – see Table 1). While relying heavily on the help from outside the family, some of those households, however, have their own means against poverty: over the last five years, 34% of them raised the agricultural productivity of their land, and 15% sold some property.

Upward Mobility with the Use of External Resources

The fourth strategy is *upward mobility with the use of external resources*. These families appear to be the most socially active. The core of their strategy is to establish contacts with useful people (65% of cases), find extra earnings (54%), improve their professional and educational level (41%), and gather useful information (23%). They are also quite willing to change jobs (39% of cases – see Table 1) and, in some cases, do not disregard small agricultural practices – 27% of such families increased the productivity of their land in last five years.

Families employing the mobility-centred strategies (both horizontal and upward), tend to have higher self-esteem and better feelings about their social status and material situation, compared with those who are less mobile. Assessing their position, these socially mobile families more frequently put themselves in above average or average strata, and less frequently describe themselves as poor. The families who appear to be less mobile tend to feel worse about their circumstances. Nearly, a quarter of those representing the first strategy describe themselves as poor or extremely poor (Table 2).

The strategy of mere economizing and cutting off expenses appears to be inefficient for improvement of families' circumstances. Nearly 30% of those families who mostly rely on economizing report a decline in their well-being in the last five years. The same is true for those who tend to rely upon social benefits and support from relatives – however, in the latter category, nearly 30% talk about improvements in the same period, while in the former group, less than 15% mention improvements (Table 3).

The families with mobile strategies demonstrate more positive attitude to the changes they met in the last time. This is especially true for those mostly oriented on horizontal mobility – they feel positive dynamics in 36% of cases, and

Table 2. In your opinion, to which of the given groups does your family belong?

	S1	S2	S3	S4
Families with above-average income	0	2	1	4
Families with average income	27	45	41	47
Not poor, but having below-average income	45	40	39	32
Poor families	22	8	16	13
Extremely poor families	2	3	3	2
Don't know, difficult to answer	5	1	0	1

Table 3. How did the material well-being of your family change over the last 5 years?

	S1	S2	S3	S4
Got better	2	9	2	10
Got somewhat better	11	27	26	17
Didn't change	44	35	37	39
Got somewhat worse	23	15	18	17
Got worse	9	9	11	9
Difficult to answer	11	6	6	8

Table 4. How do you estimate the risk of poverty for your family?

	S1	S2	S3	S4
Our family is poor now	10	8	11	6
High risk, on the verge of poverty	22	11	15	15
Moderate risk, as for the majority of the Russian people	66	75	68	68
Almost no risk	1	4	5	9
No risk at all, family will never be poor	1	2	2	2

stability in other 35% of cases. Those families that orient themselves on upward mobility are less satisfied – they report about improvements in their situation in 17% of cases. However, nearly 40% of them see situation as stable (Table 3).

The difference between those families with an economizing strategy and the others is clearly seen in their estimation of the poverty risk (Table 4). Though the majority (66%) of families following the economizing strategy says that they are at the same risk of poverty as most of the Russian population, 10% of this category tends to see themselves as already living in poverty, another 22% estimate the risk of becoming poor as high. In the other categories, expectations towards the future are slightly more optimistic. Those who orient themselves towards horizontal mobility tend to estimate their perspectives as rather stable, three quarters of them report themselves to be at moderate risk. The families that base their strategy on increasing access to external resources feel even more optimistic: 9% of them see almost no risk of poverty for themselves. However, even in this relatively well-off category, the share of those who report themselves as poor or being on the verge of poverty is twice as high as the percentage of those who feel secure and see no risk (Table 5).

The four strategies described, as we already mentioned, are not mutually exclusive – neither are they stable. They are typically combined within families, and they can change with time and with changing socio-economic conditions. It is possible to say that each strategy has its own limit of applicability, and has to be changed into another strategy when this limit is reached. It is interesting to see how different strategies are transformed under the pressure of (hypothetical) reductions in a family's well-being (Table 6).

Those who now employ a rather passive economizing approach appear to be equally passive in anticipation and planning their activities for possible bad times. More frequently than the others (in 11% of cases), followers of the first strategy mention that they don't know what they would do in a situation of hardship (Table 6). A significant portion of them (33%) rely on their ability to endure hardships not only now, but in the future as well. However, even among relatively passive families there are 45% of those who in the face of worsening conditions would move towards more active labour behaviour (i.e. look for an extra job). Another visible change that a supposed reduction of well-being can produce in these families is activation of their social contacts: 21% of the families are going to ask relatives for financial help in case of hardship, while during last five years, only 15% did so.

Families oriented towards horizontal mobility and their own resources would repeat those behavioural patterns in the face of future hardships. Their willingness to simply endure troubles is significantly less than among the first strategy followers (12 vs. 33% – see Table 6). Their way out of troubles is seen as being in the sphere of labour – in 66% of cases, they are going to look for an extra job; in 40%, their option is to change their job for a better-paid one.

Households that mostly follow the third kind of behaviour (reaction without strategy) are like the most passive representatives of the first strategy with respect to their readiness to sustain possible hardships in the future. In 34% of

Table 5. Presumed sources of help in hardship

	S1	S2	S3	S4
Specialized department of local administration	2	3	13	1
Local administration, mayor	2	2	1	3
Charity organizations	4	2	1	1
Employer	3	6	5	6
Friends, relatives	77	79	75	92
Governor, regional administration	6	7	3	0
Church	14	6	9	3
NGOs	0	0	0	0
Business sponsors	0	0	0	0
Other	4	3	1	2

Table 6. Actions to be taken if material well-being gets worse

	S1	S2	S3	S4
Sustain, endure	33	12	34	22
Look for better-paid job	18	40	33	33
Look for extra job	45	66	43	61
Demand on-time salary payments	7	11	5	4
Demand salary increase	3	8	6	9
More actively use smallholding (land)	12	15	23	29
Make money by any means	13	15	7	10
Try to take a bank loan	2	6	6	4
Offer part of a dwelling for rent	0	4	8	5
Try to sell some property	4	6	8	5
Try to borrow money from colleagues, friends and relatives	12	8	12	13
Ask relatives for financial help	21	10	12	21
Join anti-authorities meetings, rallies	3	3	1	3
Join any protest actions	2	2	1	3
Move to other city	1	1	1	1
Try to move abroad	0	5	1	3
Don't know yet	11	5	3	4
Try to marry	1	1	3	4
Give birth to a child to receive social benefits	0	1	1	1
Other	0	0	0	0

cases, they report endurance as their likely behaviour in case of troubles. However, unlike the most passive households, they tend to see broader opportunities to compensate the hardships. Concerning labour behaviour, they are oriented not only towards increasing their activities (taking an extra job), but towards a qualitative change of job for a better-paid one (34% of cases of the third strategy representatives compared with 18% of families following the passive strategy). Another possible source of sustainability for them is the land – in 23% of cases, such families are going to use their smallholdings more actively. They appear to be noticeably more self-reliant than passive families of the first type: only in 12% of cases might they ask relatives and friends for financial help (vs. 21% in the first type – Table 6).

Families of the fourth type (mostly following the strategy of upward mobility), demonstrate a mixture of possible reactions towards anticipated future hardships. As with the other groups, their main reaction would be connected with labour – they are going to change jobs (33% of cases) or find extra ones (61% of cases). Additionally, they count on their ability to work at the land (29%), on the help of relatives (22%) and on their ability to endure hardships (22% of cases). It appears that such families demonstrate not only an active strategy at present, but a readiness to employ more a versatile approach in the face of possible future troubles.

Table 7. Actions taken by family in last 5 years to prevent or overcome a hard situation, per cent

	All	Below 1 SW*	1–1.5 SW	1.5–2 SW	2–3 SW	Above 3 SW
Got another job	34	48	37	29	28	39
Changed profession	11	22	13	9	8	4
Non-workers started working	26	22	24	25	29	33
Raised professional and educational level (got extra education, took courses)	16	23	23	12	15	11
Started business completely on their own	3	6	2	2	2	7
Received help from authorities for starting business	1	2	1	2	1	2
Found extra earnings	20	24	24	18	17	22
Received rent for apartment, dacha, garage, etc.	4	4	2	3	5	3
Changed dwelling for a cheaper one or moved to live with relatives	2	4	2	1	1	2
Produced more on dacha or farmland	15	22	21	10	12	13
Sold property	7	5	10	4	9	9
Economized, spent less on leisure, entertainment	66	79	73	74	61	30
Economized on clothing and footwear	65	75	66	75	60	36
Economized on nutrition	52	67	54	64	44	24
Received material help from relatives, friends	16	26	19	15	11	12
Received help, benefits from state or municipal institutions	7	18	5	6	9	2
Received help from civic institutions, NGOs	1	0	1	0	1	1
Received important information	6	3	6	3	5	16
Made new contacts with useful people	15	16	17	12	13	24
Other	1	1	0	0	2	1

*SW = income of 1 official "subsistence wage" per person.

Poor Families' Ways of Meeting Hardships

In the previous section, we identified four different tendencies of how people behave in the event of hardships. Our interviews focused on poverty, on those who were on the verge of poverty, how they cope, what actions they have taken and what resources they use. It might be argued that it is not possible to analyse strategies without taking access to resources into account (Rivkin-Fish 2005). For analytical reasons, we have used Sen's classification of assets into resources, rights and relations to distinguish between the different actions families have used (Sen 1984).

The Use of Rights

With reforms ordinary people gained some new rights while losing others. For example, they received the right to start businesses or private farming, but they lost the right to get a job, along with different rights to services they had been entitled to in the Soviet time. The new poverty phenomenon opened up a role for social workers as a new profession along with resources allocated to social services (Iarskaia-Smirnova and Romanov 2002). Interviews reveal that those who are entitled to social benefits are active enough to claim benefits and show how families try to fit the official criteria for the poor:

> I have many friends and all of them qualified to get benefits, applied for them and got them: benefits, subsidies, children's food. No one was refused, there is nothing bad in getting benefits. You are fit, why not to take? (Entrepreneur)

The amount of help offered by state social services is, however, often described as insufficient and even ridiculous:

> Sure we get milk food for my son. We also get 100 rubles benefit, it is such a funny sum of money. And to get that you should gather tons of references, proving you really need it. Experts of the agency came to our place to check our housing conditions, if we are really poor. (Young mother)

One thing that has been mentioned in interviews is that it has become more common to ask for benefits for apartments and rents, a problem which earlier was commonly dealt with by work places (Lazareva 2009).

> If we didn't have to pay rent for the flat, we would more or less have enough, but we have to spend so much on the flat, and there is no chance that we could buy one, nobody would give us that kind of money and it is completely unrealistic that we could ever earn enough money to buy one. So we will just stay here, and then see what happens. (low-income family with a child)

Respondents also provide examples of employees who have turned to the trade union to claim support in the form of sanatorium vouchers, compensation of employees or special help with repairs:

> They get a salary, but it's not enough for them. For example, a cleaner, her workday is shorter, but still she works and earns 6000 rubles per month and plus bonuses. But if she needs to install gas consumption, and she has no husband, she is divorced and her house is cold. She wants to install gas consumption, ask for help, and we help her, give money etc. (Trade union leader)

Some of the respondents who lost their jobs describe how they use their rights to get unemployment benefit by registering at the Employment service. The low unemployment benefit, however, means that they work illegally in order to survive, rather than using their rights to get assistance in job seeking and requalification which could improve future possibilities. It happens that such a behaviour is even promoted by staff from the unemployment centre who tell they "look the other side", when they observe those officially unemployed trading on the market, because as they explain:

> Everyone knows the unemployed have no choice. One can't live on unemployment benefits.

Presumably, some of the state or regional programmes provide better opportunities. Interviews describe families using the possibility to get a grant to build their own house from the federal programme for young families from 2010.[5] Respondents typically mention how important the help from parents or relatives was when they decided to build their own house. To use the grant for building your own house, for example, you typically need help from friends or relatives who are prepared to work for free as the grant does not cover the cost of labour or building materials. This help concerned assistance in building, financial help, giving a room to live or taking care of the children, while the family was temporarily homeless.

> Parents still help us. For example my father-in-law, he's a carpenter. He helped to build a house for us. We didn't hire any builders. (Father)

We also heard about families using the "mother's capital" to improve living conditions.

> A friend of mine, they rebuild their grandmother's house. He works on weekends and on weekdays he builds, for three years already. (Young mother in divorce, living with parents)

Respondents, however, indicated that it is maybe not the poorest who claim their citizen rights (for example, the right to get support from "the young families programme" to building the foundations of their own house).

The Use of Relations

The majority of respondents recognized the importance of financial support between relatives. Some of them provided examples of how a person or a family gives away resources when their relatives are in urgent need of help, while the same person or family may accept help when their own situation turns worse. Respondents describe how relatives help in different ways, it can be occasional or regular, payment of loan, food sharing, help with children, and, for example, cohabitation after divorce.

> I give money for food rarely, I provide only food for my son, and the rest, for water or gas consumption... all that is from parents, they pay and feed us. They also pay for a loan on my car. I don't help them in this case either. Sometimes they buy pants or a sweater for Vanya, my son. (A young mother living with parents)

Some respondents mentioned that their friends helped them to seek for jobs or sponsors, but perhaps more important, they provide moral support:

> Well friends – they can give only moral support. Of course if there are some troubles with Vanya, for example to bring milk, I asked a friend Lena, she drove her at that time new car and bought it to me. Well, there are some presents friends gave Vanya, toys, many toys. We have bought only a few of them ourselves. A godmother or friends, or relatives give presents. (A young mother)

As we have seen, families in vulnerable situations could find a few strategic opportunities to improve their situation. However, as social networks such as kinship are vitally important, they are vulnerable if somebody disappears. As earlier research shows, the most vulnerable social groups, as a rule, experience lack of social and even kinship networks, while inclusion into social networks gives a person a feeling of social security, moral support (Teodorovich 2009). A lack of communication might also be connected with self-exclusion:

> As parents here are rather peculiar ..., I don't know, maybe it is because of me, I did not join the parents club. I did not mix much with them, although there are certainly matters that it could be useful to discuss with them. They are there, some are friends between themselves, it is possible to be like that. (low-income family with a child)

As supported by earlier research on poverty and isolation (see i.e. Khlinskaya Rockhill 2010; Salmi 2006; Shubin 2007), those who lack support from parents, relatives and friends, and moral support from the nearest surrounding, might face a particular risk of falling into the "poverty trap" in the event of hardships. For example, migrants from other towns are typically in such a position. And, once inside the "poverty trap", they tend to get into other traps. Such a "domino effect" concerns not only migrants, but also influences the next generation. For instance, respondents depict a migrant family from Kazakhstan:

> A child has no documents and he won't have any, because his mother moved from Kazakhstan, she's a citizen of Kazakhstan, she has no Russian passport and she won't get it soon; she has no residence permit, no obligatory medical insurance. And a child doesn't have these documents either. That's why all the troubles. We go on to help the child; he is an orphan now, because the mother is now deprived of her parental rights. It was also hard to make, because there's no passport or any Russian identity document. It was a problem for us to place the child into a local rehabilitation center, since he has no certificate of birth, nothing. So the problem deals not with education but with defining the status of the family. (Social worker)

The Use of Resources

Answering the question "what will you do if things get worse", the respondents typically answered they would try to work more. For many respondents, an extra job is a characteristic of low income families. As emphasized by a school teacher, however, low wages might imply that people are trapped using all their time with several jobs:

> You see, I know families where they work from morning till night and have not one place of work. They just have a miserable salary and as a result a low income. It doesn't mean they are lazy, they are just low paid. It could be an employee of a government-financed organization. They get into a situation they can't influence. They can work all day long but still be low paid. How to overcome it? (School teacher)

In line with earlier research (Aidis, Estrin, and MickieWicz 2007; Ericson 2009), respondents express the view that it has become more difficult to set up private businesses than before. Still, people start their own businesses in, for instance, trading or taxi-driving. Interviews describe how entrepreneurship rises in crisis years, when families' incomes are not enough to live on (most likely, not formally, registered in order to avoid taxes). The possibility to work "vaktovyi metod", which usually means that the husband goes away for specific periods, to work in, for example, the oil fields or in the forest, was mentioned, although it was pointed out that this way of working could be harmful to the family.

One effect is that families in hardship, occupied by everyday survival routines simply do not have the time or strength for any planning, for example, they don't have time to think about leisure activities:

> I suffer in the evenings, I don't know how to organize life. I come from work, I sit with my son after school, then I go out with the dog, come back, he does not do his homework by himself, so I still have to sit with him, and I still have to prepare dinner and so on. How could I take him to after school activities? I would also have liked to do sports myself. But I have no idea when to go to after school activities'. (low-income family with a child)

Respondents further indicate that plot production is important for most people:

> Small towns are still alive due to home production of food. The land feeds. Everyone here is low paid. (Social worker)

> I don't know what we would have done if we had to buy food, we have everything; we don't buy vegetables, we have got eggs, chicken of our own. (Young mother)

> It happened to be a difficult period in Autumn, we used to live on home food and used to buy only milk and bread. (Young mother)

We also hear about the use of other natural resources:

> We have our land, garden. We grow up vegetables ourselves, we pick berries and mushrooms in a forest. We make jam, pickling mushrooms. A subsistence agriculture. (Father)

Coping Behaviour vs. Strategies to Change Living Conditions

Some respondents express an ambition or at least a hope to break out of poverty, while others mention methods which are more to be understood as ways of coping with a difficult situation (Figure 2). Sometimes respondents express an ambition to break out of a difficult situation in the future, arguing that they just have to go through some temporary hardships.[6] Coping behaviour could actually be transformed into a strategy in the future. It is possible to distinguish between those who have improved their situation in the last five years, vs. those whose situation has become worse. In the first group, actions were directed towards changing a job, improving of competence, education, development of human capital, development of social networks, development of important contacts and capability of making use of information.

In the second group, actions were directed towards taking on an extra job, changing profession, saving on clothes and shoes, nutrition, leisure, working on a plot and relying on support from parents. A wider spread of actions was noted with respect to the second group. Combining the information from Tables 1, 3 and 7 indicates that those in the lowest income groups have been more active than other groups; we also see that those who are primarily saving on expenses are among those who face a worse situation. This shows that facing increasing costs by working more and saving more ("just coping") could actually cause a downward process.

Interviews outlined about how families use benefits which can be referred to as citizen rights, how they used land, their own labour and other resources, as well as their good relations with their families and friends and also work relations. We heard about those who had moved to the city, but who failed

Coping	Strategic agency
• Take extra job • Be pluriactive • Start to work, change jobs/profession • Migration - loss of networks • Plot production • Subsistence entrepreneurship • Apply for social benefits • Borrow for consumption	• Professional development • Education (for children) • Change jobs (and move to Moscow) • "Vakhtovyi metod" • Start a business • Use grants from program for building private home • Become a foster family • Move to countryside and join specialist programme • Seek information • Borrow for investment • Investment in education

Figure 2. Ways of meeting poverty

and came back. We also heard about those who moved out of the town to the countryside in order to reduce costs of living and concentrate on agriculture. But still we see that being active is not enough, not even for those who are already above the surface. Many families near the poverty line, told about various activities, struggling just to cope with hardships and trying to keep above the surface.

We discovered that some of the mentioned hardships took place outside the immediate control of those affected. Such events could start a downward process. As confirmed by earlier research (e.g. Tichonova 2005), we sometimes have to deal with the fact that people for one reason or another enter vicious circles, where something happens causing a downward trend that is difficult to break out of.

One factor that could start a downward process is the loss of a breadwinner (caused by the death of a spouse or a divorce). The situation might be especially difficult if children are small as this also makes it harder to keep a full time job. A one-parent family with no relatives is likely to be particularly vulnerable. Both experts and families confirm that giving birth to a child means increasing expenses and decreasing income, since child benefits are inadequate, reflecting the inadequacy of Russian wages to support large families.[7]

A loss of a job as well as a sharp decrease in salary appears to be an important cause of financial difficulties within families. Respondents point out negative consequences of the crisis in 2008 as heavy redundancies took place at the most important enterprises in the town. At that time, working people felt the crisis as well, due to sharp salary reductions (in some cases twice). And, only some of them were able to find alternative adequately paid jobs or to start their own businesses. The vision of the opportunities available among the clients of job centres is sometimes limited by previous work experience, especially for those whose occupation was highly specialized and not highly qualified. Many have to just cope and to be patient. As a trade union leader puts it:

> If there is no job, depression grows, and poverty comes, and a suicide, and a hooliganism, and a robbery etc. (Trade Union Leader)

The point here has not been to deepen the discussion into the causes of poverty, but rather to highlight how a single event can cause a downward mobility when people are close to the poverty line and vulnerable to any changes. It does not really matter how it starts, but we want to draw the attention to the circumstances that, if it starts, there is no clear mechanism to stop it in terms of societal structures. We hear about how people cope, but how difficult it could be to get over the threshold. Respondents indicated that it is not, maybe, the poorest who have the strength to actually apply for social benefits. We also find that we have not really met the poorest. We hear about them only through the interviews with others:

Downward trend	Upward trend
• Loss of job – depression – poverty – suicide, criminality • Migration - loss of networks • The birth of a child – increasing consumption • Low income - drinking • Drinking - low income • Falling into the category of 'undeserving poor'	• Grant from programme for building private home • Rising up from the category of 'undeserving poor' • Enter social network which activates people

Figure 3. Reasons for changes in poverty

> Alcoholism is very close. As a rule people applying are of dysfunctional families. An alcoholic has usually lost his job, and lives on the verge of poverty if not below. They are often jobless. (Psychologist)
>
> There are low income individuals who drove into poverty by themselves. Here's our tradition to drink a glass and forget about everything. (Entrepreneur)

These are the ones who don't even have proper documents, needed for receiving elementary support. Although we heard about individual social workers who describe how they have to help people step-by-step to collect documents, etc., the tendency seems to be that if they fall out of the social security system, they are likely to be lost. Rather than helping families in hardship to find ways back to normal life, social policy is directed towards saving children (Figure 3).

Conclusions

The survey that forms the base for this article provides a general picture of strategies and ways of coping across income groups. On the basis of this survey, a factor analysis was carried out in order to get a deeper understanding of the situation for the poor. It was complemented with interviews. From the factor analysis, we distinguished four basic types of behaviour for families, facing the risk of poverty:

- *non-mobility and economizing, or coping with the use of own resources of the family* – 59% of families;
- *horizontal mobility* (changing jobs) – 33% of families;
- *reaction without strategy* – 29% of families.
- *upward mobility with the use of external resources* – 28% of families.

The factor analysis shows how strategies are not totally mutually exclusive; in particular, the first one is typically used by most families, alone or as a complement to other actions. The analysis shows that families employing the mobility strategies tend to be better-off and more positive towards their current situation and possible future. Thus, social and labour mobility appear to be important factors for overcoming poverty. Social connections also prove to be important for those who are already poor or face the risk of poverty. Inclusion in social networks gives them new possibilities and may activate their capabilities and help them to be active. Social networks offer information exchange, which is important for overcoming poverty. Those families that combine work and professional mobility with being socially active appear to reach better results in terms of both survival and development. Social and labour activity of more successful families seems to be connected with their low tolerance to hardship. Such families are not willing simply to sustain, they start to react earlier than others, and react more actively, which gives them additional chances for success.

Interviewees talk about using land in order to produce food for their own consumption and also to build their own house. This is about using "mother's capital" or grants from the presidential programmes and having a capacity for manual work. But it is also about using rights to unemployment benefits and other benefits. Some respondents have mentioned as the most valuable resource "the good working family and a husband who does not drink". However, many respondents also indicate that it is not enough to be active, while some of the poorer families are not able to break out of vicious circles; even if they work more and more. They try continuously to reduce expenses just to cope, and they are particularly vulnerable to any changes. Interviews reveal that families living on the edge of poverty do not have time and energy for long-term strategies. This highlights the need for supporting structures. The supporting role of public authorities is especially important when considering the possibilities for poor people themselves to take actions.

The fact that it is visible that some people are able to break out of poverty (by their own actions) shows that it is interesting to study what strategies they have used. More specifically, this tells us something about the effects of reforms and consequences of social change. The analysis of strategies of change means that you focus on agency, which in turn feeds back into social change, challenging existing norms, changing the space for actions and imposing effects on societal development. On the other hand, coping behaviour should be associated with acting within a given space, adapting behaviour which tends to keep to existing norms and preventing societal changes. This can also tell us something about processes leading to a continuation of poverty, how and why processes of poverty are started, when and how they are leading to and reproducing patterns of poverty and when it is possible to break out of such vicious circles.

Acknowledgements

Field research in Russia has been organized and made together with Nina Ivashinenko, Rebecca Kay and Margarita Lobanova. We want to express our gratitude to them and also to several other persons who participated in research work in different important roles. We would like to express special thanks to Leo Granberg for his valuable comments.

Funding

The authors greatly appreciate the support from Lobachevsky State University of Nizhniy Novgorod, the funding from Nizhny Novgorod Scientific Research Centre for Economics, Society and Science (EON) and the research grant from the Swedish Research Council.

Notes

1. Families with many children are even more vulnerable (Social and demographic development of Russia. , UNFPA, 2010. http://akparov.ru/node/238).
2. The survey was based on a questionnaire with 500 households within different income groups, chosen to represent the ordinary population of a small town in Russia.
3. The interviews for this article were conducted in a small town, where industrial plants were closed during crises. The interview data consist of 35 semi-structured, in-depth interviews with local residents and families experiencing poverty, professionals from local social service structures, leaders of charitable and other non-governmental organizations, as well as representatives of the local administration.
4. Federal law No 122, August 22, 2004. A key task was to divide administrative and financial responsibility for providing benefits (*l'goty*) between the central level and the regions, which means that regions support two-thirds of the recipients. See Wengle and Rasell (2008), 743–44.
5. http://programma-molodaja-semja.ru/programmy.
6. The most obvious division concerns the fact that we connect strategic behaviour with a more long-term perspective, while coping draws our attention to survival and the handling of hardships in the short-run.
7. Earlier research shows, the daily calorie intake decreases with the number of children in a family (Wegren 2013).

References

Aidis, R., S. Estrin, and T. MickieWicz. 2007. Innovations and Entreprenurship Development in Russia; Comparative Perspective, UCL-SSEES, Economics Working Paper No. 79.

Ashwin, S. 2006. "The Post-Soviet Gender Order: Imperatives and Implications." In *Adapting to Russia's New Labor Market. Gender and Employment Behavior*, edited by S. Ashwin, 32–56. London: Routledge.

Avraamovoi, E. M., ed. 2003. *Adaptapcionnye strategii naseleniya, Kollektivnaya monografiya* [Adaptation Strategies of the Population]. St.Peterburg: EUSPb.

Bobkov, V. N., V. G. Zinin, and A. A. Razumov. 2004. Politika dohodov i zarabotnoi platy [Policy, Incomes and Wages]. Doklad v ramkah proekta MOT "Preodolenie bednosti, sodeistvie zanyatosti i mestnoe ekonomicheskoe razvitie v Severo-Zapadnom federal'nom okrugė [Report of the ILO Project "Overcoming Poverty, Promotion of Employment and Local Economic Development in the North-West Federal District]. Moskva: Ministerstvo Truda i Social'nogo Razvitija.

Chebankova, E. 2010. "Public and Private Cycles of Socio-political Life in Putin's Russia." *Post-Soviet Affairs* 26 (2): 121–148.

Clarke, S. 1999. *New Forms of Employment and Household Survival Strategies in Russia*. Coventry: ISITO/CCLS.

Desai, P., and T. Idson. 1998. *Wage Arrears, Poverty, and Family Survival Strategies in Russia*, Discussion Paper Series No. 9899-05. New York: Columbia University.

Ellman, M. 2000. "The Social Costs and Consequences of the Transformation Process." United Nations, Economic Commission for Europe, (UNECE), Economic Survey of Europe no 2/3.

Ericson, R. 2009. "The Russian Economy in the Year 2008: Testing the "Market Economy"." *Post-Soviet Affairs* 25 (3): 209–231.

Gradoselskaya, G. V. 2001. *Analysis of Social Networks, Cand. Sci. (Social.) Dissertation*. Moscow: Institute of Sociology, Russian Academy of Sciences.

Granberg, L. 2007. "Rural Paths in Russia." In *Reflecting Transformation in Post-Socialist Rural Areas*, edited by Maarit Heinonen, Jouko Nikula, Inna Kopoteva and Leo Granberg, 49–62. Cambridge: Cambridge Scholars Publishing.

Guariglia, A., and B.-Y. Kim. 2004. "Earnings Uncertainty, Precautionary Saving, and Moonlighting in Russia." *Journal of Population Economics* 17 (2): 289–310.

Iarskaia-Smirnova, E., and P. Romanov. 2002. "A Salary is Not Important Here: The Professionalization of Social Work in Contemporary Russia." *Social Policy & Administration* 36 (2): 123–141.

Ioffe, G., and T. Nefedova. 1997. *Continuity and Change in Rural Russia: A Geographical Perspective*. Oxford University Press.

Kay, R. 2006. *Men in Contemporary Russia: The Fallen Heroes of Post-Soviet Change*. Aldershot: Ashgate.

Khlinskaya Rockhill, E. 2010. *Lost to the State. Family Discontinuity, Social Orphanhood and Residential Care in the Russian Far East*. New York: Berghahn Books.

Kim, B.-Y. 2002. "The Participation of Russian Households in the Informal Economy: Evidence from the VTsIOM Data1." *The Economics of Transition* 10 (3): 689–717.

Klugman, J., ed. 1998. *Poverty in Russia. Public Policy and Private Responses. EDI Development Studies*. Washington, DC: The World Bank.

Kravchenko, Z. 2008. *Family (versus) Policy: Combining Work and Care in Russia and Sweden*. Stockholm: Acta Universitatis Stockholmiensis.

Lazareva, O. 2009. *Labour Market Outcomes during the Russian Transition*. PhD diss., Stockholm School of Economics.

Ledeneva, A. 1998. *Russia's Economy of Favours*. Cambridge: Cambridge University Press.

Ledeneva, A. 2008. "Blat and Guanxi: Informal Practices in Russia and China." *Comparative Studies in Society and History* 50 (1): 118–144.

Lokshin, M., and B. M. Popkin. 1999. "The Emerging Underclass in the Russian Federation: Income Dynamics, 1992–1996." *Economic Development and Cultural Change* 47 (4): 803–829.

Lokshin, M., and R. Yemtsov. 2001. *Household Strategies for Coping with Poverty and Social Exclusion in Post-Crisis Russia*. Washington, DC: The World Bank.

O'Brien, D. J., V. V. Patsiorkovski, and S. K. Wegren. 2004. "Poverty and Adaptation in Rural Russia." *Journal of Peasant Studies* 31: 457–488.

Ovcharova, L. N. 2008. "Bednost i Ekonomicheskii Rost v Rossii [Poverty and Economic Growth in Russia]." *Zhyrnal Isleovanii Sotsialnoi Politiki* 6 (4): 439–456.

Pickup, F., and A. White. 2003. "Livelihoods in Postcommunist Russia: Urban/Rural Comparisons." Work, Employment & Society 17: 419–433.

Ries, N. 2008. *Potato Ontology: Surviving Postsocialism in Russia*. March, Paper 32.

Rimashevskaya, N. M. 2004. "Bednost' i marginalizaciya naseleniya (social'noe dno) [Poverty and Marginalization of Population (social bottom)]." *Sociologicheskie issledovaniya* [Sociological Research] 4: 51–77.

Rimashevskaya, N. M. 2010. "Riski bednosti v sovremennoi Rossii [Risks of Poverty in Contemporary Russia]." *Narodonaselenie* 2 (48): 4–9.

Rivkin-Fish, M. 2005. *Women's Health in Post-Soviet Russia. The Politics of Intervention*. Bloomington: Indiana University Press.

Round, J., and E. Kosterina. 2005. "The Construction of 'Poverty' in Post-Soviet Russia." *Perspectives on European Politics and Society* 6 (3): 705–727.

Salmi, A.-M. 2006. *Social Networks and Everyday Practices in Russia*. Helsinki: Kikimora Publications.

Sätre, A.-M. 2001. "Women's and Men's Work in Transitional Russia: Legacies of the Soviet System." *Post-Soviet Affairs* 17 (1): 56–79.

Sätre, A.-M. 2010. "Women's Work in Transitional Russia: Women's Strategies for Entrepreneurship and Survival in Russian Regions." In *Perestroika: Process and Consequences*, edited by M. Kangaspuro, J. Nikula and I. Stodolsky, 330–350. Helsinki: Finnish Literary Society.

Sätre, A.-M. 2012. "Gendered Experiences in Russian Entrepreneurship, Family and Social Activities." In *And They All Lived Happily Ever after? Norms and Everyday Practices of Family and Parenthood in Russia and Eastern Europe*, edited by H. Carlbäck, I. Gradskova and Z. Kravchenko, 297–318. Budapest: CEU press.

Sen, Amartya. 1984. *Resources, Values and Development*. Oxford: Basil Blackwell Publisher Ltd.

Shanin, T. 1999. "Informal Economies and Expolary Structures in Contemporary Russia." In *Neformalnya Ekonomika. Rossiya V Mir*, edited by T. Shanin, 61–84. Moscow: Logos.

Shubin, S. 2007. "Networked Poverty in Rural Russia." *Europe-Asia Studies* 59 (4): 591–620.

Silverman, B., and M. Yanowitch. 2000. *New Rich, New Poor, New Russia: Winners and Losers on the Russian Road to Capitalism*. Expanded ed. Armonk, NY: M.E. Sharpe.

Soldatkin, A. 2013. "Bednost Kak Sosialnaya Problema Povyshenie Kachestva Zhizni Naseleniya [Poverty as a Social Problem]." In *Participatory Approach in Improving the Quality of Life*, edited by N. M. Rimashevskoi and N. N. Ivashinenko, 135–156. Nizhnii Novgorod-Moskva: Izd-vo Nizhegorodskogo gosuniversiteta im. N.I.Lobachevskogo.

Soldatkin, A. E., and A. A. Varyzgina. 2013. "Strategii Sovladaniya S Bednost'yu Sredi Naseleniya Malyh Gorodov Nizhegorodskoi Oblasti, Materialy Mezhdunarodnoi Nauchno-Prakticheskoi Konferencii." Gumanitarii v XXI veke, 18–19 aprelya 2013.Pod obshei redakciei prof. Z.H. Saralievoi: v 2 t. T.1. – N.Novgorod: Izdatel'stvo NISOC, 696s, 198–204.

Tartakovskaya, I. N. 2004. "Social'nye seti i povedenie na rynke truda [Social Networks and Labour Market Behavior]." *Sociologicheskii Zhurnal* 1 (2): 129–144.

Teodorovich, M. 2009. *Bednost' kak social'naya problema: strategicheskij podhod* [Poverty as a Social Problem: Strategic Approach]. Nizhny Novgorod: Monograph Nizhny Novgorod State University.

Tichonova, N. 2005. "Rossiiskaya bednost': masshtaby, prichiny, perspektivy [Russian Poverty: the Extent, Causes and Prospects]." *Narod MROT 21*. http://www.index.org.ru/journal/21/tihon21.html.

Walker, M. 1998. "Survival Strategies in an Industrial Town in East Ukraine." In *Surviving Post-Socialism: Local Strategies and Regional Responses in Eastern Europe and the Former Soviet Union*, edited by S. Bridger and F. Pine, 188–202. London: Routledge.

Wallace, C. 2002. "Household Strategies: Their Conceptual Relevance and Analytical Scope in Social Research." *Sociology* 36 (2): 275–292.

Wegren, K. 2013. "Food Security in the Russian Federation." *Eurasian Geography and Economics* 54 (1): 22–41.

Wengle, S., and M. Rasell. 2008. "The Monetisation of L'*goty*: Changing Patterns of Welfare Politics and Provision in Russia." *Europe-Asia Studies* 60 (5): 739–756.

White, A. 2000. "Social Change in Provincial Russia: The Intelligentsia in a *Raion* Centre." *Europe-Asia Studies* 52 (4): 677–694.

World Bank. 2011. Russian Economic Report No. 24, 3–16, Russia.

Yates, S. 2004. "Living with Poverty in Post-Soviet Russia: Social Perspectives on Urban Development." Doctoral thesis, London School of Economic and Political Science.

Single Men, Single Stories: Alternative Paths in the Transition from the Late Soviet to the Neoliberal Market Economy in the Light of Life Stories

Ildikó Asztalos Morell and Irina Tiurikova

This research investigates life strategies of physical worker Russian men, belonging to the generation of people who were the most active group in the late Soviet period, went through the collapse of USSR and the transformation to capitalism. The historical biographic perspective allows reproducing common social experiences which have formed this generation. The in-depth biographical interviews were conducted with six men of age 46–63, single, with officially low income, who started their working lives in the public sector. The research shows the diversity of men's alternative life strategies to adjust to the neoliberal economy established after the collapse of the USSR. The paper explores the biographies as representations of diverse forms of masculinities formed along gender, age, social position and marital status-based marginalization processes emerging in the transition context.

Introduction

There was a widespread expectation that with the transition into the market economy men and women in Russia, as well as in other post-socialist countries, were to be divided into "winners" and "losers" (Silverman and Yanovitch 2000). The emerging socio-political transition to market relations was envisaged as an arena for the strengthening of traditional gender relations, a kind of "gender restoration", which was to lead to releasing men's creativities previously emasculated by state socialism (Eley 1998). As Novikova et al. argue, diverse post-socialist nation-rebuilding projects "targeted the active reconstruction of men's [*traditional*] social roles and representations as well as masculinity imageries." (Novikova et al. 2003, 86, see also Kolga 2001; Watson 1996). Strengthening of images of masculinity formed a part of gender-specific expectations concerning men's and women's activity and positions within the "home – work"- system, which became popular during the late Soviet period (Meshcherkina 2002).

Thus, a successful public image was combined with expectations concerning the revival of complementary gender roles and revival of men's status as the main breadwinner and head of household (Kukhterin 2000). We can find in the printed media of the 1990s, without any doubts, many corroborations of this idea. Those "succeeding" in the emerging market relationships are seen as being the winners, and this group is most commonly represented by the portrait of a man, aged approximately between 30 and 40, a successful businessman or manager (Yurchak 2002). Meanwhile, women portrayed in magazines were urged to find their new rules in the domain of the home and beauty (Kis 2005).

The gender-specific expectations of the post-Soviet period were reflected even in research, where scholars argued that loss of jobs would hit women harder, and a dismantling of women friendly institutions of the Soviet state, such as the cut in social provisions to working mothers secured by work places, would lead to a disproportionate loss of labour by women, while prospective new jobs for women within the service sector would create insecure, low-prestige employment (Posadskaya 1994).

A contrasting image, also identified as the "crises of masculinity" discourse views men as losers portraying them as a homogeneous group, as "given up, on themselves, on their responsibilities and on the wider society of which they are a part" (Kay 2006, 207). Men are seen as troubled by apathy, defeatism and indifference (208): "Russian men have been dying earlier, drinking more, and committing suicide in greater numbers since the end of the Soviet period" (Ashwin and Lytkina 2004, 190). The situation of men in crises is often associated with men's position in the Soviet period. According to the expectations of what researchers identified as "hegemonic soviet masculinity" (Chernova 2012; Kelly 2003, 389; Schrand 2002, 45; Zdravomyslova and Temkina 2012) men were to obtain recognition in the public sphere through work, being the main breadwinners and economic suppliers of the family. In contrast, women were seen as allies of the state (Kukhterin 2000) charged with the moral guidance over both children and their men. The critiques of the triangular state-centred Soviet and in broader meaning state socialist gender model emphasized the role of the state in monopolizing "paternal power" (Aivazova 1998; Goven, 2002; Verdery 1994). Fathers were seen primarily as economic providers, through which men became disassociated from caring within the family leading to the loss of their rights as fathers (Chernova 2012; Municio-Larsson, 2012; Novikova et al. 2003; Zdravomyslova and Temkina 2012). Those men, who were not capable of achieving status and economic recognition in the public could not reverse gender roles in the family, where their patriarchal position had been relegated (Ashwin 2000). Ashwin argued that as part of the continuities from the Soviet past, men experiencing marginalization in the context of post-socialist transition, especially those unemployed, have often been doubly marginalized, due to lacking a meaningful retreat to the private.

However, Soviet systems were not all-pervasive, and an alternative (second, informal, grey) economy flourished, which gave also an alternative context for the formation of masculinities (Asztalos Morell 1999). As Zdravomyslova and Temkina (2012) argued, the conceptual divide between public vs. private is not fully adequate for describing Soviet and post-Soviet realities. The arenas of informal survival strategies (Clarke 1999) were also arenas for the formation of alternative masculinities.

An additional image of men (Kukhterin 2000) elucidates their struggle to gain recognition as caring fathers, challenging the formerly identified gender stereotypical images. Kay (2006) finds corroboration of this image in the provincial media, which portray individual men as "having a strong sense of moral responsibility", and accepting the male obligation "to protect and to serve" (209).

While recent research concerning Soviet and post-Soviet masculinity (Ashwin and Lytkina 2004; Kay 2006; Kukhterin 2000) has emphasized the importance of fatherhood for the identity formation of men either as absentee fathers or as men seeking to gain recognition for their fatherhood as providers or caregivers, less attention has been paid to being single in a broader meaning, which would include the study of the interrelation between both public and private roles of single men finding themselves outside of cohabiting heterosexual pair relations.[1]

Furthermore, there is a need to problematize the mechanisms of the creation and transfer of socio-economic and gender inequalities from the Soviet to the Post-Soviet period. The life experiences of the generation born in the 50s and 60s, starting their private and public careers during the Soviet period form a bridge between the two epochs and by this allow the analysis of these transitions. These men also give expression to the concerns of a specific demographic group, men at the latter stage of their active period, in the transition towards ageing and retirement, an age category that has not been in the focus of research before. Therefore, we focus on a group of single men who find themselves at the later stage of working life on the one hand, and on the other hand, who have already built their families and their children have become adults.

Finally, there has been an overwhelming focus in studying the interrelation between post-socialist economic and gender transition within the conditions of the main, formal economy (Sätre Åhlander 2005). It is argued that the transition to the market economy was accompanied by the increase in social differentiation and the marginalization of social groups not capable of being integrated increased. Men's economic self-realization is commonly associated with their engagement within the main (formal) economic sphere. Meanwhile, research pinpointed the importance of informal strategies for the survival of marginalized groups (Clarke 1999). Therefore, the study of the importance of men's economic self-realization in the context of post-socialist transitions needs to incorporate an understanding of their activities in the second (grey, informal) economy (Asztalos Morell 1999). Men in the focus of this study have been or still are either physical skilled workers or have used their bodies as work instruments. They combine in varying forms survival strategies based on the formal and informal economies.

Our intention was to shed light on the conditions of men who represent along different dimensions of intersecting marginalities of age, singlehood and poverty either the losers of transition or those striving after alternative masculinities. The analysis is based on interviews with six single men living currently in the Archangelsk region between the ages of 46 and 63 with a skilled work background.

Masculinities and Social Inequalities in the Late Soviet and Post-socialist Transformation Context

The accumulation of a patriarchal dividend ensuring certain privileges for men in society was central for Connell's theory (1995) of masculinities. Hegemonic masculinity refers to a narrow group of men, which we might most commonly associate with a kind of international businessman, harvesting the profits of both public careers and caring homes. However, the majority of men find themselves in different stages and forms of marginalized masculinities, which might give access to different degrees to diminishing degrees of patriarchal dividends. The specific context of the Soviet and post-Soviet transition period provides challenges for the applicability of Connell's theory. One such challange is posited by the crises of masculinity discourse which identifies men as the victims of the Soviet system. Therefore, we need to problematize the specificities of the Soviet and post-Soviet transition context as arenas for the articulation of masculinities.

State socialism challenged the economic system where the possession of economic capital was central in the generation of social inequalities. Applying Bourdieu's (1986) theory of forms of capital, Szelényi et al. (1988) argued that it was rather immaterial capital, such as cultural and social capital that played a central role. The main access route for the stratification of Soviet-type etatistic societies was through teleological and technocratic capital. Status was achieved between workers and leaders either through political allegiance (cadre) or through human (skill) capital (technocracy). However, as Szelényi et al. (1988) argued, Soviet-type societies were not all-pervasive. Alternative systems of survival emerged, where the informal economy constituted a major force. The formal and informal spheres formed interconnected, yet separate spheres for the formation of social inequalities including that of gender (Asztalos Morell 1999).

The first and the second economies were both spheres of patriarchal dividend accumulation. In the state public sphere, men's ability to access some kind of patriarchal dividend depended on their positions within the hierarchies of hegemonic Soviet masculinity. Here, the above-discussed political and cultural (human) capitals were of importance, which also gave access to valuable social contacts, since men occupied positions on the top of work life hierarchies. Nonetheless, patriarchal dividends could be accumulated even in the informal sphere. During the transition period, gender (a patriarchy dividend in form of symbolic and social capitals accumulated in both, state public and quasi-public spheres) became a resource for constructing strategies for overcoming the crises (Meshcherkina 2002).

Masculinities in the Transition of the Formal Sphere

Problematizing the social transitions of the post-socialist period a long-lasting dominating theory was that of path dependencies (Stark 1992), arguing for the continuity of social, cultural and economic patterns and the longevity, stolidity, stiffness of institutions with regard to change (Sätre Åhlander 2005). Continuity and change characterize even the gender patterns of transition. Sätre Åhlander (2005) argued that applying Kornai's theory (Kornai 1986) highlights the impact of the differential transition of the Soviet economy. During the Soviet period, certain sectors of the economy, such as military industry, heavy industry, were prioritized. They were protected from labour shortages by higher wages, and were typically male-dominated areas. Other sectors, such as consumption-related or cultural spheres, were not shielded from demand factors, and were low priority in terms of wages and had typically a high degree of feminization. Some of the former priority areas, such as military industry, maintained their protected features, while many male-dominated sectors, such as heavy industry jobs, were hard hit, when market conditions were adopted. Meanwhile, it seems that those areas, which were low priority during state socialism, were both more adjusted to hard budget control and were those, which were underdeveloped compared to the demands of society, and thus have expanded following transition. As a consequence, men's labour areas, with a few exceptions, such as energy industry and military industry, declined in importance, leading to high degree of loss of status and employment by men, while women's work opportunities were less prone to disappear and more likely to develop.

On the other hand, the former gender segregation of work was reproduced under the new conditions. The most privileged and senior positions continue to be held by men, whereas women continue to be engaged with professions unprivileged and remote from power. In the new Russian economy, this labour division was replicated and acquired new features. While the sphere of serious business was primarily occupied by men, a new "women's business" – mostly in the beauty and leisure industries – appeared (Yurchak 2002).

An Alternative Model of Masculinity as Performed in the "Quasi Public" Sphere

Chernova (2002) argues that the dichotomy of public, the domain of the political and of rationality – and so, the sphere of men – and private, the domain of the family and household – and so the sphere of women, usually used in relation to western societies, becomes ineffective when applied to research on Soviet society. The inefficiency of this approach is caused by some particular social and cultural phenomena and practices which existed in Soviet society at the intersection of the public and private spheres (Chernova 2002). To mark this sphere of interaction, E. Zdravomyslova introduces the concept of the "quasi public sphere" which means the space of communication independent from the state (Zdravomyslova 2012, with reference to Voronkov 1997). This sphere represents the space for construction and performance of an alternative masculinity – not opposite to, but existing beyond the hegemonic Soviet masculinity constructed and performed in the official public sphere determined by the state. This alternative, compensatory model of masculinity was constructed and existed in an informal, or quasi-public sphere, was produced in homogeneous men's groups, relatively independent from the state regime. In the Soviet period in these homogeneous groups, men accumulated what Connell (1995) refers to as a patriarchal dividend, which was expressed in terms of social connections. These networks served as social capital (Bourdieu 1986).

Survival strategies of the Soviet period based on the informal sector emerged from the specific conditions of the state socialist system. Although some argued, in the case of Hungary, that such strategies could lead to the accumulation of economic capital and a process of embourgeoisement (Szelényi et al. 1988), facing the facts of transition, these strategies most commonly were either reproduced within the new post-socialist context or proved non-viable, yet seldom led to breakpoints from marginal positions (Clarke 1999). Such breakthroughs might occur in cases of successful processes of intersecting accumulation of material and immaterial capital assets (Asztalos Morell 2014). Rather, the post-socialist economic elites originate from the elites of the late Soviet period (Szelényi, Szelényi, and Kovách 1995).

Our research is focused on the survival strategies of men not belonging to the normative models of Soviet and post-Soviet hegemonic masculinities, rather we focus on men who can either be considered as losers or as representing alternative paths of masculinities.

Transitions and Marginal Masculinities

Applying R. Connell's theory, we understand masculinity as a dynamic category which changes historically under the pressure of political and economic transformations and changes of ideology, etc. We also consider masculinity as a category which changes over time at the individual level. We distinguish three stages of this change: entering manhood (becoming masculinities); in manhood (being masculinities); and entering marginal manhood (ageing masculinities). The hypothesis is that the patriarchy dividend received by man because of *being* men is not a constant and unchangeable privilege which a man possesses in the same degree throughout the whole life. This dividend is accumulated, held and gets lost as far as man passes through the above stages of masculinity. As such, we consider the patriarchy dividend as functioning in both public and private spheres. It implies that even if in the sphere of private life a man continues to use this patriarchy dividend even in his old age, in the public sphere his claims to it become invalid, because regardless of his physical condition (biological age), an elderly man after 50 is no longer seen as a "man". This neutralization of the gender of elderly men in the public sphere, especially, when it concerns the issue of employment, is not uniform.

Though we focus on the masculine gender group and investigate masculine survival strategies, an intersectional approach allows us to take into consideration the fact that men do not represent a homogeneous group, different from women through certain specific privileges. The respondents themselves underline that perception and interpretation of their age by other people establishes certain limits on their life claims. Ageism turns out to be the most obvious type of discrimination towards "elderly" men; as such, the age turns out to be a relative category depending on the symbolic and economic capitals of respondents. The lower symbolic and economic capitals are, the more negatively the age level of respondents is perceived, and they are regarded by others as "elderly". Thus, in the framework of research such terms as "age", "old", "elderly" are used not in a biological, but with a socio-psychological meaning. Age itself is regarded, like gender, as a social construct.

Convertibility Between Different Forms of Capital as Survival Strategies

Ageing constitutes a factor that influences even the convertibility between various forms of capital. Bourdieu (1986) distinguishes three forms of capital which on certain conditions might be converted into each other. Depending on the field in which the capital functions, these forms are: economic, cultural and social capitals. Economic capital is the form of capital which is immediately and directly convertible into money and may be institutionalized in the forms of property rights. Cultural capital can obtain institutionalized forms, as in educational qualifications, and embodied forms, which gain expression in long-lasting dispositions of the mind and body, i.e. habitus. It might be convertible into economic capital on certain conditions. Social capital is "the aggregate of actual or potential resources which are linked to possession of a durable network of more or less institutionalized relationships of mutual acquaintance and recognition – or in other words, to membership in a group – which provides each of its members with the backing of the collectivity-owned capital".[2] In other words, social capital is made up of social "connections" which provide individuals belonging to a certain group with special privileges that represent actual or potential resources for multiplying other forms of capital.

The different forms of capital are interconnected. In certain cases, the availability of social capital represents the main condition of capitals' conversion. For instance, social capital facilitates the conversion of cultural capital (implying skills and qualifications) into economic capital, or services and goods, which can provide the owner of cultural capital with necessary living conditions. In this sense, the conversion of cultural and social capitals into economic capital might be regarded as a survival strategy.

It is important to mention some difficulties related to social and cultural capitals' conversion. First of all, the existence of a network of connections and relationships is not given. It is a "product of investment strategies, individual or collective, consciously or unconsciously aimed at establishing or reproducing social relationships".[3] Putnam (2000) had a divergent perception of social capital seeing it more as the accumulation of trust and he differentiated between bonding (within groups of similar social status) and bridging (between groups of different social status) social capital. Social mobility is seen to be facilitated mostly by the second.

Secondly, while, on the one hand, market demand for certain qualifications determines the chances of an individual making a profit from his cultural capital, on the other hand, the fact that cultural capital is embodied means it is impacted by the physiological and psychological transitions of its owner. Ageing or employee injury, reducing individual's ability for physical work, lead to a depreciation of individual's cultural capital if his/her qualification has been linked with physical labour. And vice versa, if an individual's qualification has been linked to intellectual labour, his/her cultural capital – assuming that he/she is keeping pace with transitions and changing intellectual demands – multiplies with ageing, bringing more profit to its owner. This observation is important because our respondents possess different cultural capitals which determine their survival strategies as well as their physical condition and biological age.

Method and Sampling

The research interviews were conducted by Irina Tiurikova and Lidia Kriulya, both of whom are native speakers of Russian and between the age of 20 and 30, using semi-structured qualitative in-depth interviews which were conducted with six men aged between 46 and 63 years old. The chosen men were to be single, meaning officially not married, which could also be a result of divorce or widowhood. It did not exclude having out of marriage relations, yet the chosen men were not to cohabit with their eventual partners. We chose also men who started their career during the Soviet time in the public sector. However, they were to have low first economy incomes during the post-Soviet time, which they could combine with income from the informal economy or from occasional benefits from their specific cultural capitals and qualifications. The respondents were found through social network, and first contacted by people they knew well. The interviews were conducted by the team of researchers, in the university classrooms or in café chosen by respondents. All interviews were tape-recorded and transcribed.

The qualitative methodology was chosen due to the type of research questions: *how?* (Silverman 2010). Our research questions were: *How* do single men after 50, with low income, make their living in Russia? and *How* do such categories as gender, age and class determine their survival strategies? We used in-depth biographical interview as a method because it centres on the stories the subjects tell, i.e. personal *narratives*. As S. Kvale and S. Brinkmann note, the narratives that appear during interview are "one of the natural cognitive and linguistic forms through which individuals attempt to organise and express meaning and knowledge" (Kvale and Brinkmann 2009, 155). Thus, the aim of our interviews was through the individual stories to reproduce the meanings and knowledge of one generation. By "generation" we understand on the one hand, collective identity, based on self-determination and, on the other hand, structural condition, i.e. social environment, daily routine and events which form an individual way of life.

Brief Presentation of Respondents

All of the men in our study have high school-level education achieving different diplomas qualifying them for skilled work. One of the men had even a complementary shorter education at college level. Nonetheless, the men in our study represent two broader categories. On the one hand, we find men whose working life was based primarily on hard physical work (Sergey, Vladimir and Vahtang), and on the other hand, we find men, where although their work contained a physical aspect, nonetheless, this aspect was not hard and did not consist of physical work destructive of the body and whose work contained a higher degree of white collar features (Vadim, Alexey, Evgeny).

Men with Hard Physical Work

Case 1 Sergey

Sergey, born in 1966 (46 years old) in Arkhangelsk. He graduated from the Naval College, served in tow. At the age of 30 (1996) retired from Tralflot.

Worked as a locksmith, a stoker. When working "on land" changed his employers, both in government and commercial organizations, almost once a year. Was always employed in hard manual jobs. Unemployed at the present moment. Divorced with an adult child. Lives with his mother. Most of the summer time lives at datcha. Looks about 60 years old.

Case 2 Vladimir

Vladimir, born in 1961 (51 years old) in Arkhangelsk. Higher maritime education. From 1981 to 1989 worked on a ship, went abroad (Europe, Mediterranean Sea). From 1989 docker mechanic. From 1993 worked as trucker, auto mechanic, fitter plumber, mechanic at the poultry farm. Lives alone. Has a house in the countryside where he lives the whole year. In summer works for babushkas. Has registration in the town, in the three-room flat of his brother, a person with special abilities (has no legs), an alcohol abuser. Lived with brother but moved out because of the heavy drinking habits of his brother. Income: 14.000, plus "haltura". Divorced, single. Has a son (31 years old). Does not maintain relationship with his child. Looks about 60–65 years old.

Case 3 Vahtang

Vahtang, born in 1952 (60 years old). In 1971 (19 years old) moved from Georgia to the Russian Federation, to Severodvinsk to serve in the army. After three years in the Northern fleet, he settled in Severodvinsk to work at the Northern ship-building plant as a welder. Divorced. Had two marriages. Has two children from the first marriage: a daughter (35 years old) and a son (31 years old). After perestroika, which, as he says "broke all his life", he had to retire. Tried to start a business, but failed. Vahtang is registered to his daughter's apartment, but doesn't live there. Before the moment of the interviewing he was living in the apartment of his "civil wife". Now he lives at his friend's apartment because he had a serious quarrel with his "civil wife". Looks about 60–65.

Men with More Varied Work Conditions

Case 4 Vadim

Vadim, born in 1951(61 years old) in the Ukraine. Most of his life served in the military services. A specialist in radio-electronics by profession. In 2000 was retired for the first time. Then served in the prison service (UFSIN). His second retirement took place in 2010, because of his critique of the administrator: "I can't keep silent. I can't, if I see injustice. That's why I was retired". During 10 months "was a pensioner". At present works in the prison service. Combines the official job in the prison service with a job in a kindergarten as an electrician, and "some other jobs". A widower. Nine years ago he lost his wife. Has two children: a son (25 years old) and a daughter (23 years old). Both children have university education. The family lives in a two-room apartment. Likes classical music, Russian romances and plans to move with his children to the Ukraine where he has a house and a big garden. Looks about 50 years old.

Case 5 Alexey

Alexey, born in 1963 (49 years old) in Severodvinsk. Graduated from Sevmashvtuz. After two years of studying in the institute combined studies with working at the ship-building plant "Zvyozdochka". By diploma is an electrical engineer. Since the beginning of his work, the plant he worked at the same department (workshop), and after getting the diploma, in 1986, got the position of electrician. Retired in 2005. That year, 2005, he found a new job in St. Petersburg, was accepted and resigned from ship-building but before moving to St. Petersburg broke his leg. After this accident lived with his mother and was completely dependent on her, because did not have any income. At present, works for a commercial firm as a civil electrical engineer. His parents sold their three-room apartment and the respondent could buy a one-room apartment, where he lives now alone. Has a daughter of 10 years old from the second "civil wife". Looks about 40 years old.

Case 6 Evgeniy

Evgeniy, born in 1949 (63 years old) in Leningrad (St. Petersburg). The same year the family moved to Severodvinsk. The respondent entered the institute in Severodvinsk, specialization: "Engineer – electric welder in submarine construction", did not finish. Learned dancing and passed his military service as a ballet dancer in the military choir, gave performances on tour in France, Japan, Mongolia, Bulgaria, Czechoslovakia, etc. After military service, graduated from the Kiev Circus School and returned to Severodvinsk, worked in local theatres of Severodvinsk and Arkhangelsk, gave performances on tour. During interview, underlines the importance of personal connections which always helped him to have extra income and to be well-to-do. At the moment, does not have permanent work, pensioner. From time to time organizes "corporatives" and concerts which bring him good income. Does not like word "corporative" and prefers to call himself "producer". Was married and divorced twice, has three children: two daughters (38 and 11) and one son (25). Younger children live with their mothers, but Evgeniy helps them. In relationship with young woman (approximately 40 years old). Looks about 55.

Private Life Trajectories

Five of the six men in the study had one or two divorces behind themselves and had 1–3 children. All three men with physically demanding jobs had unsatisfactory housing conditions. To be able to secure an independent living could be seen as part of the masculinity projects connected to adulthood. Sergey lives with his mother, Vladimir is moving between his disabled, alcoholic brother and a dacha in the countryside, while Vahtang is registered in the flat of his daughter, yet living in the apartment of friend. Out of these three men, two had lost contact with their children after divorce, and could be seen as examples characterizing the pattern described by the theory of the crises of masculinity. One of them was himself an alcohol abuser, while another lived with an alcoholic brother at times. The third men in this group, Vahtang, had, despite troublesome living conditions, good contact with his children and was even supporting his son financially. Thus, he could be seen as working for the recognition of his fatherhood:

> I: Could you tell, please. Do you get any financial support from your children?
>
> R: Oh well, no! My son asked me to take a credit for him. I took one, and the second time, and the third time as well.
>
> I: So, you help your son ... and your daughter?
>
> R: I don't help my daughter now. She got married for the second time. It seems, everything is fine there. (Vahtang)

In comparison, those men, who had more varied work conditions, all three had stable and independent housing, even if for one of them, Alexey, it was his parents who bought an apartment, and thus, this was not realized as part of an adult masculinity project. Two of the men in this group succeeded in remarrying and creating new families with one younger child in the new wedlock. However, both remarriages ended in divorce. The third man in this group, Vadim, is different, in the sense that he is a widower. As such, he had raised his children on his own, and by this he constitutes a clear example of men striving for alternative masculinity through recognition as fathers. Even Evgeniy is a father taking responsibility for his children, living together with one of his daughters. Alexey describes himself as a Sunday father, who nonetheless attributes importance to his role as father.

One of the men had to shoulder the role of provider and care provider even for his younger brother with disabilities who is a single man too. Weak social policy and lack of proper information about services make our respondents suspicious and sceptical concerning the willingness of the state structures to provide people with any kind of assistance.

> R: I even went to our district policemen!
>
> I: And?
>
> R: I say: "Tell them, to these mates, not to come (to my brother). Let them come once a month, or once a week ...!", but they come every day. Someone comes every day. I asked: "What do these policemen do ...?" Nothing. No movements, no movements absolutely.
>
> I: And have you applied to any other social services? Do you know any?
>
> R: But where? Where? Social Security Service? It's useless. They themselves have 50 people with disabilities for one inspector.

I: It turns out that no one really cares ...

R: No, I have their phonenumbers, but it is senseless. Once, or maybe twice they came at New Year, they give these presents ...

I: And what?

R: What do they give?

I: No, they give a present and what is happening then?

R: And that's all. Good bye. They put a tick and that's all. They bring chokolate, and something else, like a child's present.

I: There is a community of disabled people [NGO] in Arkhangelsk, and ...

R: There is ...

I: Haven't you applied?

R: No ... what for? As for me, I'm ashamed, for example. And what? The representatives of this community will come, and what? – here it is, this drunk company (Vladimir)

Such attitudes are the result of both weak and inadequate social policy and of socialization in gender-differentiated ways. In the Soviet period, the gender contract for "working mothers" guaranteed facilities for women and they began to treat such facilities as an essential part of their social rights. Men were recruited for employment and service only in the public sphere and their roles as family members were ignored. Of cause, the Soviet gender model gave some obvious patriarchal privileges for men, but not all of them were able to use such opportunities. The normative Soviet and in broader terms the state socialist model of femininity included the expectations that the state should provide support to ease the care duties of female citizens, but the normative model of masculinity did not incorporate expectations to perform care duties and therefore neither to relieve men from such duties (Asztalos Morell, 2007). Even when the rhetoric of "crisis of masculinity" became very popular, the main reason for "men's troubles" was found in the egalitarian ideology but not in inadequate social policy. Kay (2006) found in her study that men striving for recognition as caregivers find little support in a social service system viewing women as caregivers.

While men in the study differed in the degree to which they engaged with active fathering, all respondents showed their solidarity with the idea that the main social role for a man is the role of a "breadwinner". Moreover, some of them consider the implementation of this role to be so important that they began to associate it with the essential conditions of men's existence. Most clear was Vadim, who shouldered both the role of provider and care provider:

> R: And now the main question comes, indeed. Why are men dying? And men are dying, because there is no good work for them, which would give certainty that he can provide for his family. And this is the most important thing. And then, this man comes into depression ... enters into a state of depression and hopelessness. (Vadim).

However, those men who have more troublesome divorces demonstrated indirectly a kind of unconscious criticism of that normative gender model. They felt trapped into it by their former wives. Their critique took misogynist undertones, when they started to describe women as "avid" and "grasping" persons, as somebody who exploits men and doesn't pay attention to real life and physical conditions which sometimes can restrict seriously men's abilities to play the expected normative role.

Transition to the Neoliberal Market Economy

After the collapse of the USSR, many of our respondents lost their jobs or were forced to change their occupation. Our respondents show their critical position towards the core of Soviet normative masculinity – the idea of service to the state, especially in the military sphere and how the transition led to the loss of status attached to their hard work:

> R: I was in the military. 32 years in the armed forces [pause], in uniform [pause].
>
> I: And how far were you promoted?
>
> R: Well, [smiles] well, I was promoted to the fact that I work anywhere, anyhow. I do not want to remember about the service.
>
> I: Are you retired now?
>
> R: Yes, I'm retired. I do not want to remember about the service, it is a taboo, a complete taboo, and, when I took off my uniform, I felt that I've missed so much in my life!(Vadim)

The above respondent perceives himself and large sections of society composed of ordinary people as the losers from transition due to the unaccounted privatization of former state property:

> It's still needed to continue to talk about this issue, because the state is so unfair to its citizens. These are billions and millions [of Rubles] that are gone to no one knows where, most likely somewhere to someone's account. As for ordinary citizens, they have not even gardens, schools, and other educational institutions ... (Vadim)

Since we chose this specific group of men for our study, who could not be considered the winners of transition, none of them have well-paying jobs, they have similarities in their life paths since they all had to use their immaterial (cultural and social) capitals collected during the Soviet time in a new way to adjust to new economic conditions. However, we find significant differences in how men from the two subgroups managed to utilize their immaterial capital assets in the transition and post-Soviet periods. We also found that the value of their cultural capitals has changed with ageing, and saw how this distinction in value determined the difference of life paths of men from different groups.

On the one hand, men with hard physical jobs became both bodily worn out and had only managed to obtain low-paid jobs in the formal economic sector. After the collapse of the USSR, they have experienced a great degree of instability and long periods of unemployment in between formal jobs. One of the respondents, Sergey, who is only 46, is an example of this kind of life situation. He has worked all his life in the domain of hard physical labour. In the Soviet time, seaman had guarantees of being paid a good salary, access to fringe benefits and could expect to get a decent pension. After the collapse of the USSR, all these guarantees were lost. Today Sergey has not got a permanent job. The only domain he can find a job in is still in hard physical labour. Regarding his physical health condition, Sergey looks around 60, more than 10 years elder then his chronological age. The type of cultural capital he has (skills in blue-collar professions and work experience only in hard physical labour) do not allow him to find a job in any domain that would not demand physical force. These conditions make him entrapped, pushing him to get a job that would exhaust him physically more and more, and so would diminish his cultural capital.

> I say, I've recently worked in the stokehold. It's kind of private enterprise. So, I've worked there, but it's too heavy as well. I got sick and left. It's heavy labor. And already ... Well, I got sick because of my age ... and they've found a new one for replacement. (Sergey)

Another particularity of Sergey's situation which is also determined by the type of immaterial capital he has is the way Sergey can find a job. In the Soviet time, he belonged to a community of people united by the profession of seaman. Sergey had performed his masculinity in what Zdravomyslova calls a quasi-public sphere, and so he has developed his social capital through and within this group. He has created a particular type of social capital – bonding social capital -, which he is using now to find a job, but that keeps him in the same economic niche.

> R: A friend of mine promised me to find a new job, so it will be resolved after New Year. I haven't told anyone yet.
>
> I: And before? How did you change job?
>
> R: Well, how ... Someone helps, sometimes I find myself (Sergey).

On the other hand, the men involved with more varied tasks, including white-collar conditions, had relatively stable jobs, even though low paid, as in Vadim's case, or had migrated to the North in order to obtain a well-paid job, like Alexey, or had such specific cultural (producer of ballet performances) and bridging social capital as Evgeny, that could allow him to establish himself as a cultural entrepreneur. These men were also perceived, especially Evgeny, as younger than their age. Nonetheless, the case of Alexey's accident indicates that sickness or other unexpected misfortunes can easily challenge this perceived relatively privileged position. For the most, all of the men in the study, with the exception perhaps of Alexey, who migrated to the North, who found a well-paying job, complained about low wage levels, including those who had a certain stability of employment over time:

> At the state level, state employees get about 6000 RUB! 6–7 thousand somewhere. Well, kindergartens even worse ... I want to cry, 4900! Well, it's ridiculous! I would like to see how the president would live with this salary. I would have paid him extra from my pocket, that he would live with this month salary. (Vadim)

> And now it is very difficult to work in culture. I do not know how it is at the moment, but 3–4 years ago ... Well, it's hard when the salary is about 5–7 thousand. Is this money? Shame! (Evgeny)

Despite the fact that all of them were not old in the 90s, it was especially difficult to find a job according to their qualifications for those men who were involved into physical labour during and after the transition period. The main reason for this difficulty is that their cultural capital, consisting mostly of physical force, diminishes with time. However, for those whose cultural capital consists mostly of intellectual skills the age also represents a challenge: they become uncompetitive on the labour market in comparison with younger specialists and have to retire. Now, three of the interviewed men have reached the age of retirement as pensioners (60, 61 and 63), but their pension payments are rather small, and it is impossible for people of this age to live without extra-work or someone's help. The above conditions make men search for alternative survival strategies.

Reciprocal Networks as an Alternative Survival Strategy

All of the men in the study have compensated for lost abilities to obtain decent incomes and through this a patriarchal dividend from formal employment by taking "under-workings", often informally and without any contracts.

> Now almost the same exists. But you can find a job, but let's say ... but it will be very low-paid. Any work will be very low paid. Say, official work ... I work in two places officially and unofficially in one. Official work [after two jobs] will be paid about 15 000 RUB, and my informal work is paid times more. (Vladimir)

> I am an electrician, and not just an electrician, I'm doing lots of things in life. Well, I do not even know what I'm not doing. I do absolutely everything you are interested in, what is needed: to make a table — here you are! to make a door – here you are! To glaze a window – here you are! Let's say, an electric oven is broken – here you are! (Vadim)

To make the ends meet, the men have several jobs, permanent as well as temporary, so called "haltura". Usually they use widespread informal interpersonal relationships based on the principle of reciprocity to get these jobs. The respondents emphasize the importance of their relations with acquaintances and neighbours, thus the importance of informal relationships in their lives. Moreover, these relationships become more evaluated and important from the point of view of "surviving" than "formal" relationships and official employment and incomes. The value of such informal relationships increases when the social capital and wealth of respondents go down. We can find the "distillation" of such a position in the words of the respondent whose social and financial status is worse in comparison with the rest:

> ... one always needs to get acquainted. People are always useful (Vladimir)

The reciprocity can be explained not only as a means of recompense for the inadequate social policy but also as a form of resistance to the neoliberal market economy and changes in relationships initiated by it. The neoliberal market economy is the very field where the new model of hegemonic masculinity has been forming. R.W. Connell defines this model as "transnational business masculinity". If we compare this model with the attitudes which have been shown by our respondents, we can notice some significant contradictions between them. According to Connell, "transnational business masculinity" can be characterized by two main features: confined technical rationality and strengthening of consumerist attitudes. However, the attitudes shown by our respondents are at variance with such features.

The model of behaviour which we define as "reciprocal relationships" is constituted by the developing of a neighbour-circle support network. It works according to the principle: "I help you now, you will help me later". Relations are based on mutual trust, rather than formal agreements:

> I: Does it mean that relationships are based on trust?
>
> R: Yes, everything is based on trust. One has money, then gives it back, if one-has none, then one will give it back later (Vladimir)

A specific system of values is presupposed in these relationships. The most important personal characteristics in such a system are openness and readiness to participate in informal cooperation and communication.

> R: Law is law, but what can it do? At night this law doesn't work there. We have no laws there. We have our own government, we make our own laws (Vladimir)

Vladimir, who is partially residing in his dacha, finds that these kind of informal relationships are especially tight in rural areas:

> I like guys from the rural area, very much ... they're this kind of people who are good-natured, and have no conflicts, and they are so open ... The city is quite another thing! (Vladimir)

Respondents make a comparison between rural and urban inhabitants and ways of interaction in the Soviet and the today's Russia. It is remarkable that their positive estimation of the Soviet period is connected neither with politics or ideology, nor with the economy. They show the strongest nostalgic recollections about people's relations which have changed significantly with the beginning of market reforms.

> R: What I liked in the Soviet era is that people were more open, more honest, and more decent. Well, we cannot say they were liberated, but they were more cheerful, perhaps, more convivial. Now I see another trend: people meet to have fun, but there is something inside them. They do not disclose ... From 90-s, communication ceased after all ... an open, respectable communication. Well, it got down, reduced in times ... There are corporate meetings and celebrations, but what is their sense? And how much flattery there is, on the one hand, and falsehood and hypocrisy, on the other hand! There is a lot! The man is like in a mask, he does not say what he thinks; he thinks: "And what will they say? And what will the colleagues think?" and so on. In Soviet times, it wasn't like this. One cannot say that everyone said everything directly and frankly. Somewhere and something was hidden, but we discussed and talked about some other topics, about everyday things, openly with dignity and with a twist. Now I do not see it. Somehow everything is false. Fast food, this is, if I may say so. Now, it is fast food. (Vadim)

Payments in Kind or Cash?

Though the reciprocal relationships mean non-market circulation of goods and benefits they don't exclude money. Money can be an element of such circulation but it works not only as a part of the system "goods – money – goods" but mostly like "one more gift".

> R: ... you get there, and then there. One does not calculate. 700 RUB if one helps to grannies, well, 500 RUB ... Well, we are not bank owners ... What does one do? One goes to the store to buy food. (Vladimir)

However, often those who need some work done lack financial resources themselves. In such cases, barter chains are applied:

> R: Even here, in the countryside, a granny gave me something. Her husband died, well, he worked in the shipping company ... a sheepskin coat has remained after his death ... It's a little bit too big for me, why should I sell it? I know a guy who has a bigger belly than mine! How much is it?, he asks. I say, You know, it is new ... sheepskin ... A couple of bottles of vodka – sheepskin ... take it! It might cost 15 000 RUB, but ... take it. It suits you well. The same way people bring things to me. (Vladimir)

We can say that there is some kind of a "substitute" or an "equivalent" of money in these reciprocal circulations. The function of such a substitute is realized with alcohol, namely Vodka. Vodka works as a universal "currency". This role of Vodka is stressed in narratives of those respondents for whom the reciprocal relationships become a cardinal strategy for surviving.

> R: No, in the village everything is for Vodka. Money ... they do not look at it. One cuts forest, goes to the tractor driver ... I take a couple of bottles of Vodka with me and go to the tractor driver. Well, he takes this Vodka, takes the wood, we drink together (laughs). Well, it is like this there. (Vladimir)

The attitudes to drinking Vodka are rather ambivalent. On one hand, the respondent (Vladimir) admits the destructive effect of abusing Vodka (especially when he tells the story about his brother). But on the other hand, Vodka is considered as an essential part of informal relationships among men. It works not only as "currency" but also as something that creates the proper condition for communication and interaction (as a "glue").

> R: (laughs) No, drink ... One has to drink anyway.
>
> I: Does one have to drink?
>
> R: Sometimes, sometimes ... I don't say a lot. (Vladimir)

Such a neighbour-circle network consists mainly of men who help each other. But sometimes it can include women too. Those men in the study with less favourable skills, such as Vladimir, had typically more physical labour-based networks and were the ones indicating barter-type payments, e.g. working for babushka. The only one who obtained jobs resulting in formal incomes through networking was Evgeny. He has, even after his recent retirement been able to obtain assignments as a producer of performances. Thus, the type of social and cultural capital these men could utilize in their informal incomes impacted on the regularity and type of remuneration. Those with lesser resources were those paid time to time in alcohol. This in turn could be a built in element in the perpetuation of destructive lifestyles and the reproduction of their marginalization.

Conclusions

We have set out to provide an intersectional analysis of marginal masculinities in the Russian transition context. We were to analyse the survival strategies and perceptions of manhood by six men. Firstly, those men coming from skilled occupations with different degrees of physical work in branches that have lost from their prestige in the transition. Men who had skills where hard physical work was central in the occupation gave expression to larger difficulties in working life following transition. Their occupational careers were characterized by short-term very low-pay employment. Meanwhile, men with technological skills with a larger component of white-collar-type tasks and fitting better ongoing technological advancements (electric engineers) have been better off in terms of finding long-term employment. Nonetheless, both of these categories of men experienced material difficulties and had to resort to a large degree of informal income generation. Two of the men were exceptions: one who chose to migrate to the extreme North and by this realize a substantially higher salary and one, who had specific cultural skills and could obtain a satisfactory level of formal revenues by starting a private enterprise as producer.

These men differed also in their ability to run consolidated lives, where we considered as one expression of successful realization of an adult masculinity project to secure an independent living condition. The men with the most problems in finding permanent employment had also been the ones who had temporary forms of accommodation often living together with relatives. While two of the men with a higher portion of white-collar features in their occupation had been successful in remarrying during their lifetimes, the blue-collar men have fallen into singlehood following their divorces. Two of the men in the former group had viable contacts with their children, as compared to only one of the three in the blue-collar group. Two of the men in the blue-collar group had also difficulties with alcohol. Thus, three of the men in our sample were making sizeable efforts to gain recognition as caring fathers. This implied things such as continued shared living with their adult children or continued financial support for them. One of the men was a single father, although his fatherhood was the outcome of being a widower.

Looking at the type of informal work and social networks utilized for obtaining these extras, we find that all five men, with the exception of the one with specific cultural skills, used mainly kinship, neighbourhood and acquaintance networks to obtain extra incomes by helping with whatever could be needed. This could mean work for babushkas but also tasks at a day-care centre. The blue-collar skilled men indicated that their networks often included persons who had few resources themselves (babushkas), which meant often that they were to take barter items in payment. In these types of barter trades, alcohol occurred as the medium of generalized exchange, by this reinforcing certain self-destructive habits.

The analysis of our interviews provides some corroboration of the theories elaborating the continued pattern of men in crises. In particular, those men with primarily physical labour had difficulties in finding ways to create an independent living arena for themselves, create new bondage through remarriage and had been less active in the lives of their adult children. Nonetheless, we found, especially among men with a combination of white collar and physical skills, alternative patterns of masculinity. Every other man makes efforts to gain recognition as a caring father. Even if this occurs at the time of their children's adulthood, this does indicate a challenge to the view that portrays men as excluded from such contacts with their children.

The interviews indicated also the strong presence of alternative strategies for survival and through this, creating masculinities. The majority of the men in our sample found ways of securing their daily survival through channels outside of the main stream economy, even if their life stories indicate often the fragility of such survival strategies. The heavy reliance on the physical body, the irregularity and lack of social security attached to these jobs presupposes good health.

Acknowledgements

The authors would like to thank Lidia Kriulya for her contribution into research development as an initiator of the project and a lead of the research group, and considerable help with collecting the empirical data. The authors would also like to thank Olga Pospelova for her contribution into the project as a scientific adviser.

Notes

1. Other challenges include the normativity of heterosexual couple relations.
2. Bourdieu, P. The Forms of Capital.
3. Bourdieu, P. The Forms of Capital.

References

Aivazova, S. 1998. *The Russian Women in the Labyrinths of Equality*. Moscow: RIK Russanova.

Ashwin, S. 2000. "Vliianie sovetskogo gendernogo poriadka na sovremennoe povedenie v sfere zaniatnosti [The Influence of the Soviet Gender Order on Employment Behavior i Contemporary Russia]." *Sotsiologicheskie issledovaniia* 11: 63–72.

Ashwin, S., and T. Lytkina. 2004. "Men in Crisis in Russia." *The Role of Domestic Marginalization, Gender and Society* 18 (2): 189–206.

Asztalos Morell, Ildikó. 1999. *Emancipation's Dead-end Roads? Studies in the Formation and Development of the Hungarian Model for Agriculture and Gender (1956–1989)*. Uppsala: Acta Uppsaliensis 46.

Asztalos Morell, Ildikó. 2007. "How to Combine Motherhood and Wage Labour: Hungarian Expert Perspectives During the 1960s." In *Gender, Equality and Difference During and After State Socialism*, edited by R. Kay, 41–62. Basingstone: Palgrave Macmillan.

Asztalos Morell, Ildikó. 2014. "I Do Not Understand How I Became a Farmer: The Poor-peasant Path to Farm Family Enterprise in Post-Socialist Rural Hungary." *Developmental Studies* 1 (1): 88–99.

Bourdieu, P. 1986. "Forms of Capital." In *Handbook for Theory and Research for the Sociology of Education*, edited by J. E. Richardson, 241–258. New York: Greenwood.

Bourdieu, P. 2001. *Masculine Domination*. Cambridge: Polity Press, 133.

Chernova, J. 2002. "Masculinity of the Late-Soviet Period: The Bard Culture Variant." In *On Masculinity*, edited by S. Oushakin, 452–476. Moscow: Novoe literaturnoe obozrenie.

Chernova, Zhanna. 2012. "The Model of 'Soviet' Fatherhood." *Russian Studies in History* 51 (2, Fall): 35–62.

Clarke, S. 1999. *New Forms of Employment and Household Survival Strategies in Russia*. Coventry: ISITO/CCLS.

Connell, R. 1995. *Masculinities*. Berkeley, CA: University of California Press.

Eley, G. 1998. "From Welfare Politics to Welfare States: Women and the Socialist Question." In *Women and Socialism. Socialism and Women. Europe Between the Two World Wars*, edited by H. Gruber and P. Graves, 516–546. New York: Berghan Books.

Goven, Joanna. 2002. "Gender and Modernism in a Stalinist State." *Social Politics: International Studies in Gender, State & Society* 9 (1): 3–28.

Kay, R. 2006. "Heroes or Villains? Russian Media Representations of Men." In *Men Contemporary Russia. The Fallen Heroes of Post-Soviet Change?* edited by R. Kay, 19–44. London: Ashgate.

Kay, R. 2006. *Men in Contemporary Russia. The Fallen Heroes of Post-Soviet Change?* Aldershot: Ashgate.

Kelly, C. 2002. "The Education of the Will: Device Literature, Zakal, and Manliness in Early-twentieth Century Russia." In *Russian Masculinities in History and Culture*, edited by B. Evans Clemens R. Friedman, and D. Healey. Baisngstone: Plagrave.

Kelly, C. 2003. "'Khochu byt' traktoristkoi!': Gender I detstvo v dovoennoi sovetskoi Rossii ['I want to be a Tractor Driver!': Gender and Childhood in Pre-war Soviet Russia]." In *Sotsial'naia istoriia. Ezhogodnik: Zhenskaia i gendernaia istoriia* [Social History: The Female in Gender History], edited by N. L. Pushkareva, 385–411. Moscow: Rosspen.

Kis, Oksana. 2005. "Choosing without Choice: Dominant Models of Femininity in Contemporary Ukraine." In *Gender Transitions in Russia and Eastern Europe*, edited by Ildikó Asztalos Morell, Helene Carlbäck, Madeleine Hurd and Sara Rastbäck, 105–137. Eslöv: Gondolin.

Kolga, V. 2001. *EU FPV Thematic Network: The Social Problem and Societal Problematisation of Men and Masculinities*. National Report: Estonia. http://www.cromenet.com.

Kornai, J. 1986. *Contradictions and Dilemmas. Studies on the Socialist Economy and Society*. Cambridge, MA: MIT Press.

Kukhterin, S. 2000. "Fathers and Patriarchs I Communist and Post-communist Russia." In *Gender, State, and Society in Soviet and Post-Soviet Russia*, edited by Sarah Ashwin, 73–91. London: Taylor and Francis.

Kvale, S., and S. Brinkmann. 2009. *Interviews: Learning the Craft of Qualitative Research Interviewing*. London: Sage.

Meshcherkina, E. 2002. "Being of Masculine Consciousness: The Experience of Masculine Identity Reconstruction of Middle and Working Class." In *On Masculinity*, edited by S. Oushakin, 268–287. Moscow: Novoe literaturnoe obozrenie.

Municio-Larsson, Ingegerd. 2012. "Doing Parenting in Post-socialist Estonia and Latvia." In *And the Lived Happily Ever After, Norma and Everyday Practices of Family and Parenthood in Russia and Central Europe*, edited by Helene Carlbäck, Yulia Gradskova, Zhanna Kravchenko, 273–297. Budapest: CERU Press.

Novikova, I., K. Pringle, J. Hearn, U. Muller, E. H. Oleksy, E. Lattu, J. Chernova, et al. 2003. "Men, Masculinities and "Europe"." In *Men in the Global World: Integrating Post-socialist Perspective*, edited by Irina Novikova and Dimitar Kambourov, 75–102. Helsinki: Kikimora Publications.

Posadskaya, A. 1994. *Women in Russia, a New Era in Russian Feminism*. London: Verso.

Putnam, R. D. 2000. *Bowling Alone: The Collapse and Revival of the American Community*. New York: Simon Schuster.

Sätre Åhlander, Ann-Mari. 2005. "Women and Women's Work in Transitional Russia: Impacts from the Soviet System." In *Gender Transitions in Russia and Eastern Europe*, edited by Ildikó Asztalos Morell, Helene Carlbäc, Madeleine Hurd, and Sara Rastbäck, 195–219. Eslöv: Gondolin.

Schrand, T. 2002. "Socialism in One Gender: Masculine Values in the Stalin Revolution." In *Russian Masculinities in the History and Culture*, edited by B. E. Clements, R. Friedman, and D. Healey, 195–205. New York: Palgrave.

Silverman, D. 2010. *Doing Qualitative Research: A Practical Handbook*. London: Sage.

Silverman, B., and M. Yanovitch. 2000. *New Rich, New Poor, New Russia: Winners and Losers O the Russian Road to Capitalism*. 2nd ed. Amonk: M.E. Sharpe.

Stark, D. 1992. "Path Dependence and Privatization Strategies in East Central Europe." *East European Politics and Societies* 6 (1): 17–51.

Szelényi, I., R. Manchin, P. Juhász, B. Magyar, and M. Bill. 1988. *Socialist Entrepreneurs, Embourgeoisement in Rural Hungary*. Madison: The University of Wisconsin Press.

Szelényi, Sz, I. Szelényi, and I. Kovách. 1995. "The Making of the Hungarian Postcommunist Elite: Circulation in Politics, Reproduction in the Economy." *Theory and Society* 24: 697–722.

Verdery, K. 1994. "From Parent State to Patriarchs: Gender and Nation in Contemporary Eastern Europe." *East European Politics & Societies* 8: 225–255.

Voronkov, V., and E. Chikadze. 1997. "Leningradskie evrei: etnichnost' i kontekst [Leningrad Jews: Ethnicity and Context]." In *Biograficheskii metod v izuchenii postsovetskikh obshchstv* [Biographic Method in the Study of Post-Soviet Society], edited by Viktor Voronkov and Elena Zdravomyslova, 74–78. St. Petersburg: TsNSI.

Watson, P. 1996. "The Rise of Masculinism in Eastern Europe." In *Mapping the Women's Movement: Feminist Politics and Social Transformations in the North*, edited by M. Threlfall, 216–231. London: Verso.

Yurchak, A. 2002. "Masculine Economy: No Time for Follies When One is Making Career." In *On Masculinity*, edited by S. Oushakin, 245–267. Moscow: Novoe literaturnoe obozrenie.

Zdravomyslova, E., and A. Temkina. 2002. "The Crisis of Masculinity in the Late Soviet Discourse." In *On Masculinity*, edited by S. Oushakin, 245–267. Moscow: Novoe literaturnoe eboznie.

Zdravomyslova, Elena, and Anna Temkina. 2012. "The Crisis of Masculinity in Late Soviet Discourse." *Russian Studies in History* 51 (2, Fall): 13–34.

The Ukrainian Power Elite and Poverty Reductive Efforts: An Inquiry into a Selection of Elite Members' Legislative and Philanthropic Initiatives

Tetiana Kostiuchenko and Hanna Söderbaum

This study inquires the efforts of the Ukrainian political–economic elite to improve the situation for the poor in Ukraine through legislative and private philanthropic initiatives. We compare three groups: politically active philanthropists, non-politically active philanthropists and politically active non-philanthropists. Findings show that poverty reduction efforts made by the selected elite members are rather negligible. While the wealthiest business owners focus on non-poverty reductive single-shot actions, politicians seem to emphasize non-poverty reductive long-term projects. Those with both political and economic capital tend to use either both types of capital or none of them to ease the situation for the most vulnerable groups.

Introduction

At the time of independence in 1991, Ukraine had a strong industrial and agricultural resource base, a literate population with practically the same number of students, teachers, doctors and engineers as in any developed country. However, despite outwardly favourable conditions, the first decade of independence has been dubbed a disaster, a lost decade with a steady population decrease.[1] This was largely due to exogenous shocks that came with the economic collapse of the Soviet Union, implying a decrease in demand for

Ukrainian exports as well as the end to very cheap energy. This was complemented with a collapse of governance: low levels of trust, dysfunctional institutions and a weak legal system with widespread corruption (Riabchuk 2012; See further on the development of an authoritarian regime: Kuzio 2005; Way 2005; Wilson 2005). The orange revolution in 2004 brought a lot of hopes for change, but the second decade of independence still entailed a lot of economic and political problems. A substantial part of the population is struggling with their household economy.

The most vulnerable groups for ending up in poverty in Ukrainian society are the unemployed, pensioners, homeless, people with physical health problems, families with many children and the rural population.[2] In addition to this, we can see a rise of the so-called working poor as a consequence of raised prices for basic needs together with unchanged salary levels.[3] These groups are studied as "excluded" at the bottom of the economic distribution. However, there is another exclusion at the top – of a voluntary kind – when wealthy people are able to exclude themselves from society (Rowlingson and Connor 2011). Thus, when studying social exclusion related to the poor, we should take into consideration the behaviour of the wealthiest whose actions can influence the state of poverty in the country. Rowlingson and Connor (2011) argue that inequality and poverty may be criticised when the wealth of rich is not seen as based on hard work or effort (Rowlingson and Connor 2011, 440). This is based on public opinion and publications in media that create the image of this elite as undeserving.

Ukraine has seen the evolution of philanthropy foundations initiated by the political and economic elite since the mid-1990s. Several of the most important Ukrainian philanthropists also hold seats in the parliament or other politically elected institutions. These actors have both economic and political capital. They can change the situation using three types of resources – through philanthropy, legislation, and employment conditions. With regard to the limited scope of this paper we exclude employment conditions from this study and focus on the remaining two.

The overall aim of this article was to study what the Ukrainian political-economic elite does to improve the situation for the poor segments in society. In relation to philanthropy and legislation, we aim to answer the question: Do they use their political and/or economic power to change the situation for the poor? We compare three groups: politically active[4] philanthropists, non-politically active philanthropists, and politically active non-philanthropists and ask if we can see any differences in what kind of philanthropy projects they support and what kind of legal proposals they support. In order to do that we need to develop a classification scheme that can map the different philanthropy projects into a suggested division between projects aiming at poverty reduction and other projects.

We will try to find the answer to our questions by studying the self-representation of their philanthropy work by these groups and official data on their political work. Self-representation refers to their own stated objectives and programme declarations mainly found on foundation websites but also in interviews. This picture will be supplemented with viewpoints from experts on elite philanthropy in Ukraine and its impact on poverty reduction, as well as representatives from recipient organisations in civil society.

Firstly, an overview of poverty, the elite and inequality in the Ukrainian context will be given along with the description of approaches to measuring poverty applied by social scientists in Ukraine. Secondly, the methodology and selection of 18 members of the economic and political elite will be explained. Thirdly, these actors' philanthropic and charity programmes will be classified and analysed. Fourthly, their possibility of influencing reforms aiming at poverty reduction will be studied through the analysis of legislative initiatives drafted, submitted and approved by MPs. Naturally, a discussion and conclusion follows.

Measuring Poverty in Ukraine

Scholarly attempts to measure the poverty rate in independent Ukraine started in 1990s: The sociologists Kharchenko and Paniotto suggested several additional characteristics to be added into the mainstream questionnaire in order to measure the real consumption of Ukrainians whose official wages were sometimes lower than their reported expenditures. As a result, hypotheses about coping mechanisms were tested and the first data on non-registered employment were collected by the Kyiv International Institute of Sociology (Kharchenko and Vladimir 2000).

According to Ella Libanova, the director of the Institute of Demography and Social Studies of Ukraine, *objective poverty* is determined through criteria of income and access to the material and spiritual resources as approved in the country, including opportunities for children to get education, to get professional training, to receive qualified healthcare services, to have accommodation, etc. — all according to the standards of a particular country. In contrast, *subjective poverty* deals with the self-assessment of the person when she or he identifies themself as poor. It is also based on the public assessment of resources (income) necessary to satisfy the minimal needs of people in this country (Libanova 2008, 43—48). This criterion is identified during population surveys and is based on judgments of what is the minimal life standard preventing poverty. The national poverty level and poverty line are both objective measurements.

We can see in Table 1 that the national poverty line increased substantially (mainly due to inflation). The national poverty level, that is the percentage of persons below the poverty line, shifted up and down between 24 and 28% during the ten-year period.[5] According to this one-fourth of the Ukrainian population was considered poor in 2010.[6] We understand the social groups most vulnerable to poverty as families with children over 3 years (as stressed by the Ukrainian National Demography Institute), the working poor, the rural poor, the unemployed, as well as professional groups as artists and students.[7]

Table 1. National poverty level and poverty line in Ukraine 1999–2010

Year	1999	2000	2001	2002	2003	2004	2005	2006	2007	2008	2009	2010
National poverty line (in UAH (the Ukrainian currency) per person) (10)	126	156	175	192	220	271	365	430	526	778	835	944
National poverty level (in %) (11)	27.8	26.4	27.2	27.2	26.6	27.3	27.1	28.1	27.3	27,0	26.4	24.1

Notes: To calculate this indicator in national currency, a level of income is set at 75% of the median household income (for Ukraine). This is the level of *relative poverty* – a share of households in the country that live on income below the calculated poverty line.
Source: Data of the Institute of Demography and Social Studies of Ukraine provided by Director Ella Libanova.

Inequality and the Role of the Elite

While poverty has remained, a substantial problem and governmental structures have been suffering from inefficiency, corruption and subsequent budget deficits; Ukraine has since independence experienced a rise in the number of some extremely rich individuals. The economic elite gained their capital accumulation in metallurgy, agriculture, chemicals, the food processing industry, oil extraction, retail, mass media, finance, etc. Eight Ukrainians appeared in the FORBES world ranking of billionaires in 2011.

The Gini index is a measure of the deviation of the distribution of income (or consumption) among individuals or households within a country from a perfectly equal distribution. A value of 0 represents absolute equality and a value of 100, absolute inequality (Figure 1). According to Ukrainian sociologist Yevhen Holovaha), "The official statistics demonstrate that the Gini index, illustrating a gap between the rich and the poor, is close to 30 now.[8] But if we had statistics that covered the corruption level and shadow economy, we would see that this gap is even larger. Simply because the wealthy people hide their real income."[9]

Youth policy think tank researcher Yael Ohana (2007) suggests the economic elite, in absolute terms, or "oligarchs" as she calls them, have a great potential and power but that the lack of accountability makes them capricious. This group of individuals with very different preferences, she argues, may develop as a constructive force for change, but it "remains to be seen if they will overcome the temptation to play the role of 'kingmakers'". These potential philanthropists have large sums to spend, but a number of ethical debates are raised by the involvement of such actors in philanthropy:

> Motivation and accountability come to the fore in discussions of the validity of their active involvement. To the extent that the state claims not to be "in a

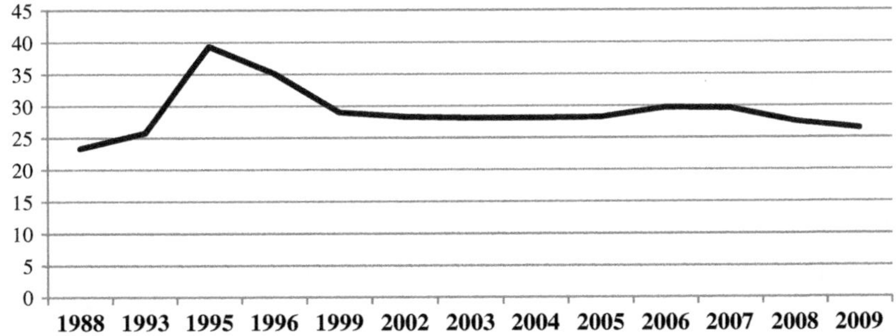

Figure 1. Gini index dynamics in Ukraine during 1988–2009(18)
Source: World Bank – World Development Indicators(19). Measure of the deviation of the distribution of income (or consumption) among individuals or households within a country from a perfectly equal distribution. A value of 0 represents absolute equality, a value of 100 absolute inequality. (World Bank 2011) Data on Ukraine is available online: http://data.worldbank.org/indicator/SI.POV.GINI, no figures for 2000, 2001, 1989–1991, 1993–1994, 1997–1998. That is why the x-axis does not refer to a timeline but instead shows the moment of measurement.

> position to say no" and independent actors are simply not consulted, the Oligarchs are de facto implied in the determination of public policy and gain even deeper footholds in the political decision making sphere (whether formalized or not).

She contends that "many actors in the culture field feel very uncomfortable with what appears to be the unchallenged ability of the very rich to determine public policy (Ohana 2007)."[10]

As far as some of the richest people in Ukraine also possess political power occupying top positions in the parliament and government, they can implement changes in legislation due to their formal opportunities and obligations. According to the International Social Survey Programme (ISSP 2009) data on Ukraine,[11] there is a strong belief among the population that it is the obligation of the political authorities to provide a decent standard of living for the poor: in 2009 survey almost 86% of Ukrainians reported that they "absolutely agree" or "agree" with the statement "The state authorities should provide a decent standard of living for the unemployed". Besides, 86% of all respondents agree that it is the responsibility of the government to reduce the income gap, and almost 78% of respondents did not support the idea that the government should spend less on benefits for the poor (answers "strongly disagree" and "disagree").

When talking about just or unjust distribution of wealth in society using the same ISSP (2009) survey data, we discover that 81% of Ukrainian citizens consider the taxation of the rich to be too modest: they believe that people with high incomes should pay a larger or much larger share of their income in taxes than those with low incomes. Moreover, the vast majority – 94% of the total sample – agrees that differences in income in Ukraine are too large. In case of "oligarchs", the richest Ukrainians, although some of them report paying millions of hryvnias as taxes to the state budget, they can, according to the above-mentioned study, be expected to do more for unsecured groups of society. Philanthropic activities are a way to make this visible to the wide public.

Methodology

When studying philanthropic and charitable establishments, focus areas and target groups are understood through the self-presentation of the foundations. This refers to the foundation's programmes or "establishments", self-presented motivation and relation to other actors, and is found partly in interviews, partly on the foundation's official websites. Where budget figures have been available, they have played a role in the analysis as well. Our investigation is based on the picture they intend to communicate; the basis for our analysis is what they choose to present. When it comes to the discussion about whether projects can be considered philanthropy or philanthrocapitalism, subjective viewpoints obtained through in-depth interviews as well as our own analysis have been the sources. Materials from the interviews conducted by Söderbaum within the framework of her doctoral dissertation have been used here. And, as already mentioned, used both as information (what kinds of projects, etc.), but still with a stress on the *self-representation* of information, and as stories for illustration of the situation.

In order to analyse the legislative initiatives of selected political elite members, we looked at all the draft laws they submitted during November 2007–August 2012 – from the start of the new term of the parliament (*Verkhovna Rada*) until the current moment. We conducted a quantitative analysis of legislation activity statistics (draft laws submitted and approved) of the laws related to poverty reduction policies, revealing the topics that politicians raised in the documents they developed while being in power.

Selection of Cases

Our sample of actors studied is selected on the basis of rankings of the wealthiest politicians[12] and lists of publicly known philanthropists.[13] First, we compared a list of the 100 persons with the highest net worth with the members of parliament, and found 10 coinciding. Then, we added two politicians whom we know have established a philanthropy foundation. Those are not in the list of the top wealthy, but are still wealthy and to a considerable part finance their foundations. In addition, to this we checked again the top net worth list and selected those who are publicly known as the funders of a philanthropy foundation and added six more to our study. All of these have been in the top 12 Ukrainian philanthropists for one or more years during 2010 and 2012. Most of the actors in this last group are also active politically, however, not in parliament and thus without legislative power. Their titles and affiliations are listed below (Table 2).

Elite Philanthropy and Poverty Reduction

In the Nordic countries, elite philanthropy played a significant role in times of economic transition from agrarian to industrial societies. When later municipalities developed and took greater responsibility, philanthropy work changed focus, away from immediate poverty reduction programmes.[14] In other types of transitions, such as the post-Soviet transition from planned to market economy, philanthropy could play a similar role of stepping in when the public sphere is insufficient or lacks ability to cope with ongoing poverty problems. Elite giving can also have the purpose of changing existing state and communal policies (SOU 1993:82, 234).

While the post-Soviet philanthropists find a function in a society with a history of a strong state, the philanthropists in the early United States were functioning while the state was still developing. These robber barons at the turn of the nineteenth century slowly developed into patron-benefactors funding huge projects within culture, education and nature preservation. Their capitalist/industrialist position as employers and philanthropists was at the time both

Table 2. Selection of actors

Wealthy POLITICIAN* and (known) PHILANTHROPIST	Wealthy POLITICIAN* (No known philanthropic activity)	Wealthy and (known) PHILANTHROPIST
• Rinat Akhmetov, MP (Party of Regions) • Boris Kolesnikov, MP (Party of Regions) • Oleksandr Feldman, MP (BYuT) • Arseniy Yatsenyuk**, MP (Our Ukraine/Front Zmin) • Anatoli Tolstoukhov**, authorised representative of the Prime Minister (Party of Regions) • Konstantin Zhevago***	• Tariel Vasadze, MP (BYuT) • Oleksandr Savchuk, MP (Party of Regions) • Ihor Gumenyuk, MP (Party of Regions) • Pavlo Klymets, MP (Party of Regions) • Vadym Trofymenko, MP (BYuT) • Oleksandr Slobodian, MP (Our Ukraine)	• Petro Poroshenko (Minister of Economic Development and Trade) Previously MP (Our Ukraine). • Viktor Pinchuk (since 2006 not in parliament) (then Labour Party Ukraine (now Strong Ukraine – Tihipko party leader) and Elena Pinchuk • Vitalii and Vladimir Klitschko (politicians but without legislative power) (UDAR) • Dmitri Firtash (strong connections with Party of Regions) • Ekaterina and Viktor Yushchenko (Our Ukraine) • Oleksandr Onishchenko

*With legislative power.
**Not ranked in the top 100 wealthiest net worth list.
***No established foundation which is why his engagements are NOT studied here.

strongly criticised and cherished. They were criticised since their philanthropy projects were running simultaneously with workers' wages being pressed to the bottom. Similar criticism has been raised against the business elite in present day Ukraine when doing philanthropy privately while professionally searching for tax havens abroad (Rothkopf 2008, 136 f.; Riabchuk 2012). Philanthropy celebrants Desai et al. claim it is hard to estimate the exact payoffs of philanthropy, but that the Rockefeller's foundation should be honoured for all the benefits of the University of Chicago, as well as the discovery of a vaccine for Yellow Fever and the formulation of penicillin (Desai and Acs 2007). Early philanthropists in the US feared the state, and responded by taking individual responsibility for social security (Katz 2006, 1316). Corporate philanthropy in the US became more and more common in the 1960s and 1970s, and tended to be directed at the communities in which a firm's plants were located and its employees lived (Katz 2006, 1307).

Mykhailo Ivanovich Tereshchenko (1886–1956) and his ancestors were the Russian Empire equivalent to the American Rockefellers. Tereshchenko inherited industries, developed his own fortune and decided to engage in philanthropy:

> I fastened on the process of building asylums for homeless in Kyiv, which would function as a haven or even hospital for injured soldiers. A wonderful premise with 1000 beds was erected on Nizhnii Val Street on Podil (a central district in Kyiv /authors' remark.). We also replenished the budget for several hospitals built earlier by our family in Kyiv, including a children's hospital and the hospital on Streletska Street, so that they could get everything that was necessary while waiting for the injured people from the war and the frontline. (Tereshchenko 2012, 3rd chapter, part 1)

The children's hospital was called Okhmatdet hospital and still exists today. Among the people studied in the current political-economic elite, here are those giving donations to the same hospital (Voronov). In general, philanthropy in Ukraine is nothing new but has its history and is probably most well-known through Tereshchenko, who stands for a reformation/social change perspective on the role of philanthropy.[15]

Some contend that "the oligarchs" in the post-Soviet states of Russia and Ukraine are cruel creatures who do not seek to legitimise even one penny of their fortunes, but that their philanthropy initiatives are pure PR (i.e. see Dinello 1998). Others (Karl 1997) argue that their wish for legitimization has grown during the last decade. The wealthiest people are concerned more now about moral purposes than economic interests given the evidence of the developed countries with philanthropic foundations established by the rich industrial elites at the beginning of the twentieth century (Karl 1997). While the first decade of the transition was about making money, the second was about spending it. Obviously spending money on the public, a culture institution open for everyone or the publication of a non-profit newspaper, can be an act of economic calculation, where legitimacy gives greater revenues from other business in return. Chrystia Freeland, in her study of the Russian oligarchs, gives an example of the importance of legitimacy, also in the 1990s. Vladimir Gusinsky funded the liberal newspaper "Segodnya" (Today) and although the paper had a continuous budget deficit, he kept flinging money into it.

> It's not that he was a champion of the free press, although he sometimes posed as such, but he had a keen interest in preserving Segodnya's reputation. If his paper was credible and influential, Gusinsky thought, then maybe some of its lustre would rub off on him. [...] "at the price of a few million dollars a year — Segodnya's annual losses — it was a bargain." (Freeland 2009, 143) Still others stress their pure altruistic philanthropic expressions. This chapter will not dig into the motives of the mega-givers of Ukraine, but instead focus on analysing the kind of projects they tend to present.

Philanthropy, Philanthrocapitalism and Charity

Charity and the modern use of philanthropy can be defined as giving money or its equivalent to persons and institutions outside the family, without a definite or immediate quid pro quo.[16] The common understanding of the difference between the two concepts according to Daly (2012) is that philanthropy is often understood as being that kind of aid that is channelled via foundations, often funded by rich individuals, while charity is the act of many equals contributing with small amounts (Daly 2012). In this chapter, we use them slightly differently.

The organisational form of foundations is unique as they are funded by endowments, run independently by a board of directors and driven by donor intent. Schramm (2006) argues they play at least two clear critical roles: Firstly, they provide a channel for wealth reconstitution and second they act as an institutional entrepreneur. In addition to these functions, they can provide public goods (Schramm 2006). "Where social problems are the result of a lack of public goods, such as those which provide health, education and personal security, foundations can help stem inequality of availability and access", argue Desai and Acs (2007, 286). A critical counterview presented by Kavita N. Ramdas distinguishes between charity and philanthropy and argues that the new kind of philanthropy that goes under the term "philanthrocapitalism" does not meet the criteria for being philanthropy, which aims at eliminating social ills at its root:

> Social change philanthropy, in contrast to traditional charity, must be measured by its capacity to question the dominant development model, to seek the root causes of inequality, and to engage in a process of self-reflection that also seeks to expand its accountability to the broader public that it seeks to serve.

(Ramdas 2011) Ramdas says that despite current philanthrocapitalism's many good intentions, this venture version of philanthropy is enmeshed in contradictions: The most obvious is that its existence requires inequality and the more unequal the world gets, "the more the public is being invited to celebrate a cherished few who benefit from this condition of inequality", and this kind of philanthropy is characterised by addressing "specific" problems with "measurable" outcomes. To give an example: funding from the Bill and Melinda Gates foundation in the health sector has contributed to the development of national-level health systems in some countries (Desai and Acs 2007, 285). "What is missing is any deeper questioning about what ails a global economic system that seems to produce endemic inequality, crushing poverty and food insecurity – all of which damage the livelihoods of hundreds of millions of people (Ibid., 394)." Teresa Odendahl's conclusion in "Charity begins at home" (1990), where she interviewed over 140 elite givers in the United States, is that their giving actually leads to a conservation of existing social classes/structures.

Another common distinction between the two concepts charity and philanthropy is that charity focuses on immediate symptomatic social problems, for example feeding homeless people or giving material aid to mothers with HIV-infection, while philanthropy, on the other hand, focus on the root causes of social problems. While the latter seeks to create long-term improvement by empowering people, charity can instead create dependency (Desai and Acs 2007, 287). Others talk in terms of almsgiving versus self-help. Natalia Dinello argues that Russian historical philanthropy is more of an almsgiving character while

Western is more focused on self-help.[17] Peter Frumkin holds that charity, because it is not systematic, demands nothing in return from the donor. Charity then is easily seen as the manifestation of the donor's need to express caring and compassion rather than as a potent tool for social change (Frumkin 2008, 6).

Both Rockefeller and Tereshchenko believed philanthropy to be a dynamic and responsive mechanism that can tailor solutions to social problems. To quote Rockefeller: "The best philanthropy is constantly in search of finalities – a search for a cause, an attempt to cure evils at their source."[18]

We leave the deep motivation, or intentions, of the current Ukrainian philanthropy elite to be investigated another time. We will, however, make a contribution to the discussion whether this may be understood as philanthrocapitalism or not at the end of the next section ("Elite giving for poverty reduction"). The critical perspective holds that philanthrocapitalism is not real philanthropy as opposed to philanthropy in its traditional meaning, actions that really contribute to social change.

In this chapter, we use the concept of philanthropy both as all kinds of giving through the foundations we study, and as distinct from charity in our classification scheme and analysis. Charity then is the concept of *short-term* projects and gifts as opposed to philanthropy's *long-term* projects and gifts. In our next distinction, we make a difference between *philanthropy* and *philanthrocapitalism*, where philanthrocapitalism connotes either to PR purposes or "not aiming at alleviating social problems at their roots".

Developing a Classification Scheme for Giving

This paper suggests a classification scheme of the kinds of giving. We classify all long-term projects as philanthropy, and all short-term projects as charity. In our study, we seek to understand what type of giving [charity or philanthropy (or philanthrocapitalism)] the Ukrainian elite are engaged in. We do this by studying their philanthropy "establishments". Firstly, we ask if giving may be regarded as poverty-reductive or not; secondly we discuss if it may be considered philanthropy or charity, where ***charity*** is defined *as short-term strategies helping out here and now/instantly,* and ***philanthropy*** should be defined *as long-term strategies reducing social ills*. As already mentioned, self-representation from websites and interviews will lie as the basis for this study. Subsequently, we will discuss philanthrocapitalism, that is are these establishments for public relations

Table 3. Classification of the establishments for philanthropy/charity activities

	Short-term giving strategies (Charity)	Long-term giving strategies (Philanthropy or philanthrocapitalism)
Poverty-reductive	A	B
Not poverty-reductive	C	D

and/or supporting the status quo, or are they "genuine" and aiming at system change. We classify the establishments according to Table 3:

Elite giving for Poverty Reduction

Ukrainian private philanthropy foundations have been established since the mid-1990s, with the number escalating in the mid-2000s. The sums donated grew continuously until the financial crisis in 2008, which hit Ukrainian business hard. Now, at the beginning of 2010s, we see still an increased interest in these kinds of engagements, even though some foundations struggle with funding.

Using the frequently referred to International Classification of Non-profit Organisations (ICNPO) system developed by Anheier and Salamon (1992), the most prevalent activity spheres of the Ukrainian private philanthropy foundations studied are Culture and Recreation, Education and Research, Health, and Social Services. Development and Housing is quite popular too, while establishments within Philanthropic intermediaries and Voluntarism Promotion, Religion, Law, Advocacy and Politics, International Activities and Ecological projects are rare. Business and Professional Associations, Unions do not appear at all. One foundation is engaged in migration projects, with the purpose of informing Ukrainian emigrants about migration while still at home. It appears in diagram 2 as "Not elsewhere classified" (Figure 2).

Twelve elite givers' establishments are recognised in Diagram 2. The numbers indicate the amount of philanthropists engaged in the different areas. The units of analysis are the projects, so called "establishments" within each foundation.[19] The basis of classification is an establishment's principal activity area. If the establishment is engaged in health research, the principal activity is then labelled research since research is its principal activity (Anheier and Salamon 1992, 267—309). If the principal activity is HIV information campaigning, the principal activity will be labelled Health. Units are thus differentiated according to the types of services or goods they provide.

The Ukrainian foundations under this study are both grant making and operative, however, mainly operative. Where grant making is concerned, individuals rather than other non-profit organisations are the recipients.

The total amount of yearly budgets in recent years by the twelve philanthropy foundations[20] appearing in the diagram above, was 530,3 million UAH.[21] The average yearly budget was 44,2 million UAH and the single philanthropist with the largest budget summed up to 198 million UAH.

This short presentation aims to give a clue of what spheres they are engaged in, as well as the amounts donated. Instead of focusing on exact amounts for specific targets, we will now take a deeper look at some of the foundations, and the self-representation of their work. The ICNPO classification above is insufficient for our aim, which is to analyse the degree of poverty reduction programmes in the philanthropy foundations.

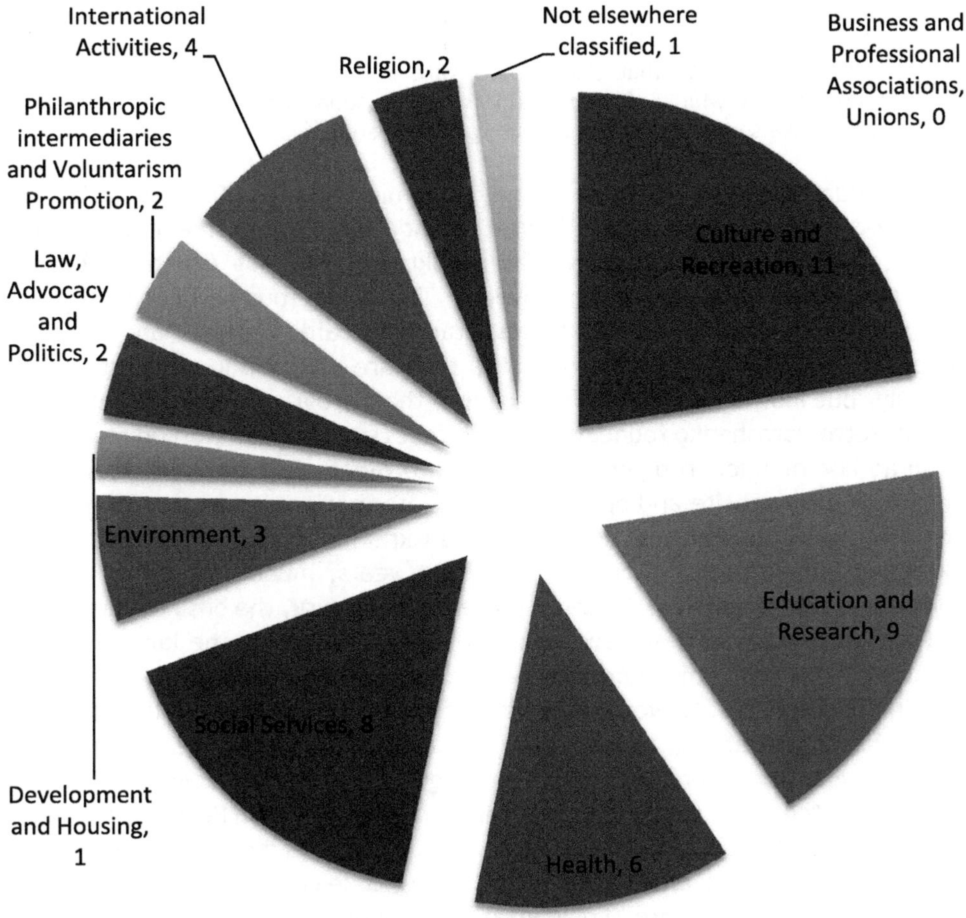

Figure 2. Ukrainian mega philanthropists' activity spheres according to ICNPO classification (by number of organisations in the sphere)
Source: Survey based on self-representation of foundations as of March 2012.

Currently around ten of the selected elite members channel their philanthropic (or "giving") activities through their own established foundations. From a sustainability and evaluation/accountability perspective, foundations as an organisational form constitute more stability than whimsical one-time donations, according to a Ukrainian philanthropy professional and former employee of the Pinchuk foundation. However, the same professional expresses his concern about them too, and even questions their being foundations at all.

> I guess that these foundations, even the case of Akhmetov, are too dependent on the wish of their owner, so that you cannot predict what will happen in five years. None of them have done any endowment. I would really put an endowment as a criterion for Ukrainian philanthropists. If you think that an organization should do some public good, then just endow it; make it independent. Just establish the foundation, give money, endow the foundation well and articulate the goal for this endowment. Now your role is zero. If you want to

> have a puppet, and to please some of your emotions, it shouldn't be called philanthropy, but something else. Since I don't see any endowments going on in that area I think that Ukrainian private philanthropy is very unstable, it depends on the whims of their founders, and as soon as a harshening economic situation we shouldn't expect blooming in that area.[22]

Most foundations were affected by the economic crisis in 2008 that hit Ukraine extremely hard. However, the largest foundation, Development of Ukraine, funded by the wealthiest individual in Ukraine, did not cut their budget, according to an interviewed employee.[23] The same foundation has since its establishment used three strategies: targeted aid, "stars" and systemic change. The interviewed employee says they are not working against poverty directly, but indirectly through for example their programme for orphans.[24]

The Petro Poroshenko foundation has since its start in 1998 worked much more in an ad hoc manner, replying to needs and projects that they like to support. Their lack of a website and open accessible information decreases transparency and evaluation possibilities, according to a Ukrainian philanthropy specialist at Ukrainian Philanthropists Forum.[25] In recent years, much of the foundation's budget has gone to an infrastructure project in Vynnytsa, the business hometown of Petro Poroshenko. They have rebuilt the bay and set up the largest musical fountain in Europe. This enormous resource-consuming project has resulted in cuts in other spheres. However, the gifts of sweets to children at Christmas time are something that has always and will always stay put, according to the director. Another example focused on targeted aid is the Aleksandr Feldman foundation, though engaged in longer-term programmes than Petro Poroshenko.

It seems as if the focus of the larger foundations has moved from their business core regions, to encompass all Ukraine. At least this seems to be what they wish to communicate. Looking at the expenses of particularly targeted aid, we can conclude that the core business region of each particular philanthropist still receives a large share. This is particularly the case with Petro Poroshenko (Vynnytsia) and Aleksandr Feldman (Kharkiv), but not so much less with Rinat Akhmetov (Donetsk).

The ideology behind each of the founders is much noticeable in both relation to the state and other groups in civil society. While Arseniy Yatsenuyk and Rinat Akhmetov both run think tanks aimed at reforming politics and the government, the Petro Poroshenko foundation has no interest in supporting the government, "which has no future anyway" … In April 2012, Poroshenko was appointed as the Minister of Economic development and Trade, and although Akhmetov is the founder of the think tank Effective Governance, his own seat in the parliament is left empty, and according to the interviewed employee at his foundation Development of Ukraine, Akhmetov is not interested in making social change through political structures; he is looking for that through his foundation instead. According to him, politics is too time-consuming. He will not participate as a candidate for Member of Parliament in the next election as he wants to be able to spend more time on his foundations. The interviewed employee at the foundation confirms that Rinat Akhmetov wants solely to engage in philanthropy starting after the next elections in October 2012, instead of being in parliament. "Well he is doing *something* in parliament ... " "Politics and philanthropy should be separate from each other." More than one time during the interview, he emphasises that he does not know what happens in the government, that he is not following politics. He says Ukraine is a social state, and that "we shouldn't increase that, because those programmes make people lazy."[26]

Considering now transparency and information, it is clear that not all those needing help know about the foundations. A culture activist in civil society said Open Ukraine's culture travel grants always go to the same crowd, and that he never heard about the grants until he was asked to be involved in a project sponsored by the foundation. "I never knew about them before!" he says with a great gesture of surprise as he is acknowledged to hold such information as one of the main culture event bloggers in the capital of Ukraine (who has now moved to Poznan because of the "banditry" that has captured his motherland).[27] A graphic designer wanting to study a Master's programme abroad said despondently about the Pinchuk university scholarships "those are all predestined, they all go to his crowd, somebody's son or daughter".[28]

Classifying Ukrainian Elite Giving

Establishments that can be understood as somewhat poverty reductive are ad hoc, short -term "targeted aid" and catastrophe aid. These projects (the terms "establishments" and "projects" are used interchangeably) are often directed towards vulnerable groups, however not always (necessarily), as those receiving aid at catastrophe incidents are not exclusively poor. "Targeted aid" is often targeted towards patients with a special disease, orphans, pensioners or families with many children. However, the programmes directed towards large families are not targeting only the poor, and they may be ineffective. A project criticised by many was implemented in the middle of the first decade of this century, when large families were bought big homes, the argument being that many of these families did not need bigger houses, but instead other facilities.

> Another big project, which I was involved in, was promoted by the president and supported families with many kids. At one occasion he, President Yushchenko, gathered more than 60 oligarchs and big businessmen and pushed them to sign off an agreement that they would take one or several oblasts and would give apartments or houses to families with more than 10 kids. Sure the incentive was very good from the president's side. But I was involved in this on behalf of the Pinchuk foundation and instead of checking what was the interest of these families; the President thought that he knows better. But in many cases, before implementing this program, we made a survey, we contacted these families in the oblasts that Victor Pinchuk was

> taking care of, Dnepropetrovsk and Lviv, and we realized that only half of them really needed a house or bigger apartment. Some of them needed big cars because they have 10 or more kids, they cannot fit them in the usual cars, or they had some health issues with their kids so they needed special equipment or so on, or they had very talented kids so they needed violins or something else. (... These parents are often either alcoholics or prostitutes, or they belong to some religious groups.) So, basically half of them, at least in those oblasts that I know about, were from Baptist or Evangelist groups. They have big families but they also had support of communities so they didn't need houses. Still, since president said it's only about houses, we couldn't really have much of room for creative philanthropy. The presidential administration was pushing hard and it was really a stupid way of doing philanthropy.[29]

Other establishments that fall into this category (A or C) are those which channel grants and scholarships to students and artists, not helping them from extreme poverty but rather giving them an opportunity to engage in their profession or to travel. However, these may be given to persons with (more or less) financial stability. Where students are required to support their own education abroad to the tune of 50 per cent, when they will be given the remaining 50 percent, this cannot be considered as being poverty reductive, even though these types of scholarships may be argued to lead to a rise out of poverty. We define all these examples as charity.

Establishments that can be defined as philanthropy may instead be the kind of programmes that Tereshchenko engaged in as "the first oligarch" during the first decades of the twentieth century: Long-term development of Ukraine.

Projects categorised in this category (B or D) would be long-term projects aiming at reform in the education sphere, health care, including medical equipment (even though this kind of financing supports both rich and poor), as well as targeted aid to public institutions (Kolesnikov e.g.), and information campaigns directed towards low income groups in society (about HIV/AIDS, about migration issues, etc.). Targeted aid to institutions can be understood as philanthropy, if it is aimed at reforms rather than helping out at severe situations. All these projects are products of a broader idea of reforming society (keeping in mind that what we look at here is self-representation). They may, however, lead to larger income gaps, or they may entail economic growth with trickle down effects. They may also function as an effective reform spark really targeting the social ills at its roots.[30]

Projects and programmes that in our understanding lie outside of the still quite broad framework for poverty reductive establishments are (D) cultural and ecological projects, as long as those are not in grant-form targeted to poor-income groups in society. However, we want to make a comment on the role of culture for changing norms and creating new ideas in society, which in the long run most probably indirectly would bring some prosperity to groups not affluent today. An employee of the Borys Kolesnikov foundation exemplifies: "a competition in architecture for the library can change people's minds".[31] Another example is Pinchuk's idea about the role of the Pinchuk Art

Centre, illustrated in a video clip shown at the Davos Philanthropy Forum 2011: how a visit to his art centre changes the minds of any audience that it opens up for new ideas among the Ukrainian citizens.[32]

Other establishments outside the understanding of povertyreductive ones are (C) occasional gifts, such as sweets and chocolates to children at Christmas. This type of providing assistance to vulnerable groups is almsgiving and can according to Dinello be traced back to the Soviet Union as well as the Russian empire and the ideology of orthodox Christianity (Dinello 1998, 113–115) (Table 4).

We see in Table 5 a slight focus difference between those givers who also hold political power and those who do not. Those without tend to give most to short-term projects while those with political power tend to support more long-term projects. Almost no-one in either group gives directly to poverty reducing projects.

Philanthropy or Philanthrocapitalism?

A previous employee at the Victor Pinchuk Foundation is critical of current mega-giving "philanthropy" in Ukraine. His line of argument goes well with the notion of philanthrocapitalism.

> I guess that the culture of organized philanthropy is very low, and is degrading. I see that the best managers, program managers, in philanthropy are leaving for business, because they cannot survive in philanthropy or they don't see any perspectives in the future, or I know of several cases when very good managers are leaving for Russia or elsewhere. They just don't find the place here. We had a booming time in 2003–2008 but now it's gone. And philanthropy is slowly moving into the corporate world. It was moving into the middle and small business world. But the crisis this year killed small and middle business. I guess we will need to reinvent private philanthropy, real philanthropy, in five to ten years once again. And it could be a smarter philanthropy, more rational, more responsible.[33]

Table 4. Examples of classification of philanthropy and charity activities

	Short-term giving strategies (one-time donation) (Charity)	Long-term giving strategies (Philanthropy or Philanthrocapitalism)
Poverty-reductive	A: Yushchenko: Emergency help, new houses to big families	B: Akhmetov: Health system reform programme
Not directly poverty-reductive	C: Poroshenko: Chocolate gifts for children at Christmas, Music fountain in Vynnytsa	D: Pinchuk: Pinchuk Art Centre, Yalta conference (Arts, education), Yatsenyuk: Open Ukraine

Table 5. Differences between politicians + philanthropists and philanthropists only

ELITE MEMBER'S SURNAME	A, B, C and D establishments	Predominating type of establishment
Known philanthopists ***with*** political (legislative or executive) power		
Akhmetov	B C D	**B**
Kolesnikov	C	**C**
Feldman	A C D	**D**
Yatseniuk	D	**D**
Tolstoukhov	D	**D**
Poroshenko	A C D	**C**
Known philanthropists ***without*** political (legislative or executive) power		
V. Pinchuk	C D	**D**
E. Pinchuk	A B (if HIV-affected counts as poor)	**A/B**
Klitschko	C	**C**
Firtash	C D	**C**
Yushchenko	A D	**A**
Onishchenko	C D	**C/D**

Note: The typology was formed in September 2012 based on information available, before the parliamentary elections in Ukraine in the end of October 2012.

The only foundation he finds to be of genuine character is The Renaissance foundation,[34] previously the George Soros foundation, as well as one establishment within the Victor Pinchuk Foundation: The Pinchuk Art Centre as is discussed as follows:

> The Renaissance foundation is really strong at needs assessment, at understanding what are the stakeholder groups interested in etc. And that's what I tried to sell to the Pinchuk foundation, but I failed with this. Wherever you see a philanthropists' real, genuine interest, philanthropic interest, it's a rare occasion. Here in Ukraine the case of the Pinchuk Art Centre is a genuine philanthropy project. He is personally interested in it, he believes that that is good for the country. And that is what we have – something brilliant, unusual, and a mind-opening, counter-isolating organization. But there are a number of other events like bringing pop stars to sing and so on - its absolute bullshit, its not philanthropy but it raises attention to philanthropy. It's a game you never can judge a lot of this. But at the end when we take the balance sheet of the annual report we can see, is it 50/50 philanthropy PR or not?[35]

Reconnecting to the discussion by Ramdas, this venture version of philanthropy is enmeshed in contradictions: The most obvious is that its existence requires inequality and the more unequal the world gets, "the more the public is being invited to celebrate a cherished few who benefit from this condition of inequality". This is certainly relevant for most of the foundations. Tolstoukhov's foundation Arts Support Fund, the smallest one in financial terms of the foundations included in the study, is, however, not as dependent on this inequality, but would instead benefit from more financial sources, from individuals. The Arts Supports Fund is special in this sense, that it functions on the basis of various donations, where Tolstoukhov himself donates solely the venue. However, on this basis, one could argue that this foundation is different from the others. And if so, Yatsenyuk's foundation may be also an outcast from the others studied, as his Open Ukraine also seeks funding from external donors, to a substantial part.

Ramdas also argues that the kind of philanthropy phrased as philanthrocapitalism is characterised by addressing "specific" problems with "measurable" outcomes. Akhmetov's foundation Development of Ukraine, stresses these strategies. The interviewed employee at the foundation declares that the basis on which they prolong programmes or establishments is always evaluation and efficiency. On the question whether they will prolong the PhD programme in mass media studies at Kyiv-Mohyla Academy, he answers:

> I don't know. It will be decided after evaluation. We will ask: What are the results? Are those reflecting the ones we posed at the start of the program? What did we gain from this program, what have people in general gained from it, what has Kyiv-Mohyla Academy gained from it, what are the results? If it looks good, we will keep on, no doubt. However, we do not aim at keep on financing things forever and ever. We want the activity to become independent, so that we can focus on other things, other spheres. That is why we work with state structures – we build, the state takes over, and we go on to another sphere ... [36]

The same employee also stresses efficiency when asked why they are not engaged in establishments concerning human rights or ecology:

> Firstly, to have five directions is already too many. If you don't focus, you will have problems. (...) The stricter the focus the better results. Secondly, System Capital Management (owned by Rinat Akhmetov) is engaged in ecological projects (so we do not need to). Thirdly: distribution of resources, I give money to this and that and that, what is the result? If I've got extra money, where should I spend it? The answer is – in those programs we already have, because that would lead to higher effectiveness. Not always, but it is my task to try to figure out how to do that.[37]

Their cultural programmes are also discussed in terms of efficiency. Overall, the foundations run both philanthropy and "philanthrocapitalistic" programmes. Some run only one or the other. Smaller ones which are dependent on external funding tend to be more "genuine" than the larger ones which rely on one funder.

Legislative Activities for Poverty Reduction

Defining Legislative Initiatives with Regard to Poverty Reduction

Poverty reduction activities run by wealthy people who also have access to political power include not only philanthropy as discussed above. The other side of the coin is changing of the legislation – some of the philanthropists and a number of wealthy Ukrainians possess the positions of deputies in the national parliament or in other authorities of the state or regional level. Below we provide examples of the selected legislative initiatives (LIs) with regard to poverty reduction submitted as by the known philanthropists as well as by the other MPs who are not publicly famous as millionaires.

Legislative initiatives (LIs) refer to actors on the political arena submitting draft laws and being included in the discussion during parliamentary sessions. In a broader perspective, this connects poverty alleviation policies and efforts with the principles of governance on a state level implemented by the elites. In this regard, "state-society" relations are regulated by the legislation developed by the state actors – parliamentarians and ministers – and focused on the poor as a social group. That is why, when studying activities of members of the political elite, we should keep in mind their legislative efforts and the content of the draft laws they submit for approval. Besides, insofar as some of the top-politicians appear in the rankings of the wealthiest Ukrainians, we assume they can contribute to poverty reduction with the legislation as well as with philanthropy/charity projects. That is why the analysis of legislative initiatives submitted by the elite members from our sample were analysed not only with regard to poverty reduction and welfare system development, but also within the framework of legal regulation of philanthropy in Ukraine. These two areas are connected; however, the analysis of the selected draft laws is conducted separately for each topic.

According to the Constitution of Ukraine (article 93), legislative initiatives can be submitted by the President, deputies of the Parliament, Cabinet of Ministers and the National Bank of Ukraine. One of the important forms of the legislative initiatives is a draft law: it is developed by one or several authors and submitted to the Parliament for discussion. In order to be discussed, the draft law should be included into the agenda of the plenary meetings of the parliamentary session taking place monthly. After the draft law is discussed, it can be returned for reconsideration to its authors – together with suggestions and comments from the other deputies; thus, the process of legal approval is rather long, because it can take several months or even years. Not all the legislative initiatives result in laws – some of them are returned to the authors and never submitted again. For the draft law to be accepted, a simple majority of the parliamentarians should vote for it after the first, second or third reading.

So, categorization of the legislative initiatives (LIs) relevant for either philanthropy activities or poverty reduction is taken as follows:

- LIs directly connected with philanthropy/charity activities;
- LIs directed on improving the quality of life of vulnerable groups:
  - social benefits, allowances, retirement/pension payments
  - employment
  - affordable accommodation
  - healthcare provision
  - education and training.

Developing Legislation on Philanthropy Activities

As mentioned above, elite members who both possess economic and political power can provide influence on poverty reduction through their legislative activities in the Verkhovna Rada of Ukraine. Specifically, Members of the Parliament are those who initiate discussion around changes in the current legislation or adoption of a new law.

With regard to philanthropy, there is a need to adopt laws that would regulate such activities and specify its types, forms, taxation if any. However, there is no single mechanism yet which we can apply for the regulation of philanthropy or charity activities, either among the donors or among the recipients.

A similar situation is observed with regard to poverty reduction. Some of the current laws that allow vulnerable groups to receive support from the state or private donors are not living up to people's needs and are in need of reconsideration. So, parliamentarians who at the same time run philanthropy/charity activities are capable of improving the current legislation on poverty reduction, though not all of them focus on this topic in their legislative initiatives.

We see that only one parliamentarian (Feldman) involved in philanthropy used his political capabilities to adopt new laws with regard to philanthropy/charity. This person submitted two draft laws – one was on philanthropy organisations and the other on reducing the tax burden for the recipients of philanthropy support – together with his colleagues Yuliya Liovochkina (the sister of the Head of the Presidential administration Serhiy Liovochkin), Oleh Zarubinskyi and Lesia Orobets. Both initiatives were submitted in April 2010. For the moment, two years after their submission, neither of them has been included in the agenda and discussed during a parliamentary session. Thus, we can hardly assume that these initiatives will become law in the foreseeable future.

Developing Legislation on Poverty Reduction and Welfare System Improvement

The legislative acts representing policy addressing poverty alleviation in Ukraine were analysed by Popovych (2008) who focused her attention on the

Poverty Reduction Strategy of Ukraine adopted before the Orange Revolution, and three more policy documents: The Programme of Activities of The Cabinet of Ministers of Ukraine "Towards People" (No. 115 dated 4 February 2005), the Action Plan attached to the programme "Towards People" (No.324, dated 6 May 2005) and The Programme of Activities of The Cabinet of Ministers of Ukraine "Ukrainian breakthrough: for people – not for politicians" (No. 14, dated 16 January 2008). However, all these framework documents give little understanding of how particular deputies or ministers participated in the development of the poverty reduction efforts – only their legislative initiatives can provide relevant information.

The other part of the LIs deals with the social welfare system, specifically with poverty reduction and assistance to vulnerable groups. Two out of the seven parliamentarians and philanthropists (on grey background) listed in Table 1 were relatively active in submitting law projects related to social welfare improvement and/or poverty reduction, specifically Oleksandr Feldman ("Block of Yulia Tymoshenko") and Arsenii Yatseniuk ("Our Ukraine Block"). Those few legislative initiatives under their authorship dealt with the following issues:

- reduction of communal payments for individuals
- renovation of the public health system
- state support to children with disabilities and people disabled from childhood
- protection of children's right to accommodation
- guarantees for people who adopt children
- state support for orphans (i.e. for obtaining education, etc.)
- protection of children whose parents work abroad (to avoid social orphanage)
- social benefits on vehicles for large families and pensioners
- the system of retirement payments and its reform
- provision of first employment for youth, employment for vulnerable groups of citizens
- increase of social benefits and salaries, etc.

The vast majority of those initiatives were single-authored. However, none of the initiatives listed above was processed successfully for becoming a law – they were either not included into the session agenda or postponed for discussion.

As for a qualitative analysis of the LIs that refer to welfare improvement and poverty reduction, the draft laws touched it in various ways as displayed through selected examples below.

Thus, we conclude that the wealthiest Ukrainians who combine philanthropy/charity activity with legislation development directed on welfare improvement were not very successful in the latter. One of the reasons for this can be lack of support among the other deputies; another reason is a long and bureaucratized process of changing the legislation. Besides, as seen from the legislative initiatives that were analysed, there is a lack of joint and coordinated efforts of these politicians in changing the legislation in order to reduce poverty (perhaps a lack of real desire to generate radical changes). Submitting single draft-laws cannot change the whole system; it only gives an impression of continuous activity while in power.

Discussion and Conclusion

Negligible efforts are made by the Ukrainian political and economic elite to change the situation for the poor through private philanthropy and legislative initiatives. Through their philanthropy, they target only a few of the most vulnerable groups; families with many children and to some degree homeless and people with physical health problems. Other groups such as the unemployed, pensioners and the rural population that have ended up in poverty are not targeted. The studied actors' legislative initiatives are marginal. The ones that try hard still have no success, because of single-actions with no support and no substantial results. The legislative efforts of the politicians in poverty reduction are also selective and not numerous – they target some of the vulnerable groups, but suggest minor changes through the draft laws; besides, the adoption of the new legislation takes a long time, so they become outdated. Their philanthropic establishments according to the ICNPO classification scheme are mainly focused on culture and recreation, education and research, social services and health. This classification does not say much about particular efforts in poverty reduction, which is why we developed another classification scheme determining the distinction between long-term (which we defined as philanthropy) and short-term (which we defined as charity) projects, as well as looking at whether they had a povertyreductive character or not. Here, we found mixed results, but that most establishments within the foundations of politicians were focused on non-poverty reductive long-term projects, while non-politicians to a larger degree focused on non-poverty reductive short-term projects. Wealthy business leaders may be more inclined to stay tune with the population among whom they operate. They give one-time gifts or rebuild a church or put up in their hometown the largest music fountain in Europe. This type of giving is more similar to the role of businesses in the Soviet Union. Politicians seem to put slightly more stress into long-term projects, and a reason for that, relevant to a few of the studied actors, may be actual engagement in the development of education or the health care system.

Regarding philanthrocapitalism, effectiveness is of key importance to some foundations, while others do not stress it. But what is more important in the notion of philanthrocapitalism, as expressed by Ramdas, is the stagnation of the current regime, of current societal structures. The establishments that we classified here as "philanthropy or philanthrocapitalism", what are they actually? We would argue it is more philanthrocalitaism in this sense, after having studied their classification according to ICNPO. Those, which would belong to philanthropy as opposed to philanthrocapitalism would be in "Law, advocacy and politics", as they are based on democratic values that ensure equality among human beings. We saw very few establishments of this sort.

The group of the richest not noted as philanthropists are less active in legislative actions in general, fewer draft laws are submitted, and almost no draft laws related to welfare improvement or poverty reduction. Those with both political and economic capital in most cases use either both kinds of capital or neither of them to ease the situation for the most vulnerable groups. Yatsenyuk and Feldman, who are the most active in these issues in the parliament, also have their own philanthropy foundations. Some (both politicians and non-politicians) with a philanthropy foundation argue that the political system is too slow, and therefore, they do not work with legislative initiatives but instead focus on private philanthropy, where quicker results can be obtained. From a path-dependency perspective, it is possible to interpret this as a leftover from Soviet institutions and the caring red directors who were both chiefs and providers of social services. However, a lot of worldwide philanthropy can be interpreted similarly, even though it has no Soviet past.

The actors that we have focused on have gained their fortunes in business activities. In relation to this, they have more power to make a change, and especially to target one of the groups, the working poor. This would be interesting to look into more closely through employees' view of work opportunities, employment safety and salary levels.

Notes

1. The number of inhabitants was nearly 52 million at independence, while closer to 48 million in 2002, and by 2010, even though the birth rate had slightly increased and some emigrants has returned after the Orange Revolution in December 2004, the amount of inhabitants was 45,7 million.
2. However, rural and urban poverty differs greatly, as the informal economy is more important in the countryside and the small plots for growing basic foodstuff complement formal income. See e.g. Williams and Round (2007) and Ledeneva (1998).
3. See further on the working poor phenomena: Smith et al. (2008).
4. With executive or legislative power.
5. Unfortunately figures from before 1999 are unavailable.
6. Libanova (2008). A subjective poverty measure would stretch the number of poor even higher; some state that about 70% of Ukrainian people considered themselves to be poor.
7. Should orphans be considered poor? Ella M. Libanova, who means they are in most cases very well fed, does not support the point of view that orphans should be considered poor. "It is hard to say whether these children are poor or not, as they are obviously given food... If you count their expenses – then they are not poor." Interview, 19/3 2012, Ella M. Libanova, Director, Ptoukha Institute for Demography and Social Studies, National Academy of Sciences of Ukraine.
8. This can be compared with e.g. Russia: 42 (2010) Sweden: 23 (2005), the US: 45 (2007). Source https://www.cia.gov/library/publications/the-world-factbook/fields/2172.html
9. Interview to the "Delo" newspaper dated 23 August 2012. Full text is available online: http://delo.ua/opinions/v-chem-sila-brat-ili-paradoksy-pokolenija-rovesnikov-nezavisimos-183742/ (last accessed on 28 August 2012).

10. Cultural Actors of Change in Belarus, Ukraine and Moldova. pp. 4, 10. http://youth-partnership-eu.coe.int/youth-partnership/experts/yohana-forbrig-/yohana-forbrig-.html
11. Survey conducted by Kyiv International Institute of Sociology (KIIS) in June 2009 within the framework of International Social Survey Programme (ISSP). In total, 2012 respondents were surveyed representing the population nation-wide. The data-set is available for downloading free of charge via the link: http://info1.gesis.org/dbksearch19/download.asp?db=E&id=37859.
12. The ranking as published in the magazine "Korrespondent" No 22 (459) on 10 June 2011.
13. The list of the famous Ukrainian philanthropists as published in the magazine "Kontrakty" No 17–18 (988–989) on 25 April 2011 and magazine "Korrespondent" published Dec 16th 2011.
14. See e.g. SOU (1993:82).
15. Further research is needed on the impact of Tereshchenkos initiatives, especially with regard to employment conditions.
16. Giving without expecting something in return. See e.g. Desai and Acs (2007, 283).
17. In some old orthodox texts she reads that "Labour not to be rich". Even in the Soviet Union, this kind of philanthropy existed: many workplaces were transformed into disguised almshouses, as nobody worked but they still received enough for a living (Dinello, 1998, 113–115).
18. Referred to by Desai and Acs (2007).
19. For further discussion on choice of notion, see Anheier and Salamon 1992, 281 f.
20. Viktor and Elena Pinchuk have one foundation each. Some individuals have more than one foundation, but are here presented as one unit. Firtash does not have a foundation, but is exceptionally included here as the amount he donates is large when compared with many foundations.
21. Akhmetov: 198 (million UAH (according to Korrespondent the figure is slightly higher)); V. Pinchuk 167,1; Feldman: 45,1; Firtash 44,8; Poroshenko: 23; E. Pinchuk: 21,8; Kolesnikov: 11,2; Klitshcko: 10,1; Yushchenko: 4,1 (2010); Yatsenyuk: 3 (2010); Onishenko: 1,9; Tolstoukhov: 0,2.Total: 530,3 million UAH (average: 44,2 million UAH, median: 22,4 million UAH).Largest: 198 million UAH.Smallest: 220 000 UAH (Note that Tolstoukhov does not appear among the largest philanthropists).
22. Philanthropy specialist and previous employee, Victor Pinchuk Foundation, 26 October 2011.
23. Employee, Development of Ukraine (Rinat Akhmetov foundation), 23 March 2012.
24. Employee, Development of Ukraine (Rinat Akhmetov foundation), 23 March 2012.
25. Philanthropy specialist, Ukrainian Philanthropists Forum, November 2011.
26. Employee, Development of Ukraine (Rinat Akhmetov foundation), 23 March 2012.
27. Culture activist, June 2012.
28. Student, August 2012.
29. Philanthropy specialist and previous employee, Victor Pinchuk Foundation, 26 October, 2011.
30. This can however be problematized as to how long is the "long" in long-term, and may it in some time perspectives even lead to larger income gaps? Or even if it does initially, will they have trickle down effects? These are very complex questions often impossible to answer which is why we will not attempt to do so here.
31. Employee, Kolesnikov foundation, mail conversation, 14 November 2011.
32. Video no longer available on the foundation's website.
33. Philanthropy specialist and previous employee, Victor Pinchuk Foundation, 26 October 2011.
34. This foundation is not included in this study as the founder and main funder of this foundation is of international origin.
35. Philanthropy specialist and previous employee, Victor Pinchuk Foundation, 26 October 2011.
36. Employee, Development of Ukraine (Rinat Akhmetov foundation), 23 March 2012.
37. Employee, Development of Ukraine (Rinat Akhmetov foundation), 23 March 2012.

References

Anheier, Helmut K., and Lester M. Salamon. 1992. "In Search of the Non-profit Sector II: The Problem of Classification."*Voluntas: International Journal of Voluntary and Nonprofit Organizations* 3 (3): 267–309.

Daly, Siobhan. 2012. "Philanthropy as an Essentially Contested Concept." *Voluntas: International Society for Third-Sector Research* 23: 535–557.

Desai, Sameeksha, and Zoltan J. Acs. 2007. "Democratic Capitalism and Philanthropy in a Global Economy." *Jena Economic Research Paper* No. 2007-056.

Dinello, Natalia. 1998. "Elites and Philanthropy in Russia." *International Journal of Politics, Culture, and Society* 12 (1): 109–133.

Freeland, Chrystia. [2000] 2009. *Sale of the Century – The inside Story of the Second Russian Revolution*. London: Abacus.

Frumkin, Peter. 2008. *Strategic Giving: The Art and Science of Philanthropy*. Chicago, IL: University of Chicago Press.

Karl, B. D. 1997. "Philanthropy and the Maintenance of Democratic Elites." *Minerva: A Review of Science, Learning & Policy* 35 (3): 207–220.

Katz, Stanley N. 2006. *Handbook on the Economics of Art and Culture*, Vol. 1. Amsterdam: Elsevier.

Kharchenko, Natalia, and Vladimir Paniotto. 2000. "Poverty Profiles and Coping Mechanisms in Ukraine." In *Poverty in Transition Economies*. Routledge Studies of Societies in Transition, edited by Sandra Hutton and Gerry Redmond, 91–108. London: Routledge.

Kuzio, Taras. 2005. "The Opposition's Road to Success." *Journal of Democracy* 16 (2): 117–130.

Ledeneva, A. V. 1998. *Russia's Economy of Favours: Blat, Networking and Informal Exchange*. Cambridge: Cambridge University Press.

Libanova, Ella. (2008). *Bidnist' naselennya Ukrainy: metodologiya, metodyka ta praktyka analizu* [Poverty of the Population of Ukraine: Methodology, Methods and Practice of the Analysis]. Kyiv: KNEU.

Odendahl, Teresa. 1990. *Charity Begins at Home – Generosity and Self-interest among the Philanthropic Elite*. New York: Basic Books.

Ohana, Yael. 2007. "Culture and Change." [in Ukraine.] East European Reflection Group (EE RG) Identifying Cultural Actors of Change in Belarus, Ukraine and Moldova. http://www.labforculture.org/en/directory/contents/region-in-focus/ukraine/culture-and-change-in-ukraine.

Popovych, Oksana. (2008). "Good Governance and Policy Addressing Poverty Alleviation in Ukraine." Thesis for obtaining MSc in Public Administration, University of Twente, the Netherlands.

Ramdas, Kavita N. 2011. "Philanthrocapitalism: Reflections on Politics and Policy Making." *Symposium: The Politics of Philanthrocapitalism. Soc* 48: 393–396.

Riabchuk, Mykola. 2012. *Gleichschaltung – Authoritarian Consolidation in Ukraine 2010–2012*. Kyiv: K.I.S.

Rothkopf, David. 2008. *Superclass – Hur den globala makteliten styr världen* [The Global Power Elite and the World They are Making]. Stockholm: Leopard Förlag.

Rowlingson, K., and S. Connor. 2011. "The 'Deserving' Rich? Inequality, Morality and Social Policy." *Journal of Social Policy*. 40: 437–452.

Schramm, K. 2006. "Law Outside the Market: The Social Utility of the Private Foundation." *Harvard Journal of Law and Public Policy* 30 (1): 355–415.

Smith, A., A. Stenning, A. Rochovská, and D. Świątek. 2008. "The Emergence of a Working Poor: Labour Markets, Neoliberalisation and Diverse Economies in Post-socialist Cities." *Antipode* 40: 283–311.

SOU 1993:82. *Frivilligt socialt arbete: Kartläggning och kunskapsöversikt* [Voluntary and Social Work: Mapping and an Overview of Current Knowledge]. Stockholm: Fritze.

Tereshchenko, Michel. 2012. *Pervyi oligarkh. Neobychnaya istoria zhizni moego deda, kake e rasskazala by mne moya babushka* [First Oligarch. Unusual Story of My Grandfather's Life as It Could Be told by My Grandmother]. Kyiv: Nika-Tsentr.

Way, Lucan A. 2005. "Authoritarian State Building and the Sources of Regime Competitiveness in the Fourth Wave: The Cases of Belarus, Moldova, Russia, and Ukraine." *World Politics* 57: 231–261.

Williams, C. C., and J. Round. 2007. "Re-thinking the Nature of the Informal Economy: Some Lessons from Ukraine." *International Journal of Urban and Regional Research* 31: 425–441.

Wilson, Andrew. 2005. *Ukraine's Orange Revolution*. New Haven, CT: Yale University Press.

International Social Survey Programme 2009: Social Inequality IV. (ISSP 2009), data for Ukraine (collected by KIIS).

Interviews

Ukrainian philanthropy specialist, Ukrainian Philanthropists Forum, November 2011.

Culture activist, June 2012.

Employee, Development of Ukraine, March 23, 2012.

Employee, Petro Foroshenko Foundation, October 31, 2011.

Ella M. Libanova, Director, Ptoukha Institute for Demography and Social Studies, National Academy of Sciences of Ukraine, March 19, 2012.

Employee, Kolesnikov Foundation, November 14, 2011 (Mail interview).

Philanthropy specialist and Previous employee, Victor Pinchuk Foundation, October 26, 2011.

Student, August 2012.

Websites

http://www.klichkofund.org.ua/
http://www.ukraine3000.org.ua/eng.html
http://antiaids.org/ru
http://pinchukfund.org/en/
http://www.feldmanfund.org
http://www.feldmancollection.org/
http://www.openukraine.org/
http://foundart.org.ua/ru/about
http://sofy.kiev.ua/aboutru.htm
http://www.fdu.org.ua/en

Policies Against Poverty in Russia — A Female Responsibility

Ann-Mari Sätre

This article analyses how social policies in Russia can give poor people opportunities to improve their life situations given the persisting norms of a moral and practical female responsibility for social welfare. Women working in the social sphere have created their own support networks for helping people to take part in state programmes and to become entitled to support in one way or the other. Their agenda is clearly larger than the directives they might be subject to from above. They use relations to create resources. Analysing the agency of women who are professionally working in the social sphere supports distinguishing their potential roles of empowering the poor from their controlling roles. Empirical data are based on qualitative interviews with social work experts, social workers, social pedagogues at schools, teachers, doctor's assistants, local politicians and deputies of commissions or local village councils in two Russian regions.

Introduction

The Soviet ideology defined poverty as a social phenomenon associated with deviant groups. Nevertheless, support was allocated to particular groups, based on social characteristics according to strict centrally set rules (Yates 2004). These groups included single parents, families with many children, people with disabilities, war veterans and pensioners. In the 1990s in the aftermath of the perestroika process, poverty became acknowledged as a kind of new phenomenon related to reforms (Ovcharova 2008). The poor was comprised of the same vulnerable groups as before, but in addition with a vast swelling of working poor and those affected by unemployment (Klugman 1998;

Lokshin and Popkin 1999). Contrary to mainstream discourses in previous research, many of the poor are young people whose situation became worse as a result of their poor adjustment after the global economic crisis in 2008 (Rimashevskaya 2010). Another factor is that there seems to be a rather large group vulnerable to small changes in the economy (Sätre, Ivashinenko, and Teodorovich 2012; 19).

Resources allocated to poverty relief are insufficient when reflected against the fact that social benefits payments are generally too small to cover basic expenditures. The situation where many people living in poverty are employed reflects the imbalance between wages and the cost of living (Rimashevskaya 2010). It has also been argued that there is no clearly formulated state policy for combating poverty and that support is seen as a form of compensation for increased costs (Round and Kosterina 2005). The introduction in 2005 of the National Programmes for Health, Education, Housing and Agriculture (the so-called Presidential Programmes) suggest, however, an increased attention to social policies in Russia.

After the next section, outlining the theoretical and research basis for this article, the following sections highlight the role of National Programmes in reducing poverty in Russia; the interrelation between hierarchical structures and informal decision-making with respect to social support; and the effect of the continuing responsibility of women for social welfare, before the conclusions are drawn. The empirical data are based on interviews from four communities in the Archangelsk region in 2002–2013 and three communities in Nizhegorodskaya oblast in 2011 and 2013–2014.

Theoretical and Research Basis

This article analyses how social policies in Russia can give poor people opportunities to improve their life situations through their own actions. The analytical framework is based on North's (1990) categorisation of four main kinds of institutions which influence the way a society develops: legal rules; organisation forms; enforcement; and behavioural norms. "Institutions" are all the restrictions that humans have created to regulate interaction in society. While formal rules can be changed by political decisions, informal rules, such as behavioural norms that are rooted in society, are not quickly changed.

Although North (1990) highlighted the need for "agency" (action) for change, he did not incorporate the interrelationship between agency and the institutional framework. In this article, the agency dimension is added, drawing on Sen's (1984) capability approach. Sen's analytical framework also connects agency to the issue of empowerment and seeks not only to answer the actual needs for a resource (e.g. money, housing), but also to identify the kind of support needed to transform resources into goods and services (Sen 1984). The core of the empowerment concept lies in the ability of the individual to control her own destiny, that is, the agency aspect. The aim here was to highlight the role of social workers and others who work with social issues in encouraging the poor to actively use possibilities to improve their own life, through the policies combating poverty in two Russian regions.

The impact of two kinds of informal institutions are highlighted, firstly, the survival of a general hierarchical structure of organisations from the Soviet system, and secondly, the survival of the norm that women are responsible for the organisation of social welfare. It is suggested that, while the first could provide an obstacle to encouraging the agency and empowerment of the poor, the second could promote it.

Poverty Research in Russia

Scientific interest in the problem of poverty in Russia increased at the beginning of the 1990s simultaneously with the radical transformations in Russian society. In the 1990s, poverty research focused on homeless adults and street children (Rimashevskaya 2004). Sociological questionnaires began to be used to identify the poor and to map poor peoples' access to hot food and their purchases of inexpensive clothing (Ivashinenko and Iudin 2000).

There is some earlier research on Russia that associates poverty with informal institutions. A few studies highlight how the survival of a collective spirit (Shanin 1999) or paternalistic behaviour of employers (Granberg 2007) can facilitate the everyday life of poor people. Others focus on how Soviet norms such as connections (*blat*) (Ledeneva 1998, 2008) and inter-family networks can help people to combat or cope with poverty (Desai and Idson 1998; Ioffe and Nefedova 1997; Shubin 2007) and possibly also contribute to entrepreneurship as a tool for change (Sätre 2010). There is also a debate related to surviving norms as to whether the reforms have led to increased activities in the informal economy (Ellman 2000; Kim 2002).

Then, there are those who focus on the surviving negative attitudes towards the poor: that poor people are lazy, incompetent or criminal (Khlinskaya Rockhill 2010; Varyzgina and Kay in this publication). There are those who highlight how poverty is associated with shame which makes people want to hide their poverty (Kay 2011). Some draw attention to the attitudes of politicians and to the relation between the state and poor people (Round and Kosterina 2005). Others focus on the tendency among social workers to distinguish between the deserving and non-deserving poor as a way to cope with inadequate resources (Iarskaia-Smirnova and Romanov 2012; Round 2004). Ashwin (1998) provides experiences of how "forced collaboration" has led to a rejection of general ideas of cooperation to meet common problems.

There is an emerging body of the literature on household strategies, looking either at coping as a way to meet poverty, or at survival for the day (Abbott and Wallace 2009; Clarke 1999; Pickup and White 2003; Ries 2008; Sätre, Soldatkin, and Varyzgina in this publication; Shevchenko 2002; Walker

1998). While it is important to reject the view of the poor as passive victims, it is equally important to keep paying attention to important political questions such as what gives people access to the resources which can enable them to provide for themselves (Clarke 1999). To sum up, although earlier research on poverty in Russia demonstrates that there might be some potential for agency, it provides little guidance as to how agency could advance in the Russian context. There is a body of earlier research that refers to features from the Soviet system that might prevent the kind of agency that would encourage cooperation outside the family. Consequently, although this literature provides information about hindrances to agency which is aiming at overcoming poverty, it also identifies factors, which should be changed in order to make such agency possible. This study aims to provide a contribution in this field.

An Institution Centred Approach to Poverty

An *institution* centred approach to poverty is concerned with the interaction between formal and informal institutions and the processes which link them (North 1990). Attention is paid to the working of a society as a cause of poverty rather than individual failings (Sen 1984). Adhering to North's approach, slow-changing institutions explain why people working in non-priority sectors would be unable to support themselves and their too low salaries would thus be seen as an integral part of the functioning of the economic system (Gaddy 2007; Kornai 1980; Sätre 1994).[1] Soft budgets imply that over-employment has survived, while a large part of Russians live with wages that are barely enough to cover basic expenditures (Remington 2011; Rimashevskaya 2010). In manufacturing many workers had to face a cut in their wages as a consequence of the economic crisis in 2008–2009 due to the fact that management did not reduce the number of employees (Kuznetsov et al. 2011). In effect, some features of the Soviet system have survived the reform measures from the 1990s, which explains why a large part of the Russian workforce is still employed in unprofitable large scale enterprises. Low salaries in certain professions, such as teachers and doctors who are employed in non-commercial organisations, seem to have survived (*Rossiyskiy Statisticheskiy Yezhegodnik* 2008). At the same time, privatisation implied that firms are not obliged to secure welfare for employees as in the Soviet time, while individuals have to pay for services that they did not have to pay for previously (Lazareva 2009). Ordinary people have been affected by changes in the rules for the communal infrastructure and housing reform (Round and Kosterina 2005). A new law on the monetisation of social benefits, which converted in-kind benefits into cash allowances and transferred responsibility for welfare from central to local authorities, was introduced in 2005.[2] This meant that ordinary people lost access to free local transport and local telephone calls, trips to sanatoria, free medicines and other benefits.

Changes in legal rules have also given rise to a responsibility for self-financing at the local level.[3] Although social policy continues to be financed by the state, it is organized in a partly new way (Kay 2011). There are a number of laws that directly or indirectly transferred responsibility from the state to individuals or families (see Kravchenko 2008). The situation some people end up with is chronic poverty where expenses are constantly higher than income (Rimashevskaya 2004). This also means that local authorities have to deal with the fact that the level of welfare remains low for the vast majority of the local population (Wegren 2011).

Federal and Regional Programmes to be Implemented at Local Levels

In 2005, the Kremlin launched National Programmes, focused on healthcare, housing, education and agriculture (Smyth, Lowry, and Wilkening 2007). These programmes, which were to be implemented by provincial governors, were financed by the funds which the Putin administration built up for stabilisation purposes with the help of incomes from oil and gas exports (Appel 2008; Chebankova 2010; Treisman 2010).[4] Individuals have to apply to take part in these programmes. Although it is difficult to tell to what extent the programmes have actually been implemented, interviews with low income families have revealed that they have benefitted from participating in the foster families programme, young specialists' programme, programmes for building private homes, programmes for young families, programme for setting up businesses, etc. Others have improved their living standard using the grant for building their own houses or used mothers' capital for building bath rooms.

But there are also programmes which a village or a community could succeed in taking part in, which reduce poverty in an indirect way, such as improving roads, renovating houses and building sports centre. A local head tells about how he manages to keep the young in the village by providing them with jobs through taking part in such programmes (interview Urban Village, September 2013). In 2012, a vice-mayor in another community describes how unclear rules from above make any long-term planning difficult (interview Community Centre, May 2012). She likes the idea behind the law on self-governance, but as funding is so poor, hopes are focused on putting in some small money from the community budget and getting ten times as much back from the region.

Another example is that of a mayor in a rural community and the director of the department for cultural affairs, both females, trying to encourage agency by advising people how to apply for funds for projects (interview Community Centre, November 2003). Similar activities are reported in another community, and also at later visits, when officials promote cultural activities, education and local development groups, to make people more self-content, thus imposing a change in the mentality of people towards seeing possibilities and taking action (interview Community Centre, May 2011, 2012). Local politicians are actively taking part in starting cultural organisations, trade unions and women's clubs. They also promote the establishment of social NGOs, which are used for applying money from welfare funds at higher levels (Sätre 2014).

Interviews reflect how female politicians have initiated social projects, cultural activities and small businesses in villages. One example is the "house of culture" which receives children from distant villages. A vice head reported that she had been able to receive support from a charity fund for a youth project directed towards those from problem families (interview Urban Village, May 2012). Another head told how they try to participate in all the state programmes (Urban Village 2013). Interviews also support the assumption that local authorities are able to mobilize the resources of local entrepreneurs for combatting poverty in Russia. This is about local politicians making use of their own human capital, as well as improving the skills of the local population through projects and educational programmes (see Sätre 2013).

But there are also places which are not doing well at all. A local politician emphasizes that differences on the lowest political level are wide within the same community. "Some do not have any money of their own, due to the lack of firms. This means that they have to live just on subsidies which are inadequate." One head tells me that she uses her own salary if the budget is not enough (interview May 2011). I hear about another local head who is crying over the miserable situation in her villages, and how she already spent her own salary on urgent matters'.

In 2012, the vice-mayor responsible for social policy emphasizes that poverty is the responsibility of the state:

> Social services is part of the state, they decide who is entitled to support, who is classified as poor (*maloimushchie*), and thus how to distribute benefits, this money comes from the federal level. The community can pay for transport to the hospital for somebody from distant places or for a pregnant woman, given that the person is classified as entitled to support. We build houses for social living and pay for weak elderly. Then we have programs for preventing infant mortality, and for rehabilitation of mentally sick children, for which we can get support from rich individuals or firms. (Interview May 2012)

A Formal System for Distributing Social Benefits

The financial distribution of social benefits was, and is, the main means of regulating poverty in Russia (Ivashinenko in this publication). In the 1990s in the aftermath of the perestroika process, the pressure on social welfare provision increased considerably. The poverty phenomenon opened up for social work experts as a new profession along with resources allocated to social security (Iarskaia-Smirnova and Romanov 2002). Means-tested schemes became the dominant form of social support, which meant that targets for support were diverted from families to general groups (Kravchenko 2008). Rather than targeting the "most needy", support is seen as a form of compensation for increased costs (Round and Kosterina 2005). That subsequently led to a decrease in the number of groups eligible for welfare provision. Efforts are required in the sense that benefit recipients have to apply for benefits themselves from social services.

Interviews at the social services in a few different places in the two regions tell about the formal procedures, what you have a right to if you are classified as poor, a family with many children, handicapped, etc., and there are also many documents telling about the size of the different benefits and about the adjustment of these to compensate for price increases. Social services provide groups entitled to support with information about their rights.

Natalia, a social work expert in one of these places, gives a picture of the situation (interview Urban Village, September 2013). The social services have an office in each main village. Those who get support from social services are families with children and single parents. Their number has not changed, it is more or less the same as ten or five years back. Social services work with those who apply for benefits only. They pay for child care and school lunches, sanatoria, and medicines for orphans and families with many children. Orphans from the children's home get a free meal and also help after they finish school. They get clothes and a flat when they turn 18. They pay only ten percent of the fee for summer camps. Single parents can send their children to the summer camp for free. There is no longer any children's home in Natalia's community. One has been turned into a rehabilitation centre, where the children should be temporary only. Another one had been closed a year ago, as in accordance with the new policy, children are to be placed in foster families. The foster families get a rather small salary, along with a sum for food and petrol, for each child. These children can visit the sports centre for free. They can for example borrow skates there. The children can also go to the arts school for free. The poor can further get help from social pedagogues at school. There is also free advice from juridical experts available for these families.

Natalia tells how festivals, sponsored by private organisations, aim to reach children and youngsters from poor circumstances. Nine operations have been financed by an individual duma delegate. She mentions the collections of money that have been arranged to help people who have been subject to some unfortunate happenings. A further method is the exchange of toys and clothes. Social services collaborate with the job centre and the church. Social workers often develop personal relationships with their families, which means that they help privately if the relation is good. On the question of who is poor, Natalia says "it is those who do not have enough to eat. The reason could be that they drink, but also that wages are so low. Salaries within agriculture are not enough to support three children."

Enforcement of Rights

The interviews with aid-seekers indicate that some of the problems they face are related to the functioning of institutions. Maybe the laws exist, but the enforcement of these are not working well. It could also be the case that laws prove to be inconsistent, as was not uncommon in Soviet times (Braguinsky and Myerson 2007). At that time when inconsistent plans were part of "taut planning", this might have fostered an attitude that it was possible to fulfil only the most important plans, given that they were ranked as high priority (Davis 1989). Another side of this was the attitude among people that you do not expect that you are actually protected by the law (Shlapentokh 2006). Interviews, for example, with a man suffering from epilepsy, provide examples of a low faith in authorities, not seeing any point in applying for support no matter what "rights" you might have on the paper:

> Why, me getting help from social services, ha, ha, ha ... (Man 2012)

Unclear rules along with a lack of health insurance or work place insurance are problems related to the working of institutions. This is reflected in sad stories in the interviews by individuals who feel cheated when they are not compensated in cases of accidents, thefts, storms and fires. If people do not believe that they are protected by the law, they blame bureaucrats or individual persons working at the social assistance centre rather than systemic factors (Kay 2007).

Both benefits recipients and social work experts provide evidence of perceived arbitrary treatment and a perception that the poor do not get access regardless of what "rights" they have "on paper" which supports results of earlier research (Round and Kosterina 2005). Many types of support depend on income, "if you happen to be just above the threshold, you are not entitled to support" (interview with Social Work Expert, August 2010). It appears that social work experts devote considerable time to advising people who are asking for help about what rights they have, according to federal and regional laws and legislation. Interviews reveal a view of benefits recipients' rights to obtain certain medicines for free frequently being violated, presumably contributing to the uncertainty that some of the recipients have talked about. Thus, if enforcement is perceived as being arbitrary this might indicate that the attitudes of social work experts can make a difference.

Hierarchical Decision-making

Rules on benefits are regulated in documents. Interviews give the impression that social work experts try to comply with the legal framework and that they try to follow directives from higher levels. One consequence is that some social work experts devote most of their time to categorizing people with the help of more or less sophisticated calculations of what people are entitled to, rather than helping people to change their situations. They mention various problems in present work practices (interview with Social Work Experts 2010–2013):

> Sometimes there are problems of an administrative nature such as the fact that a husband is registered in another place.
>
> I am ashamed that the child allowances are so low and that the only subsidies we can offer people in need are very low.
>
> There is too much paper work.
>
> The minimum standard of living is far too low.
>
> The shortage of child care is preventing people from earning incomes, as those who work do not get places for their children in kindergarten.
>
> I feel powerless and cannot make a difference.
>
> We cannot help people really in need of help.

Some interviews reflected desperate attempts to cope with a difficult job where resources are inadequate to support those who are entitled to it. For instance, one respondent said she tried to help disabled people and disadvantaged families she visited to change their life situations, but this was only in her free time (interview with Social Worker, June 2012). The resemblance to situations in the Soviet system of having to deal with impossible tasks by means of informal solutions is apparent.

The survival of hierarchical decision-making is likely to impede or slow down developments towards taking social workers' views into account. On the other hand, non-priority in the Soviet system also meant that those responsible for social welfare had to be entrepreneurial in a sense (Sätre 2001, 2012). In broad terms, the Soviet system might be characterized as having prioritized industrial development over social infrastructure.[5] Concentrating on the formal aspect, while industry was completely integrated in the state system of planning, social services were only partially integrated, leaving social issues partly outside of the planned target system to be dealt with in the informal sphere (Lapidus 1975). Participants were left to look for entrepreneurial solutions outside the hierarchical structures for planning. Social welfare services were likely to have had insufficient resources in the Soviet times and in contemporary Russia they continue to face the same situation (Iarskaia-Smirnova and Romanov 2002). There are examples of staff being innovative and entrepreneurial as their allocated resources have been insufficient to carry out their obligations.

One of the social work experts mentions that income is not the sole basis for deciding about support, but that they also visit benefits recipients' homes in order to get a better understanding of their standard of living. There are cases of children being taken away from their parents as a result of initiatives from a social work expert going to court.

One of the social work experts however mentions that they cannot refuse to give someone moral support. There also seem to be many programmes around to help families, specifically directed according to categories of recipients. Social work experts describe how they work to strengthen families with social problems, and how this work is facilitated if there are educational activities at hand. "A plan for each family" sounds like solutions could be different depending on needs, rather than dependent on what category families belong to. It is suggested that education and sanitary measures to improve health would help families to take care of children. Interviews tell about how letters are written to firms and farmers to ask for material help or money (interview with Head of Family Department at Social Services, September 2013). This is mainly for new year's presents or for other celebrations, she says. Outside of her job she has started a club for families with handicapped children. One social work expert talks about their struggles to allocate services that are in short supply such as child care and housing to the poorest, preventing those with money being first in the queue. "If we cannot afford needed measures, we write projects."

Such examples show that the social work expert has an objective really to help people to help themselves, to find a solution showing how to get out of their situation, at least when they have serious problems and need to get up above the ground. Such an approach, not limiting judgements about support strictly to official incomes, implies a widened possibility, which is compatible with the capability approach.

In any case, the more acute situation in the 1990s was reflected in the fact that social security could give mothers contributions directly into their hands (interview with Former Vice-mayor, October 2008). "This kind of immediate help is no longer given, as people are no longer starving." (interview with Vice-mayor, May 2012). On the other hand, there are new groups who have been able to buy on credit or have lost their jobs or stable source of income in other ways who are in need of material support. One social work expert says she wonders what some people live on!

To conclude, social work experts express disillusion about not being able to help the poorest, that they feel powerless and that they just obey instructions from above, which give them little possibility of coming up with alternative solutions on how to organize their work. What they express is that they can influence the allocation of help, but not its content. Nevertheless, interviews indicate that social work experts might be prepared to take initiatives in order to end up with what they believe are better outcomes. Some of them have ideas, and they even experiment with some ideas, on how to empower poor people, but their own agency and capability is constrained.

Women's Agency to Increase Poor Peoples' Assets

The capability approach to analysing poverty highlights relational aspects rather than incomes or ownership as such (Sen 1984). This means that exchange entitlements are highlighted. Social work specialists' ability to promote welfare development thus depends on their ability to transform whatever income or assets they have into useful necessities for the poor. As a result of the low priority given to female-dominated sectors in state policy, women had to develop entrepreneurial skills, and these skills have survived from the Soviet system (Sätre 2001, 2010). Women use them in their formal positions as responsible for social policy and in informal positions, when taking responsibility voluntarily in social work. Adhering to North, this is about the survival of responsibilities which take the form of work, of having an ability to find practical solutions to everyday problems. To act they need to have access to some assets, and also to be able to use these assets. Assets are, according to Sen (1984) classified into three categories: resources, including all kinds of capital (also social capital, human capital, cultural capital), rights and relationships. This means that incomes or assets are not enough to overcome poverty; agency in one form or the other is also required.

Interviews show that in practice, many people through their own agency have been able to improve their life situations. But we have also come across those who are not able to improve their situation no matter how active they are. Such families may work more and reduce expenses just to cope from day to day, staying poor and being vulnerable to changes that could start a downward process (Sätre et.al fc). The supporting role of public authorities is especially important when considering the possibilities for poor people themselves to take actions.

That people come to claim what they believe are their rights provides a sign of some form of empowerment. However, this provides little knowledge of actual empowerment processes of poor people in general as previous research also indicates that the poorest and most in need of support might not come to ask for it (Round 2004). These are the ones who local people often describe as alcoholics, incompetent or simply unwilling to work (Varyzgina and Kay in this publication). This opinion is given through the interviews with professionals in the social sphere; those working in commissions, at schools, at hospitals and at the local administrations. Therefore, this article also looks into actions by others who are actively working in the social sphere, how they use formal and informal resources, rights and relations to prevent or combat poverty. In particular, the aim was to show how they through their agency are in fact able to increase poor peoples' assets, by referring to how they create resources, rights and relations, respectively, for the poor.

Head of Commission

Elena is the head of the commission who tells how they work together, both with an NGO which gives psychological help to parents of drug abusers and alcoholics and with a charity fund. I hear about how the charity fund provides social support, for example the woman in charge there arranged that a poor family got a new roof, by means of sponsorship money she received. She describes how the head of the charity fund always calls to ask if she has some family for the things she has collected; food products, covers. On the other hand, she tells how she calls the head of the charity fund if there is an extreme need for something:

> She always finds somebody who is prepared to give something even for those hopeless families. We have to work with both punishment and carrots. First, we try to help as much as possible. Then, we check whether the money was actually used as it was supposed to be. If not, we have meetings. If such meetings do not give the intended results there is the option to sue the parents, which is something we really do not want to do. This is only if nothing else works. (Small Town 2011)

She describes how they work in close connection with the tutor and that she also cheques with the leader of the NGOs about whether a parent is on the list for psychological support. If not, the family is put under treatment. She sets out how they have all known each other since the mid-1980s. She emphasizes how important the social pedagogues are, they work with the families with school children. For the smaller pre-school children, there are the doctor's assistants who work with problem families, they visit those with small children. As the children of problem families do not attend child care, it is especially important that health authorities keep control over the situation in those families. These medical specialists are also members of the commission, she says.

When I asked a vice-mayor about collaboration between the local administration, social security and NGOs, she called in five women, who represent NGOs with roots from the Soviet time. As one of the heads at the lower level put it: "As the state cannot apply for funding from the national programmes we have to mobilize the NGOs. This is facilitated by working in the villages, where everybody knows each other; the same people are involved in all the NGOs" (Village, May 2011).

The School

The head teacher of the school in a small community remembers how difficult it was to work in the school in the 1990s, that teachers took on great responsibilities, and how they were able to get support from the Red Cross "at least they do not die from bad spirits as in the 1990s" (Interview, October 2013).Today, about a third of children are on the list from social services. These are living without running water and toilets, they get help from the school. The head teacher tells how she herself was able to get toilets for the school. The Red Cross gives clothes, also for adults, they can come to the school and give them. For the last eight years, the Norwegian Red Cross has paid for the children's school lunch. They benefit from a programme which provides school children with free milk. The school drives the children to the swimming hall, if they do not have enough money, they ask the monastery for support, or the head teacher herself applies for project money through the Russian Red Cross. The monastery provides meat and other food products to poor families through the school. In addition, the monastery provides protection for three girls. They have to get a social passport for the children. The head of the school told about two young school girls who became pregnant, and that they were able to receive project money for "bad girls" through the Red Cross. The school tries to follow up the families who are believed to be risk of falling down (Interview Village, October 2013).

Those on the list of social services get a free school lunch, the social services pays. The head teacher tells about how the school tries to provide additional support if both parents are drinking. They have formed an emergency group with the tutor and social services (interview Village, May 2011).

Teachers

Teachers tell about how they observe the children and have to make a list of cases where "it is visible that a child is without a winter jacket in the middle of the winter or of those who just have tea and pirogi for lunch" (interview Village, September 2014). These are the signals, then you go to visit the family, and it is visible right away whether this is a problem family. "Chinese clothes is one sign of poverty, you can see it, it is obvious, the fence of the house, the windows ..., children without their own bed, the kind of job, the housing, how they spend vacation, if they steal, damages on the car" (Village 2014).

The school can perhaps provide families with psychological help, a teacher says. But the school does not have any money, it does not get any financial support from social services; however, they work together with the school board to find solutions to some of the problems. They get a list of the poor families, so that they can pay special attention to them. They get pens and other material needed for school work for free, food three times a day and summer camp for free. The older children from these families are first in the line to earn a little money, if they organize work brigades to clean the town. They collect money if someone dies or if there is a fire, there are parents who pay for those who cannot pay. Some parents help with sports equipment and premiums, for example books. They collect toys. "but many of them do not want to get anything as they do not want to show that they are poor, but it can be seen, the clothes" (interview with Educator at School, November 2011).

Social Pedagogue at School

The social pedagogue is the one at the school who knows about the life conditions of families. According to her (we can call her Tatiana), the situation has improved in the last three years, but there are still villages where people have never worked, where they live on just potatoes. Since 2011, there has been a regional programme for building new houses for families with bad housing. There are four families with children from the school who benefitted from this programme. These were people without permanent jobs who had been drinking. According to Tatiana, this implies a better situation for the children as they now live close to the school. But they do not pay for electricity, which means that this is closed. Some of the parents have had temporary jobs, but some have been out of jobs for longer periods. Tatiana thinks it is very important to check these families, she has to pay visits regularly to make sure they do not start drinking again. The parents have to go to the job centre. The job centre regularly gets in touch with Tatiana. Low income is a signal, she receives information if someone unemployed gets a job. Tatiana regularly pays visits to the social services. Before school starts in the autumn, she has to contact families to check if they are prepared for the new school year. Do they have clothes for the children, is there a need to for the school to help with documents. Perhaps, they need the school to verify the documents needed to receive benefits. If the children do not have shoes, they can get help through the school. Perhaps Tatiana has to come along to see that they really buy shoes with the money they received. She helped a woman to get treatment for addiction to alcohol, but paid for this from her own pocket. She collected the necessary documents, so that a child could go to a summer camp. For her, there is a problem if those who drink do not register that they just do not care to do it although their children are in real need of all the help the family can get. Tatiana has to interfere. The sole tool she has is to talk, she emphasizes. She tries to talk to these families, she tries to explain, motivate them to do something, at least register. For Tatiana, it is important to involve parents in the school, it is important that they are social, that they do not isolate themselves. She wants to provide them with responsibility, so they take part, that they participate in the work to make furniture for the school, painting the walls to make the school look fine. Tatiana feels that if she loses control, there is a risk that the family will be weakened and that their situation will turn to the worse. It appears that the social pedagogue is an important resource for the poor families. But there are many families for Tatiana to follow, "apart from the 29 families who are classified as poor entitled to support (one-third of the families with children at the school), there are another 16 families who are not even registered, They are so fragile, those with a garden can at least get carrots, onions and potatoes, but some of them do not even have a plot," she says.

The interview with the Social pedagogue at a school in a provincial town of the Nizhegorodskaya oblast gives a similar picture, she describes how she has to teach some families to handle money. She describes how the effects of the closing of plants, or the reduction of work places in her town has hit the school where she is working. The number of families with either the mother or the father working with the *"vakhtovyi metod"* (a form of temporary shift-based work) has increased. Many work from morning to night without being able to improve their situation, she says. Low wages, minimal wage increases which are far from compensating for increasing costs. In her school, the number of families on the social services list increased in 2011 to 130 out of a total of 337 families, which was 30 more than the year before. But perhaps part of the increase was due to better information from the school about benefits from social services. The work place has to provide information about income, and the first step is to register.

At the same time, there are many families which are not included on the list, she knows them. Those who work unofficially or have temporary jobs and those who drink and do not work at all. She is just about to visit one such family. The mother is a conductor, and the father is a builder. The pattern is often like this, she says:

> They have a drinking week, the commission becomes involved, they are then back to work, if they get back to drinking once more, that is, they lose their jobs. Then, all the doors are closed. It is really difficult to get back to work as you have to show both a working book and a health book. Nobody wants to employ somebody who drinks.

The social pedagogue in the college is helping the girls from the children's home, making them capable of managing. "As orphans they are entitled to get a flat at the age of 18. You have to do everything with them; buy clothes and food, show them how to use the stove and the fridge, fill in the forms for applying for a social passport." (Interview Small Town, May 2013).

Social passports are made at the beginning of the school year. The teacher counts how many children with single parents they have in the class, how many with unemployed parents, how many families with many children, if they work. In one of the classes, there is, for example, "seven such asocial families, who everybody knows." The information is passed on from the previous school. But it also shows on the children. She visits these families immediately. Then, she keeps them under control. She sees herself as a link to the social services. She is to keep them updated of novelties from the social services. That they can get certain benefits, subsidy for the rent, new year's presents. They have to fill in the documents twice a year, and they receive money twice a year as well. It means child benefits, money for school lunches, extra money if the families have three children or more and money for the bus. Money for school uniforms, clothes and school books. The school has to report about problems to the authorities. The most difficult are parents who do not take care of their children. Those who stopped drinking, and then start again, she has to check them all the time, she says. "The deserted children. How difficult it is to see all the drinking everywhere." Compensation is paid for the cost of housing, lighting, child care, food, clothes and shoes. But the compensation is too small, only part of the year is covered, no discount is provided, children can only buy tea and pirogi. She focuses her attention on those with the smallest incomes, who barely make it from day to day. She advises them to visit the social services. But as they do not have the strength to fill in all the documents, she helps them. But it has become really complicated. Nobody wants to talk about their poverty.

Doctor's Assistant

The doctor's assistant is the leading medical worker in communities, a lower level doctor. Marina is a doctor's assistant who also feels that the only real tool she has is to talk (interview with Doctor's Assistant, Village, October 2013). She tries to talk to people, to explain, it is about 20% of the families who have real problems, "those without a head, who do not come to the doctor." Therefore, it is especially important that she visits them, she says. As a doctor's assistant, she can write out medicines. But the poor do not have any money for medicines. She reports to the pharmacy once a month. Sometimes, if the parents do not pay for the medicines, she pays herself. The problem with children of such families is that they are often sick as they generally do not get the nourishment they need, they do not get enough vitamins. Maybe, she can help so that they get treatment at the community centre, a maximum of two weeks based on financing from the state. She also has to report to the commission for social welfare at the local level. Occasionally, they intervene and force the family to leave the child in child care. The commission comes quite often, it could happen after a phone call from a neighbour. Marina can choose whether to take a child to the hospital, or talk to parents if they are sober. If the child is taken to the hospital, it will be subject to a medical investigation and thereafter placed in a temporary children's home. Only if there is no other solution they will be placed in the permanent children's home. The commission only looks into the sanitary conditions of families with alcohol problems. They can help with money and pay bills. It was Marina's own idea to put out boxes for the collection of money for a family under special stress. So, they received money enough to buy curtains. Another idea was to pick berries together, sell them, and buy books to the school with the money.

Marina emphasizes how important it is to talk with the families about how their children could get enough nourishment that they can get food for free from the child care. Neither NGOs nor the church help only relatives and neighbours who help by giving clothes. Marina told about how the commission took a child from a mother who had started to drink, and refused to reveal who was the father. The child was taken to the hospital and then to the children's home for one year. After some talks with the mother, she pulled herself together, and she got her child back. It is obligatory to follow the children's development over the first year. It happens that Marina visits a family every week, if she thinks that it is needed.

A doctor at the hospital in the small town tells about how they actually have a doctor's assistant in all the main villages. In this particular community, there is on average one doctor's assistant per thousand inhabitants. They are important as they are the ones who know about the pre-school children. As the poor families do not usually have their children in child care, the doctor's assistant becomes especially important.

Deputy

He is a lone father with three sons. He has some sort of disability, it is evident when he is walking. Classified as an invalid, he regularly gets a certain sum of money from the social services. According to the rules, there are many jobs he is excluded from, although he himself thinks he is able. The social services turn to him. He thinks poverty has something to do with mentality. "People do not make a budget. They postpone bills, they think, why should they pay? They just use whatever money they have. The debt just grows, eventually they have to sell their flat ...". He himself was brought up in a children's home, he started to walk only when he was eleven-years old. But the director provided him with books, and he learnt that when he was 18 it was time to leave, but he did not know how to manage, eventually he learnt through his own experiences. Now he is helping others. He is the leader of an NGO for handicapped people. All the others call him, and he tries to answer, he cheques through the internet if he cannot answer right away. He helps with documents, and advises on simple economic matters. He knows the problem families where women started to drink (Small Town 2013).

The Children's Home

Olga has been the head of the children's home since 1997. The children there have become fewer and fewer. Concretely, Olga supports the new policy to put children in foster families. The reduction from 68 residents in 1997 to 28 in 2013 means a better situation for children. In the previous hospital, there is now one building for girls and one for boys. Only four of the children are orphans, the others come from homes where parents are unable to take care of them. The children's home gets extra payment if she finds foster families for the children. Most families prefer girls, as they are believed to cause less trouble. This is reflected in the figures, only eight of the 28 children at this children's home are girls.

Their financial situation is really bad, but they make sure that the children get fruit and milk every day. They get sponsoring money from a local hockey team and from a firm. Olga tells how the director of the firm has been engaged in a number of ways, he sponsored journeys and festivals, clothes, summer camps, boots, pens, etc. He was also Santa Claus. But then he was accused of something, and now, he has disappeared. Students visit now and then, entertaining the children with performances. The governor provides them with money for furniture, library and equipment for sports. The director of the children's home tells how they won competitions and that they received money through a fund.

The woman who was the director for a children's home for eight years in the 1990s tells about how she took all the children to her home village in the summer, so they could get some fresh air for ten days. She taught them how to cultivate a garden.

Social Service Centre

They are financed by federal money. Also here, I hear about financial problems, and how they have to apply for funds from the regional level. Sometimes they get money from firms or charity funds. This year they have opened a home for homeless youngsters. At the visit in the social service centre, the social work expert Lidia tells how many families are under special control in the community. About a quarter of those who are on the list, entitled to support, are believed to be at special risk. Lidia tells that the doctor's assistant sometimes calls her in acute situations when parents have been drinking several days in a row. Then, she contacts the tutor, who goes and takes the children. Sometimes, she says, children are returned to the families, but only if parents can show that they are capable, and that they have cleaned the home. When I ask how the social services can help, she answers that they provide families with wall paper, and they have provided support for summer camps. They try to help with clothes, they buy school books for the schools who ask social services for help. The social services in turn try to get help from sponsors. They put announcements in the newspaper about special events, with a list of what they need. Firms contribute with either money or products. In the second floor, they have a "*priem*" where people can leave what they want to give to the needy. People can come there to collect things. But they also drive to the villages to leave collected items for the families there.

She talks about the different problem families, and how she tries to help them. She shares the responsibility with the tutor. Upon recommendation from the medical commission, she arranged that two children were sent to the rehabilitation centre for a couple of weeks, as they were undernourished. She goes to the families and tries to talk with them. She suggests treatment, summer camp or sanatorium and provides them with tickets. She collects parcels for distribution, she collects documents and helps families to fill them in. She visited the home of a family where both parents are drinking. As she could not note any improvement the last time, she visited them she had to report to the tutor. Lidia thinks the situation has become worse as many young parents have fallen into heavy drinking. "They do not take care of their children, they do not ensure that they children get proper food," she says.

Lidia confirms the development towards children from problem families being placed in foster families. She refers to the programme which was launched by Putin in 2008. They have to check these families, so that they do not take the children just to receive money.

The Library

In a small town, we hear about how the library takes a key role in providing information to inhabitants about their rights. This is also through a state programme. Every community library has such a function, but this one is focused on how to increase the social resources of the youth. This library also provides a meeting place for the club for foster families (interview, September 2014).

A woman reported about how the librarian at the community centre told her about the new possibility to take children from the children's home. There was a great interest, in 2006 there were quite a few families who were queuing to take children, but most later cancelled their application, so they were the first (interview with a Foster Family, Village, October 2013).

They had some problems with the boy they had taken from the children's home, they needed a psychologist. From the children's home, they could always get advice on the phone, but the tutor did not help them, he said:

> They just follow the party line, they are so hierarchical, they have solely a control function. (Foster Family Village 2013)

When he complained through the library he got help. The librarian forwarded the complaint, and the tutor was directed to change their way of working with families. The librarian is acting through deputies, but she can also call directly to Moscow.

Reflections

It appears that the Russian government has implemented social policies which have given people opportunities to improve their own life situations, implying that it would be beneficial for them be to be active. Such policies deal with poverty issues through developing welfare and improving life conditions in a general sense, but are perhaps directed towards certain groups; the young, families with many children or the like. Consequently, actors in the social sphere try to find resources, not only to cope with everyday problems of poverty but also to construct strategies based on participating in state programmes, to reach more satisfying circumstances in the future.

I have been to various authorities and met those who in one way or another work with social policy, striving to prevent or combat poverty. One component has been the introduction of a benefit system aimed at compensating people for increasing costs. This is easily documented in terms of how it should work.

Interviews have provided a fuller picture of problems of implementation. It was possible to reveal certain patterns. Going back to North (1990), this is about the effects of hierarchical structures, low trust in authorities and problems of enforcement. It appears that it is difficult for social services to allocate help to the most needy. The poor have to apply for benefits themselves, but many do not fulfil the requirements.

But informal institutions are also about persisting norms of a moral and practical female responsibility for social welfare. It is about surviving entrepreneurial behaviour necessary to deal with shortcomings resulting from the low-priority status of social issues in the Soviet system and about education. Also, the division of work comes from the socialist heritage, which leaves non-priority sectors as women's responsibility. This is about work that is not clearly regulated in the official documents. In this article, I tried to complement this picture through the help of interviews with those in certain key professions such as social pedagogues at the schools and the doctor's assistants, but also with those who in their profession have a role involving working closely with problem families and assisting the poor in other ways. Interviews tell about how social workers, social pedagogues at schools, teachers, doctor's assistants, deputies of commissions or local village councils, local politicians and others have tried to help people take part in state programmes and become classified to be entitled to support in one way or the other.

Interviews were conducted with directors of children homes, rehabilitation centres, schools etc. to get information about policies. Referring to Amartya Sens's framework of capabilities, I have focused here on the agency of women who are professionally working in the social sphere. This has been helpful as it draws attention to whether they contributed to increasing resources, rights or relations of the poor. It facilitates distinguishing their potential roles of empowering the poor from their controlling roles.

Although social policy in part continues to be financed by the state it is organized in a new way. It is indicated that women who are responsible for social welfare have to find sponsors by themselves, for their regular activities. Being responsible for organizing social welfare, women working in the social sphere have created their own support networks for this. They use relations to create resources. Their agenda might be unclear, it is clearly larger than the directives they might be subject to from above. They are also actively working to increase available resources by for example applying for projects, striving to participate in state programmes and collecting charity. This means, however, that solutions are likely to be more heterogeneous than before. My study provides information about how this happens, how women continue to take responsibility for social welfare, how they react, and about their efforts. The empirical material supports the broad picture and supports the finding that Soviet culture taught people to find solutions which are needed in contemporary Russia.

Acknowledgements

The field work has been supported by the Swedish Institute, Aleksanteri Institute, University of Helsinki, Lobachevsky State University of Nizhniy Novgorod, Nizhniy Novgorod Scientific Research Centre for Economics, Society and Science (EON) and Swedish Research Council. Field research in Russia has been organized and made together with Leo Granberg, Nina Ivashinenko, Liya Kalinnikova, Rebecca Kay, Margarita Lobanova, Alexander Soldatkin and Alla Varyzgina. I want to express my gratitude to them and also to several other persons who participated in research work in different important roles. I would like to express special thanks to Leo Granberg for his valuable comments.

Funding

The author greatly appreciates the funding from the Centre for Russian and Eurasian Studies (UCRS), Uppsala University, the research grant from the Swedish Research Council and the research collaboration grant from the Swedish Institute.

Notes

1. The continued dependency on natural resources is reflected in employment patterns as well as in relative wages in the 1990s (Sätre 2001). In the first decade of the new century, average wages continued to be highest in the gas industry and oil extraction, and lowest in agriculture and the consumer industry (Remington 2011, 102–103). State Committee for Statistics 2005, 107–109, 2008, 122–124.
2. Federal law No 122, 22 August 2004. A key task was to divide administrative and financial responsibility for providing benefits (*l'goty*) between the central level and the regions, which means that regions support two-thirds of the recipients. See Wengle and Rassell (2008), 743–744.
3. Federal law No 131 "On the General Principles of Organisation of Local Self-governance in the Russian Federation" came into force on 1 January 2006. A key task involved increased responsibility for self-financing of costs along with the introduction of a fourth level of administration (*poselenie*) within each community.
4. According to official figures, the accumulated assets of the Stabilisation Fund were more than twenty times higher in 2007 than 2004 (State Committee for Statistics 2008, 33). The fund, which was established in 2004, was split into a Reserve Fund and a National Welfare Fund in 2008.
5. One sign of this is the low priority in the Soviet time that was attributed to social production and social services in the distribution of budgets (Voronin 2002, 53).

References

Abbott, P., and C. Wallace. 2009. "Patterns of Participation in the Formal and Informal Economies in the Commonwealth of Independent States." *International Journal of Sociology* 39 (2): 12–38.

Appel, Hilary. 2008. "Is It Putin or is It Oil? Explaining Russia's Fiscal Recovery." *Post-Soviet Affairs* 24 (4): 301–323.

Ashwin, S. 1998. "Endless Patience: Explaining Soviet and Post-Soviet Social Stability." *Communist and Post-communist Studies* 31 (2): 187–198.

Braguinsky, S., and R. Myerson. 2007. "A Macroeconomic Model of Russian Transition." *Economics of Transition* 15 (1): 77–107.

Chebankova, E. 2010. "Public and Private Cycles of Socio-political Life in Putin's Russia." *Post-Soviet Affairs* 26 (2): 121–148.

Clarke, S. 1999. *New Forms of Employment and Household Survival Strategies in Russia.* Coventry: ISITO/CCLS.

Davis, C. 1989. "Priority and the Shortage Model: The Medical System in the Socialist Economy." In *Models of Disequilibrium and Shortage in Centrally Planned Economies*, edited by C. Davis and W. Charemza. London: Chapman & Hall.

Desai, P. and Idson, T., 1998. *Wage Arrears, Poverty, and Family Survival Strategies in Russia.* Discussion Paper Series No. 9899-05. New York, Columbia University.

Ellman, M., 2000. *The Social Costs and Consequences of the Transformation Process, United Nations, Economic Commission for Europe (UNECE).* Economic Survey of Europe no 2/3.

Gaddy, Clifford G. 2007. "The Russian Economy in the Year 2006." Post-Soviet Affairs, 23, 1: 38–49.

Granberg Leo. 2007. "Rural Paths in Russia." In *Reflecting Transformation in Post-socialist Rural Areas*, edited by Maarit Heinonen Jouko Nikula, Inna Kopoteva, and Leo Granberg, 49–62. Cambridge: Cambridge Scholars.

Iarskaia-Smirnova, E., and P. Romanov. 2002. "A Salary is Not Important Here: The Professionalization of Social Work in Contemporary Russia." *Social Policy & Administration* 36 (2): 123–141.

Iarskaia-Smirnova, E., and Romanov, P. 2012. "Single Mothers – Clients or Citizens? Social Work with Poor Families in Russia." *And They All Lived Happily Ever after? Norms and Everyday Practices of Family and Parenthood in Russia and Eastern Europe*, edited by H. Carlbäck, I. Gradskova, and Z. Kravchenko, 207–230. Budapest: CEU Press.

Ioffe, G., and T. Nefedova. 1997. *Continuity and Change in Rural Russia.* Boulder, CO: Westview Press.

Ivashinenko, Nina. "Searching for a New Approach to Face Poverty on the Local Level: A Case from a Small Russian Towns." *Debatte: Journal of Contemporary Central and Eastern Europe*, in print.

Ivashinenko N., and A. Iudin. 2000. "K voprosu o sotsial'no-imushchestvennoi strukture' Kuda idet Rossiya? Vlast", obshchestvo, lichnost'/Pod ob. red. Zaslavskoi T.I. Moskva, Intercentr,– c. 301–308.

Kay, R. 2007. *Gender, Equality and Diversity During State Socialism and after.* New York: Palgrave MacMillan.

Kay, R. 2011. "(Un)Caring Communities: Processes of Marginalisation and Access to Formal and Informal Care and Assistance in Rural Russia." *Journal of Rural Studies* 27 (1): 45–53.

Khlinskaya Rockhill, E., (2010) *Lost to the State. Family Discontinuity, Social Orphanhood and Residential Care in the Russian Far East.* New York: Berghahn Books.

Kim, B.-Y. 2002. "The Participation of Russian Households in the Informal Economy: Evidence from the VTsIOM Data." *The Economics of Transition* 10 (3): 689–717.

Klugman, J., ed. 1998. *Poverty in Russia. Public Policy and Private Responses.* Washington, DC: EDI Development Studies. The World Bank.

Kornai, J. 1980. *Economics of Shortage.* Amsterdam: North Holland.

Kravchenko, Z. 2008. *Family (versus) Policy: Combining Work and Care in Russia and Sweden.* Stockholm: Acta Universitatis Stockholmiensis.

Kuznetsov, B., T. Dolgopyatova, V. Golikova, K. Gonchar, and A. Yakovlev. 2011. "Russian Manufacturing Revisited: Industrial Enterprises at the Start of the Crisis." *Post-Soviet Affairs* 27 (4): 366–386.

Lapidus, Gail W. 1975. "Political Mobilization, Participation, and Leadership: Women in Soviet Politics." *Comparative Politics* 8 (1): 90–118.

Lazareva, O. 2009. "Labour Market Outcomes During the Russian Transition." PhD diss., Stockholm School of Economics.

Ledeneva, A. 1998. *Russia's Economy of Favours*. Cambridge: Cambridge University Press.

Ledeneva, Alena. 2008. "Telephone Justice in Russia." *Post-Soviet Affairs* 24 (4): 324–350.

Lokshin, M., and B. M. Popkin. 1999. "The Emerging Underclass in the Russian Federation: Income Dynamics, 1992–1996." *Economic Development and Cultural Change* 47 (4): 803–829.

North, D. 1990. *Institutions, Institutional Change and Economic Performance*. Cambridge: Cambridge University Press.

Ovcharova, L. N. 2008. "Bednost I Ekonomicheskii Rost V Rossii [Poverty and Economic Growth in Russia]." *Zhyrnal Isleovanii Sotsialnoi Politiki* [Journal of Social Policy Studies] 6 (4): 439–456.

Pickup, F., and A. White. 2003. "Livelihoods in Post-communist Russia: Urban/Rural Comparisons." *Work, Employment & Society* 17: 419–433.

Remington, T. 2011. "The Russian Middle Class as Policy Objective." *Post-Soviet Affairs* 27 (2): 97–120.

Ries, N. 2008. *Potato Ontology: Surviving Postsocialism in Russia*. March, Paper 32.

Rimashevskaya N. M. 2004. "Bednost' I Marginalizaciya Naseleniya (Social'noe Dno) [Poverty and Marginalization of Population (Social Bottom)]", *Sociologicheskie issledovaniya* [Sociological Research] 4: 51–77

Rimashevskaya, N. M. 2010. "Riski Bednosti V Sovremennoi Rossii [Risks of Poverty in Contemporary Russia]." *Narodonaselenie* [Population] 2 (48): 4–9.

Round, J. 2004. "From Inclusion to Exclusion: Barriers to the 'Formal' Post-Soviet Russian Labour Market." *International, Journal of Economic Development* 6 (2): 76–97.

Round, J., and E. Kosterina. 2005. "The Construction of 'Poverty' in Post-Soviet Russia." *Perspectives on European Politics and Society* 6 (3): 705–727.

Sätre, A.-M. 1994. *Environmental Problems in the Shortage Economy: The Legacy of Soviet Environmental Policy*. Aldershot: Edward Elgar.

Sätre, A.-M. 2001. "Women's and Men's Work in Transitional Russia: Legacies of the Soviet System." *Post-soviet Affairs* 17 (1): 56–79.

Sätre, A.-M. 2010. "Women's Work in Transitional Russia: Women's Strategies for Entrepreneurship and Survival in Russian Regions." In *Perestroika: Process and Consequences*, edited by M. Kangaspuro, J. Nikula, and I. Stodolsky, 330–350. Helsinki: Finnish Literary Society.

Sätre, A-M. 2012. "Gendered Experiences in Russian Entrepreneurship, Family and Social Activities." In *And They All Lived Happily Ever after? Norms and Everyday Practices of Family and Parenthood in Russia and Eastern Europe*, edited by H. Carlbäck, I. Gradskova, and Z. Kravchenko, 297–318. Budapest: CEU press.

Sätre, A.-M. 2013. "Women's Work, Political Strategies and Survival in Rural Russia." In *Post-communist Transition and Women's Agency: Russia and the near Abroad*, edited by Cynthia Simmons, 63–85. Dordrecht: ROL Publishers.

Sätre, A.-M. 2014. "Paid and Unpaid Social Work in Russia: Is Women's Social Work Opening up Opportunities for Empowerment Processes?" *International Social Work* 57 (5): 523–534.

Sätre, Ann-Mari, Alexander Soldatkin, and Alla Varyzgina. "Families' Ways of Coping with Poverty in Small-Town Russia." *Debatte: Journal of Contemporary Central and Eastern Europe*, in print.

Sätre, A.-M., I. Ivashinenko, and M. Teodorovich. 2012. *New Groups of Poor and Prospects for Using a Participatory Approach as a Strategy for Poverty Reduction in Russia.* Södertörn Working Paper Series 2.

Sen, Amartya. 1984. *Resources, Values and Development*. Oxford: Basil Blackwell.

Shanin, T. 1999. "Informal Economies and Expolary Structures in Contemporary Russia." In *Neformalnya Ekonomika. Rossiya v Mir*, edited by Shanin, 61–84. Moscow: Logos.

Shevchenko, Iulia. 2002. "Who Cares about Women's Problems? Female Legislators in the 1995 and 1999 Russian State Dumas." *Europe-Asia Studies* 54 (8): 1201–1222.

Shlapentokh, V. 2006. "Trust in Public Institutions in Russia: The Lowest in the World." *Communist and Post-communist Studies* 39 (2): 153–174.

Shubin, Sergei. 2007. "Networked Poverty in Rural Russia." *Europe-Asia Studies* 59 (4): 591–620.

Smyth, Regina, Anna Lowry, and Brandon Wilkening. 2007. "Engineering Victory: Institutional Reform." *Informal Institutions, and the Formation of a Hegemonic Party Regime in the Russian Federation, Post-Soviet Affairs* 23 (2): 118–137.

State Committee for Statistics. 2005. *Rossiya v Tsifrakh* [Russia in Figures]. Moscow: Goskomstat Rossii.

State Committee for Statistics. 2008. *Rossiya v Tsifrakh* [Russia in Figures]. Moscow: Goskomstat Rossii.

State Committee for Statistics. 2008. *Rossiyskiy Statisticheskiy Yezhegodnik* [Russia Statistical Yearbook]. Moscow: Goskomstat Rossii.

Treisman, D. 2010. "'Loans for Share' Revisited." *Post-Soviet Affairs* 26 (3): 207–227.

Varyzgina Alla, and Rebecca Kay. "Perceptions of Poverty in Small Town of Russia." *Debatte: Journal of Contemporary Central and Eastern Europe*, in print.

Voronin, Yo. 2002. "Prioritety Byodzhetnoi Politiki." *Ekonomist* 7: 52–57.

Walker, M. (1998), "Survival Strategies in an Industrial Town in East Ukraine." In *Surviving Post-socialism: Local Strategies and Regional Responses in Eastern Europe and the Former Soviet Union*, edited by S. Bridger, and F. Pine, 188–202. London: Routledge.

Wegren, Stephen K. 2011. "Private Farming in Russia: An Emerging Success?" *Post-Soviet Affairs* 27 (3): 211–240.

Wengle, S., and M. Rasell. 2008. "The Monetisation of L'*goty*: Changing Patterns of Welfare Politics and Provision in Russia." *Europe-Asia Studies* 60 (5): 739–756.

Yates, S., 2004. "Living with Poverty in Post-Soviet Russia: Social Perspectives on Urban Development." Doctoral thesis, School of Economic and Political Science, London.

Searching for a New Approach to Face Poverty on the Local Level, a Case Study in a Small Russian Town

Nina Ivashinenko

This paper re-examines poverty in a small Russian town, drawing attention to the public attitude towards the poor and the readiness of local society to be involved in the process of helping these people. The Russian official measurement and general approach to the study of poverty are not adequate to targeting the involvement of wider social groups in poverty reduction. This process needs a new approach for investigating poverty in Russia and the implementation of new social security services. A new approach could be based on interaction between people in difficult situations, local society, authorities and other stakeholders. This paper examines the opportunity to employ the idea of a participatory methodology for providing social security in the Russian Federation.

Introduction

According to official Russian statistics, at the beginning of 2012 the number of people leaving under the minimum subsistence level was estimated at 13.5% of the Russian population. They are therefore officially recognised as poor. However, a lot of Russian and international researchers have drawn attention to the way in which poverty is measured and managed (Rimashevskaya 2010). By the end of 2011, the average monthly child benefit was approximately 12% of the minimum subsistence level. It is true that the amount of social benefits per child increased, but the discussion here will focus primarily on the question of whether this is enough to support a normal life or not. According to economic analyses, budgeting for social benefits can result in less money being available than is required, because the economic situation can change (so prices can increase) in the time between the calculation of the budget and the distribution of funds (Ivashinenko 2007a). The last financial crisis made it very clear that governments in many countries could not predict financial decline and could not protect their citizens against socio-economic difficulties, especially the poorest who are more vulnerable and less financially stable (Mourougane and Furceri 2009).

Nobody disagrees with the necessity of providing sufficient financial support to the poor, but poverty is not just an economic problem associated with a lack of resources; poverty is a social issue which relates to social assumptions and deprivation (Benda-Beckmann et al. 1988). Poor groups living in risk of poverty need not only social benefits but also social recourses such as social support and understanding (Ivashinenko 2007b). Public opinion on poverty is a very important part of national culture and highlights the dominant values in a particular society: the value of cooperation and solidarity, or competition and individualism (Lapin 2003). For a long time, Russian society was recognised as a collectivist society based on old orthodox Christianity or Soviet type integration. Post-Soviet studies conducted by Lapin demonstrated that market oriented economies have increased the process of individualization and anonymity. By and large, many traditional forms of social integration have been lost and Russian society needs a new mechanism for social integration.

Poverty is one of the most important social problems which must be addressed in order to encourage this process. A lower risk of poverty could be achieved by combining the efforts of public and private resources, formal and informal networks, governmental and non-governmental stakeholders (Read and Thelen 2007; Kay 2011). This problem cannot be addressed only with governmental support. Further than more resources, what is needed is a self-preventing mechanism against the processes which lead to poverty. At the core of such a mechanism would be that social capital among the potential poor (and supporting network) would increase and that the empowerment of marginalised people could take place. Building adequate mechanisms to prevent poverty and reduce social insecurity is becoming a highly significant social issue (Daly and Lewis 1998; Kingfisher 2000). The participatory mechanism, which combines the various resources of the state, communities, socially responsible businesses and poor people themselves, is seen as one possible social solution (Kapoor and Jordan 2009).

Participation became part of mainstream policy discourse and practice in the field of International development in the 1980s and 90s when it was strongly promoted by the World Bank and other key institutional players (Hickey and Mohan 2004, 5–9). Almost simultaneously it also became popular as "community consultation and engagement" in approaches to poverty reduction and urban regeneration in "first world" contexts such as Great Britain, Australia and the United States (Goode and Maskovsky 2001). In either guise and in a range of contexts, the proclaimed goals of participation have been to enhance the empowerment and facilitate the transformative potential of marginalised people (Hickey and Mohan 2004, 3). It has been suggested that participatory approaches are better suited to engage with "real needs" and to develop context specific solutions in which poor people themselves could take part at all stages. Yet in the early 2000s strong criticisms emerged warning of a "tyranny of participation" in International Development (Cooke and Kathari 2001). It was argued that policies and projects claiming to empower the poor and allow their voices to be heard might in fact simply facilitate "the illegitimate and/or unjust exercise of power" (Cooke and Kothari 2001, 4), or reinforce existing hierarchies and exclusions (Mosse 2001, 17). Meanwhile, studies of poverty in Western Europe and North America highlighted intersections between the increasing dominance of neoliberal governance and the pathologisation of poverty as dependency (Goode and Maskovsky 2001, 5). Here, participation and correct demonstrations of active "agency" are read as preconditions for "deservingness" (Taylor 2007, 300—305) and in some cases become institutionalised in defining eligibility to state support (Kingfisher 2001). Moreover, it has been argued that participation might act as a mechanism for handing down those problems, which states are unable or unwilling to resolve, to poor people and impoverished communities, without the injection of sufficient resources and political support (Goode and Maskovsky 2001, 20).

Nonetheless, in the context of widespread welfare retrenchment the political commitment to participation remains (Taylor 2007, 298) and has been exported in policy advice to many of the countries which once formed part of the state-socialist bloc. This persistent reality has led some scholars to call for the development of a more nuanced approach to understanding both the potential and the pitfalls of participation. In their response to Cooke and Kothari's earlier work on "tyranny." Hickey and Mohan argue for more detailed, empirical and theoretical engagement with and analysis of participation in specific contexts rather than generalised stances "for" or "against" (Hickey and Mohan 2004, 4). Participation itself has been subject to deeper scrutiny and a range of forms of participation with their own potentials and limitations have been identified. Cornwall for example, discusses participation, "less as a singular, coherent, set of ideas or prescriptions [than] as a configuration of strategies and practices on constantly shifting ground" (2004, 81). She reminds us that spaces of participation can range from those "claimed" or created by movements from below, to those which are produced through established mechanisms of power, into which various actors and groups may be "invited," or not (ibid.). Power's work on social disadvantage in the UK stresses that initiatives are usually experimental, draw on existing organisations and networks, but require significant and consistent support in order to be successful. She suggests that a "patchwork approach based on bottom-up experiments and services" is required (1560). Whilst work of this kind continues to negate over-idealistic claims it does so by shifting the focus of analysis away from any expectation of "pure" participation or idealisation of "community" (Taylor 2007, 300) to one which acknowledges participation as always imperfect, partial and contested, but nonetheless seeks to understand and appraise its transformative potential in a range of contexts and for the diverse actors involved (Taylor 2007; Tippett et al. 2007). In the empirical argument which follows, we make no claims to the emergence of an all-inclusive or perfect participatory mechanism, but rather seek to understand for whom which areas of potential exist.

Public and academic debates about the advantages and disadvantages of the participatory approach reflect the moving cycle of attitudes towards this concept, from raised expectations to negotiation. The participatory approach, which was created as a result of the interrelation between the macro transformation of the democratic idea and reform of society on a micro level, one where learners are involved in learning processes, at present has many applications and academic scholarship employs various interpretations (Kapoor and Jordan 2009).

In spite of criticism of the participatory approach, it is generally recognised that modern social technologies, which ignore participatory principles in the process of goal oriented social changes, are limited in their social resources. Nowadays, widely employed social technologies have a clearly distributive character and spend resources rather than creating additional ones which could be done as a result of social interactions.

The participatory approach could address several complex issues, such as; organising intercommunication, the overlapping education of official bodies and social security service clients, making decisions and their subsequent implementation which could force citizens to use their own potential and resources for poverty prevention and to assume a shared responsibility for these decisions (Teodorovich 2009). However, a participatory approach does not propose that governmental responsibility be redirected so that socially vulnerable groups take more responsibility and their commitments increase. At present, community consultations do not have the status of compulsory requests to direct state social policy. One of the significant preconditions for the implementation of participatory interactions is that all stakeholders have relevant features and attitudes to starting work which are oriented towards increasing the social security of the whole population.

An investigation into the potential of employing participatory approaches for poverty prevention issues was conducted within a complex research programme and was carried out in a small Russian town called Pavlovo.

For the purposes of the investigation a mix of methods was used including:

- Household surveys involving 500 families with the sample chosen to represent the general structure of the Pavlovo population.
- 17 Open-ended semi-structured "expert" interviews with professionals involved in welfare policy implementation and provision, the leaders of

local NGOs and advocacy groups, and local entrepreneurs involved in "socially responsible business" programmes.

- 18 Ethnographic interviews with families experiencing poverty.
- Participant observation – researchers attended regular activities and events organised by a range of state and non-state support structures, NGOs and advocacy groups working on poverty issues in the town.
- In addition, one participatory consultation event was organised bringing together a range of stakeholders from policy makers, social service professionals, current and former welfare recipients etc. This workshop was facilitated using Ketso.

Pavlovo has a population of around 60,000. Compared with the social-demographic structure of other Russian towns, Pavlovo can be classified as a typical small town that allows one to extrapolate these research results to other Russian towns officially designated "small."

Poverty and its Direction of Improvement

Russian society has lived through a series of transformation crises and has experience of overcoming social risks, including poverty. At present, according to our results in Pavlovo, the poor avoid using the word "poverty" when describing their everyday life and prefer referring to difficult circumstances. At the beginning of perestroika, about half of the Russian population considered themselves to be poor. In contrast, nowadays, according to our results, only 2% of Pavlovo's dwellers recognise their life situation as very poor and 12% of Pavlovo's population answered that they live under the poverty line.

The comparison between self-estimations, which were given by respondents, and an analysis of household budgets, demonstrates different combinations between real life situations and attitudes towards poverty problems. Only 20% of Pavlovo's population were considered never to have experienced poverty. Two thirds of respondents perceived that their situation in poverty was temporary and one third regarded it as long-term. This means that the majority of people know life difficulties from their own experience. More than half of Pavlovo's people considered poverty to be a very important issue and 42% saw it as an important problem for Russia.

It can be seen from our results that there is a strong correlation between types of dynamic poverty and networks in which respondents are included. Thus respondents who have long-term experiences of living in poverty are included in networks linking relatives and friends who also have similar long-term experiences. In contrast, social insecurity among representatives from networks with high levels of social resources is lower than among other sectors of the population. However, a third of the population has been included in heterogenic networks where the long-term poverty experience of one member is compensated for by the absence of such experiences for others.

Help from relatives and friends remains a dominant source that could be used by 77% of the population if a difficult situation arises. Assistance from governmental bodies would be required by just 8% of people. Neither enterprises, nor non-governmental organisations really have the authority, in the opinion of the public, to improve the social security of the population. The serious gap in the interaction between governmental and non-governmental bodies indicates the poor development of such institutional support systems for the population, which could not only provide assistance in difficult life situations, but also build opportunities for increasing social mobility.

On one hand, the population considers the state to be responsible in a number of ways for the existence of poverty in Russia. In public opinion, the dominating point of view focuses on a macro level solution and links life quality of the population directly to state social policy, such as salaries and regulation of prices (Table 1). However, 20% of people believe that the poor are responsible for their difficult life situation, either due to alcoholism or a disinclination to work. Both points of view are quite far from the participatory concept of involving people in social networks as a means to overcome poverty. In the first case, people delegate all responsibilities relating to poverty prevention to government bodies, in the second case they blame the poor, as a consequence of their antisocial behaviour (More detailed explanations can be found in Kay and Varyzgina).

By and large, people do not perceive non-monetary support of the poor as an effective tool for overcoming poverty. Only 7% of respondents estimate that providing wider access to social services and building social networks are valuable resources for poverty reduction. However, this could indicate an opportunity for a new stage in poverty prevention programmes. Administrative distributive measures which are targeted at overcoming poverty dominate public opinion among other effective actions.

Nevertheless, more than half of the population considers an increase in access to educational facilities as a major factor in effective social mobility. Developing various public organisations which could assist people is considered an effective measure by 39–48% of those surveyed. One quarter of respondents believe that involving poor people in the decision-making process seems to be effective too. On the one hand, this number of respondents is significantly less than the proportion of people who support predominantly governmental regulation of poverty reduction. On the other hand, one quarter of the population are ready to participate enough for the start-up of public consultations which could be followed by the creation of real local projects targeted at poverty reduction. However, these social tendencies could build a social base for the implementation of participatory techniques for overcoming poverty.

The most popular kind of grassroots social assistance is passing toys and unneeded clothes to charities. More than half of Pavlovo dwellers are willing to participate in these actions. Readiness to participate in public discussion about poverty issues and decision-making stays in second place with 22%.

Table 1. The most effective measures of overcoming poverty in Russia, %.

Measures	1*	2	3	4	5
Government actions					
Increase pensions	2	7	31	30	28
Increase government control over minimum wages	3	8	33	29	27
Strengthen government control over the anti-monopoly regulation of prices	4	8	37	26	26
Increase social benefits for all categories	3	10	33	32	21
Targeted financial assistance to people in real need	3	10	42	28	16
Opening a new national project against poverty	7	14	38	30	11
Increasing budgets for supporting poor people	4	11	40	33	11
Equality of capacity					
Increase access to quality education for poor people	4	11	33	36	16
Opening social shops	6	17	42	25	10
Instituting food cards for the poor	23	25	38	11	2
Participatory approach					
Establishing non-governmental organisations which could assist people in difficult circumstances	6	12	35	32	14
Establishing special private charity foundations	7	13	39	27	14
Establishing special government charitable foundations	7	14	40	25	14
Creating a regional government programme for poverty reduction	6	11	36	33	13
Establishing non-government control of governmental policy for overcoming poverty	6	13	42	26	13
Establishing an organisation for channelling assistance from rich people to the poor	9	12	41	26	12
Engaging public impact to enterprises who could donate to poverty programmes	8	15	44	24	9
Increasing the social responsibilities of business	6	12	45	27	9
Creating programmes for mutual assistance of poor people by their peers	18	15	42	17	8
Involving the poor in decision-making of policy, planning measures and participation in particular actions against poverty	13	11	49	***17***	***8***

Note: 1 — Not effective; 2 — less effective; 3 — difficult to say; 4 — more effective; 5 — most effective; *p=0.05.
The tables reveals a breakdown in answers to the question «Which measures in overcoming poverty do you consider as more effective?».

Sixteen percent of dwellers are ready to share their experiences in overcoming poverty, which could be built into the main body of participatory groups. In addition, 12% of people living in Pavlovo demonstrate a willingness to be included in voluntary assistance for the poor. They can give to charity, but are unwilling to participate in voluntary work or common activities, and they do not want to engage with the authorities. Despite that, voluntary work is perceived as being counterproductive by a majority of respondents, so 38% of people interviewed categorically do not want to participate in any type of unpaid work. Analysis of the structure of citizen activity, targeted at poverty reduction, reveals that, at present, people trust spontaneous, informal assistance more and try to avoid contacts with formal organisations, which might be helpful for uniting common efforts.

Directions of Integration and the Sprouting of Grassroots Activities in Solving Problems of Poverty Reduction

Analysis of in-depth interviews with people living in difficult life situations and with experts reveals several strategies for social integration of different social groups which could be employed by local communities for poverty reduction:

- Supportive relationships with relatives.
- Spontaneous grassroots organisations.
- Activities of informal groups focusing on particular targets.
- Involving wealthy people in charitable support for the poor.
- Using the resources of registered charities.
- Employing the administrative resources of all Russian projects.
- Using the resources of official government bodies.

Networks of relatives remain as the most important resource for social security. The respondents seldom remember these, while describing their well-being, but mention them very often when talking about closer relationships. The lack of support from friends and relatives is sorely perceived by people who were born outside Pavlovo but moved there later. It seems that they are less *integrated* in local society than native Pavlovo people.

The lack of *embeddedness* is revealed in various difficulties such as a deficit of financial support, accommodation, job opportunities, and childcare facilities especially after school hours or during illness.

> I suppose there is support from neighbours. I asked once, and the person agreed to help me. I asked again and again, but it annoyed me, I can't ask more, because I am nobody to her, my child is also nobody to her, I don't want them to get fed up with me: I've asked once, then the second time – they may think I am going to abuse their help ... Nobody helps me, no assistance at all. It is very hard. (Mother who moved to Pavlovo 4 years ago)

Double streams are observed, so grown children live together with old parents using their living facilities and share pensioners' credits because they are paid regularly. On the other hand, children provide family food budgets so many intergenerational families have common food budgets.

> We live with my mother-in-law, we usually pay for meals. We also help my mother, she is not in a good situation, we give money to her. (Family)

The significance of these relationships is often not realised, and the understanding of the importance of this support will only come when it is lost.

Spontaneous grassroots activities, without special organisational support, more often exist in social groups which have similar interests, such as looking after small children, or attending additional educational activities for kids.

> We have tiny networks, we have all had our children at the same time, we know each other well, we are friends. Children's clothes that were worn a little and remain in good condition, we often exchange. (Mother with many children)

Nevertheless, exchange of resources is more common in middle class families, whose social self-identification does not depend on using second hand things. For them using such arrangements is not a sign of lacking money to raise their children. Grassroots activities need the existence of special places for informal meetings, such as surgeries or children's study groups, where people can communicate without social barriers and boundaries dividing people into rich and poor.

Activities of ***informal groups,*** focusing on particular targets, are close to the top-down type of charity which mostly depends on leaders and their personal and external resources. Leaders' initiatives very often are the main factor for engaging with the activities of other members. Changes in leadership result in a changing of the types of activities that the groups are currently involved in

> In principle, somebody has to take the initiative. It seems to need to be somebody who will push others. If there are no active people, groups, society, nothing at all will happen in future. (Social specialist)

Also leaders can appear as a result of their own initiative, as they may be given the duties of leaders' in the frame of wider projects organised by NGOs or faith communities.

> We asked our parishioners, and 3 people decided to help us in this matter — three ladies who are not old yet, under 60. They started visiting people. I was too busy at the time to properly follow it up, and at some point I thought that this initiative had finished. So I called them in after about 4 months time and suggested that we should make a visit to the hospital, and these ladies answered me that all these months they did go to the hospital and visited people. I was pleasantly surprised! (The third sector activist)

> There was a group of ladies, five of us. We also would go and make visits to the hospital, to organise taking confessions, offer Holy Communion, just to socialise. We worked simultaneously, and I didn't quite understand at that time what they were doing: some people coming, distributing books. And then

> in God's will I was introduced to this group and even was put in charge of it. However once I spoke to the group I realised that I just couldn't be in charge of them, I could only pray for them. So we have been friends for 4 years now. They really help people. They would come to this ward, talk to all the patients, depending who would like to engage in this contact. They socialise with people and try to help them. Somebody might need a wheel chair, somebody might need medication, somebody else might simply need just social contact. This is a very good initiative, and they have helped a lot of people. It cannot be called a church initiative, as a priest I don't organise anything. I just provide spiritual guidance, advice. They do everything themselves. We also provide them with a room in our Church of the Ascension where they can have their meetings. (The third sector activist)

One specific feature of leadership in small informal groups could be the absence of a strong management hierarchy. Employing the resources of other public institutions informal leadership reduces the risks of bureaucracy in social assistance processes but could increase the risk of a new power asymmetry.

The issue of resourcing for a participatory approach remains significant. Governmental bodies have the largest amount of financial resources for solving poverty problems. However social assistance causes many problems of stigmatisation, increased dependence and other aspects which create barriers for the implementation of a participatory mechanism in poverty reduction (Kay 2011). This could happen also in NGOs, but participation practices could reduce this risk.

However, social integration which is based on grassroots activities without resources could be possible only for solving a very limited range of targets. Supporting informal groups through charitable funds, NGOs and governmental bodies can be considered one way to bridge grassroots activities with other social resources.

Charitable activities can be realised in various forms with different grades of formality between communities and rich people who would like to help. Charitable assistance could be provided with traditional financial support to citizens initiatives, by transferring money to particular organisations. Also, it could be directed to create institutional conditions which help to implement poverty reduction programmes, such as anonymous alcoholic groups which are open for all and give some help to needy people.

> It happened that an initiative group emerged, comprising a small number of individuals, who would like to raise an issue, change something as a result and, if possible, get more people involved. Then it is possible to achieve a result. For example we have a branch of Alcoholics Anonymous in our district. And when they were trying to do something without extending it beyond themselves, very few people knew about them. Actually it was started by a private entrepreneur who decided to stay "off the record," and no one actually knows who this person is. He found a young lady, a psychologist with a university degree, who then specialised in addressing these particular problems (actually this additional training was paid for by this anonymous entrepreneur) This good

> man is keeping an eye on how the things are progressing, allowing the young psychologist to attend various courses for which he pays so that she's well qualified to address the problems of people with alcohol abuse. And she unites people who need her help. (Social specialist)

Charitable assistance to create an infrastructure to help people to increase their social security prevents poverty and opens a wide range of new opportunities for them.

This way seems to be more reliable for socially vulnerable people because the contact with this infrastructure is not compulsory for them, so upstream initiatives would be preserved and overcoming administrative barriers needs less effort. However, current Russian NGOs in general have little social capital and a low level of trust from people. In contrast, in a small town people know each other better and current NGOs have more authority than charitable organisations in large cities (Blonin, Ivashinenko, and Strelkov 2008).

NGOs are traditionally perceived as elements of an open society. However, as can be seen from our analysis, they are not free from the problems caused by the formalisation of the relationships between members (Blonin, Ivashinenko, and Strelkov 2008). On the one hand, by registering officially, NGOs have more opportunities to access and use additional resources for their activities. On the other hand, this can preserve an existing hierarchy in an organisation. Concerning a participatory approach, some types of charitable activities have become more interesting. In spite of the fact that in general the potential for trust in NGOs is not high, there are in Russia some specific organisations which are able to act as an integrator of separate initiatives because they have power via authority. One of these examples was a social fund, for the rebuilding of burnt houses. This charity helped people to collect donations from other people and businessmen and also to control its distribution.

> Let me give you the following example: on the 30th December 2010 there was a fire which completely destroyed a property where a large family of 9 members lived ... They came to us, absolutely devastated as they were really poor – Mum worked on a farm for RUB 4500, the boys were in building and construction ... People responded very generously and in the end we built them a new house using only the money which was collected by people. Now the electrical work is being finalised, and that's it – house warming party! (Social fund manager)

NGOs increased the amount of donations for families who needed help. Also, they received some assistance from their neighbours. This project, according to our observation, could only be done by NGOs because their staff had special knowledge and skills.

Creating local initiatives, which employ the ***resources of projects covering all Russia***, are rather new in Russian voluntary activities. In these cases, the main resources for the local communities have been information and methodological assistance rather than financial support.

> This group was created, some experience accumulated, and last year this group called Mercy – was nominated and received a Presidential grant and became part of the relevant network project to disseminate their experience over the territory of Nizhny Novgorod Diocese. Several workshops were held where various best practices were discussed, and using this experience we visited disabled children for Christmas (40–50 families) with presents and greetings. Everyone enjoyed it very much – both sides! We had about 20 volunteers, who were directly involved in these visits, and we had all the fairy tale characters there – Grandfather Frost and his Granddaughter, the Snow Maiden, even highwaymen! (Local priest)

As can be seen from the investigation of public opinion, people have not rejected the use of voluntary measures. They usually struggled with the forms which were employed by formal organisations. These were associated with compulsory events such as *subbotniki,* which were popular in Post-Soviet times. The changing of forms of voluntary activities could result in an increase in the popularity of charitable events among the general population. People are more willing to participate in work when it is not associated with previous Soviet social models, which were quasi-charitable but, in reality, compulsory.

The organisation of ***grassroots activities based on various official bodies*** also depends on the type of voluntary work. Experts from social security services mentioned that attempts to create new groups of parents based on existing external school activities faced resistance from the members. Government initiatives are perceived as being foisted on the parents and as being artificial. People tend to have less trust in governmental initiatives.

> We tried to act through a "top down process" effectively imposing several initiatives, but it didn't work. Then a "bottom up process" took place where participants helped each other to acquire various skills in sewing. Right in the 90s. One person started making clothes for all her children and advised another one how to do it. There's fewer activities now, but it doesn't mean that everything disintegrated. (Social Services Officer)

Bottom-up activities based on NGO work appear more natural and face fewer barriers than top-down-initiatives to stimulate bottom-up integration of the community process. Currently, mechanisms of constructive feedback between governmental bodies and the population are insufficient. The official bodies do not have special regulations for supporting local initiatives. Differences between functioning principles have caused difficulties in the dialogue between active people and civil servants. The idea and opportunity for supporting vulnerable people is the initial factor for the existence of informally structured active groups.

The main criterion that is used by official bodies to estimate the effectiveness of activities is control of expenses, which is often difficult to provide for informal groups. As a result of that, governmental bodies with the main financial sources do not have effective mechanisms of feed-back with local community. Good will from officials is important, but not enough for creating effective feed-back from people in need, because the effectiveness of these interactions is decreased by micro-cultural distinctions, shortage of trust, lack of communication and team work skills, as well as by asymmetric interaction. Development and implementation of participatory techniques within public consultations allows the commencement of a productive dialogue.

Organisation of Public Consultations: KETSO

Participatory techniques seem to provide the best way of involving people in the decision-making processes that influence their lives. A participatory approach is based on the assumption that members of a local community should be involved in the solution of significant problems, which should be fixed with consideration of their interests (Greenwood and Levin 2007). The participatory approach is used for community development and a wide range of problems, from ecological issues to poverty reduction and increasing life quality. KETSO is one example of such techniques which has developed the principle of Design Ways, created for the organisation of communication between professionals and locals (Neighbourhood Initiative Foundation 2003), and also the methodology "Future Search," widely employed for strategic planning (Tippett, Handley, and Ravetz 2007).

The main target of these methodologies is to create conditions which allow for group decisions where every member contributes equally to the efforts to form a new idea. KETSO employs a metaphor about trees, which organise group thinking. The tree has a branch which is associated with the direction of the discussion (Weisbord et al. 1993). At first, every participant makes their own decision then they write it on the leaves and afterwards show other people and discuss with them. All ideas and thoughts are collected in a common picture, which allows coordinated group thinking and enriches the participants with new ideas. The discussion involves several teams each of which has the possibility of comparing their points of view with others and exchanging successful ideas. Ranking of the ideas given provides the basis for group and intergroup discussion. During the research project in Pavlovo, two community consultations using KETSO were conducted with people and experts who represented various organisations which support vulnerable people.

The Role of Community Consultation in Creating a Participatory Process

During the process of doing in-depth interviews, it was revealed that those organisations which provide social services for the population do not interact effectively due to interdepartmental barriers. The levels of governmental hierarchy build a lot of barriers, which are usually overcome by employing personal networks and relationships between civil servants from different departments. The organisation of consultations for the community on the problem of improving the quality of life in Pavlovo was an attempt to bring together different specialists who represented a wide range of official bodies.

Initial analysis of the interviews revealed the following primary topics for discussion: human resources, financial resources, projects/initiatives and structures. During group discussions, the theme of spirituality and culture was raised. Given this fact, it can be argued that social security is a complex phenomenon which is also linked to values.

During the discussion, governmental discourse dominated the debate about the activities of structures that affect the life quality of the population. The main debates and global purposes of poverty reduction have concentrated around this topic. In spite of the fact that in individual interviews financial issues were very popular, in group sessions these aspects did not provoke special discussion because they were perceived as obvious and did not need comments.

Most discussion occurred around topics about initiatives and projects. Participants in group discussions revealed what kinds of things were associated with this direction. As a result of that, the first group started with an idea about a federal programme that supports small mono towns, then followed to an idea about the necessity of improving town infrastructure. Instead of that, the second group paid more attention to existing local initiatives, such as school clubs for funny and quick-witted students. Both groups formed very similar ideas about improving town life. In addition, the second group noted the necessity of collaboration between the state and the general population in the decision-making process.

Two overlapping group discussions showed how the process of knowledge exchange takes place. The representatives of official bodies have more deep and detailed information about different structures. Hence, they have more ability to structure current resources. In spite of that, the representatives of NGOs, schools, medical services and enterprises were less concerned about the possibility of the implementation of their ideas and paid more attention to new ideas and initiatives. After the group discussions these ideas were submitted by civil servants who preferred to transform creative views into pragmatic measures.

After the common sessions, participants exchanged not only information but also social resources. The representatives of NGOs felt that they could be heard by the official bodies and receive positive feedback for their initiatives. In spite of that, representatives of the official bodies also received social approval and understanding of the necessity and demands of their work instead of the traditional criticism that is directed at civil servants' work.

Conclusion

In Russia, social security is provided by a complex matrix of interrelated but completely separate factors which exist as almost independent processes. The institute of social assistance, which holds the main responsibility for the current situation in the sphere of social security and social help, functions separately from other organisations which could potentially be useful for poor people. On the other hand, in real practice people are underpinned by social networks and almost never mention the state as a real source of assistance and support. Several key targets of the modernization of the social environment and its innovative development involve creating links between the various social institutions which provide social security services for the population in forms which are demanded and expected by the people.

The small Russian town preserved some type of social integration such as relatives' and friends' support of poor people. However, social capital provided by these social networks is not adequate for overcoming poverty. The forms of social integration which existed after perestroika highly depended on the institutional context and the development of different sectors. Effective social integration needs the development of the third sector, social responsible business and governments interested in the support of social society (Read and Thelen 2007). Our research revealed the seeds of an intention to cooperate among all researched areas.

Nevertheless, the main condition for the organisation of effective collaboration is the correct choice of adequate collaborative forms which allow for the provision of resources, support and the implementation of grassroots initiatives. The understanding of local initiatives, gained by investigating public opinion, is important but is insufficient because their translation from top to bottom can cause their rejection. Even if a grassroots initiative is perceived by official bodies and will then be implemented, it will probably face artificial barriers.

Full participation of the active groups in decision-making and the process of implementing their ideas is an important condition for effective social change. The participatory approach could be especially fruitful for making and implementing decisions with reference to the integration of the local community and could stimulate a synergetic effect by involving people in poverty reduction programmes.

It is essential that many forms of participation, such as decisions at micro levels, cannot be copied automatically. However using the recommended scenario it is possible to transfer from one group to another as a model. The organisation of community consultations employing a participatory approach could be the first stage in starting an interacting project between the state and communities, which is directed towards increasing the population's quality of life. The implementation of these social technologies requires further investigation and a review of the practices, which will allow the advantages and disadvantages of participatory approaches for poverty reduction in Russia to be revealed.

Acknowledgements

I want to express my gratitude to our research team: Ann-Mari Sätre, Rebecca Kay, Leo Granberg, Mikhail Teodorovich, Alla Varyzgina, Alexander Soldatkin and Margarita Lobanova, who participated in research work in different important roles.

Funding

The author greatly appreciates the support from Lobachevsky State University of Nizhni Novgorod, the research grant from the Swedish Research Council, the funding from Nizhny Novgorod Scientific Research Centre for Economics, Society and Science (EON) and the research collaboration grant from the Swedish Institute.

References

Benda-Beckmann, F. von, K. von Benda-Beckmann, E. Casino, F. Hirtz, G. Woodman, and H. Zacher, eds. 1988. *Between Kinship and the State. Social Security and Law in Developing Countries*. Dordrecht: Foris Publication.

Blonin, A., N. Ivashinenko, and D. Strelkov. 2008. "Problemy I perspektivy razvitiya grazhdanskogo obshcestva v Nizhegorodskoj Oblasti: integratsiya NKO. [Problems and Prospects of the Development of the Civil Society in the Nizhni Novgorod Region: The Integration of NGOs]." *Sociology, Psychology, Philosophy Vestnik NNGU* 2: 250–258.

Cooke, B., and U. Kothari. 2001. "The Case for Participation as Tyranny." In *Participation: The New Tyranny?* edited by B. Cooke and U. Kothari, 1–15. London: Zed Books.

Daly, M., and J. Lewis. 1998. "Introduction: Conceptualising Social Care in the Context of Welfare State Restructuring." In *Gender, Social care and Welfare State Restructuring in Europe*, edited by J. Lewis, 1–24. Aldershot: Ashgate.

Goode, J., and J. Maskovsky. 2001. *The New Poverty Studies: The Ethnography of Power, Politics and Impoverished People in the United States*. New York: New York University Press.

Greenwood, D. J., and M. Levin. 2007. *Introduction to Action Research: Social Research for Social Change*. Thousand Oaks, CA: Sage.

Hickey, S., and G. Mohan, eds. 2004. *Participation: From Tyranny to Transformation? – Exploring New Approaches to Participation in Development*. London: Zed Books.

Ivashinenko, N. 2007a. "Mehanizm snizheniya bednosti: dostupnost' sotsial'nogo servisa [Mechanisms of Poverty Reduction: Availability of Social Services]." *Sotsial'naya I demograficheskaya politika* [Social and Demographic Policy] 6: 3–23.

Ivashinenko, N. 2007b. "Modelirovanie zatrat na preodolenie bednosti [Modelling of Cost for Overcoming Poverty]." *Vestnik NNGU 2007*. 3 (8): 32–40.

Kapoor, D., and S. Jordan, eds. 2009. *Education, Participatory Action Research and Social Change: International Perspectives*. New York: Palgrave Macmillan.

Kay, R. 2011. "Social security, care and the 'withdrawing state' in rural Russia." In *Gazing at Welfare, Gender and Agency in Post-socialist Countries*, edited by M. Jäppinen, M. Kulmala, and A. Saarinen, 145–168. Newcastle upon Tyne: Cambridge Scholars.

Kingfisher, C. 2000. *Western Welfare in Decline: Globalisation and Women's Poverty*. Philadelphia: University of Philadelphia Press.

Kingfisher, C. 2001. "Producing Disunity: The Contrast and Incitements of Welfare Work." In *The New Poverty Studies. The Ethnography of Power, Politics and Impoverished People in the United States*, edited by J. Goode and J. Maskovsky, 273–292. New York: New York University Press.

Lapin, N. I. 2003. *Dinamika cennostey naselenia reformiruemoi Rossii* [Dynamic of Values of Population in the Reforming Russia]. Moscow: Editorial URSS.

Mosse, D. 2001. "'People's knowledge', Participation and Patronage: Operations and Representations in Rural Development." In *Participation the New Tyrany?*, edited by B. Cooke and U. Kothari, 384–393. London: Zed Books.

Mourougane, A. and D. Furceri. 2009. *Financial Crises: Past Lessons and Policy Implications*. Paris: OECD.

Neighbourhood Initiative Foundation. 2003. *Planning for Real*. Accessed October 13, 2003. http://www.nifonline.org.uk/S

Read, R., and T. Thelen. 2007. "Social Security and Care after Socialism: Reconfiguration of Public and Private; Focaal." *European Journal of Social Anthropology* 50: 3–18.

Rimashevskaya, N. M. 2010. "Riski bednosti v sovremennoi Rossii [Risks of Poverty in Modern Russia]." *Narodonaselenie* 2 (48): 4–9.

Taylor, M. 2007. "Community Participation in the Real World: Opportunities and Pitfalls in New Governance Spaces." *Urban Studies* 44 (2): 297–317.

Teodorovich M. 2009. *Bednost' kak social'naya problema: strategicheskij podhod* [Poverty as Social Problem: Strategic Approach] Monograph. Nizhni Novgorod: Nizhny Novgorod State University, 480 p.

Tippett, J., J. F. Handley, and J. Ravetz. 2007. "Meeting the Challenges of Sustainable Development – A Conceptual Appraisal of a New Methodology for Participatory Ecological Planning." *Progress in Planning* 67: 2–98.

Weisbord, M. R., and 35 contributing authors. 1993. *Discovering Common Ground: How Future Search Conferences Bring People Together to Achieve Breakthrough Innovation, Empowerment, Shared Vision, and Collaborative Action*. San Francisco, CA: Berrett-Koehler.

Index

For Product Safety Concerns and Information please contact our EU representative GPSR@taylorandfrancis.com Taylor & Francis Verlag GmbH, Kaufingerstraße 24, 80331 München, Germany

Batch number: 10726294

Printed by Printforce, the Netherlands